To George L. Harrison

a great American sportsman and a true friend to this country in good times and, more especially, in bad

My dear George,

I asked you if I might be allowed to put your name at the head of this book for several reasons. One is that we are old friends, sharing the same views, loving the same things and with, I think, a similar sense of humour. Another is because you, too, cherish the memory of my beloved Scotland and knew it when conditions were very different to what they are now. Another is because we have both travelled among the untrodden ways, felt heat and cold at their extremes, and seen the stars shine at night from the openings of our tents.

But chiefly I dedicate it to you because you are an American and I am British, and I believe that the only hope for a tortured world lies in the closest alliance and co-operation in everything that counts, between our two countries. You and your family have been true and sincere friends to us. You enjoyed some of our good times; you did not forget us when things were bad. I will not embarrass you by recounting the many generous acts of which I am aware. They are but a fraction of the unknown. But I should like to tell you how proud and pleased I was when I heard that, as a small token of recognition from some of those who wished to mark their appreciation of your generosity, you had chosen a picture from my brush showing the hills of my native land.

This is not an entirely new book. Some of it has appeared in *A Highland Gathering* and *Big Game*. All the materials composing these were destroyed in the war. As they are still in demand, I was asked to revise them and to add some new matter and drawings for this volume, and here is the result. I hope you may enjoy turning its pages. That they may bring back memories that you would not willingly lose, and that you will accept the dedication with my admiration and affection, is the sincere wish of

Your old friend,

FRANK WALLACE.

Little Wyrley Hall,
  Staffordshire.

CONTENTS

CONTENTS

FULL-PAGE PLATES

ACKNOWLEDGMENTS

My best thanks are due to Lady Gordon Cumming of Altyre for permission to use the picture of Roehillocks, R. Findhorn, which appears as the frontispiece and on the jacket of this book.

Thanks are also due to the editors of the *Field* and *Country Life* for permission to reproduce certain pieces which originally appeared in them, also to the *Illustrated London News* for the quotation on page 206.

F. W.

HUNTING WINDS

I. SOME PERSONAL REFLECTIONS

"While I and my like tell old, old, stories."

LABUNTUR ANNI—Hilton Brown

RECENTLY I was discussing with my son a friend of his whom I had met. "Clever chap!" I remarked, "I thought him very intelligent."

"He liked you!" said my son.

Thinking him even more intelligent, I purred and made appropriate noises. "Yes," he went on, "he thought you a very good period piece!"

I stopped purring, for, to tell the truth, I did not quite know what this comment implied. Period pieces connote a certain antiquity and though I realised that I was getting on I had not quite accommodated myself to the belief that I was regarded as an antique. Thus it was brought home to me, and looking back I felt that no one but an antique could have enjoyed the experiences that had been mine. So I have tried to set down here some of the things which have made my life a happy one. Those who come after me may enjoy sport and travel, but it will not be the same sport and travel which have fallen to my lot. The world has shrunk, and though there are still some open spaces to visit (or to avoid) the journey to them occupies in these days hours, whereas in my youth it took months. Last week I attended a point-to-point. Formerly I should have arrived there in my own car. Now I had to hire a taxi. The Hall where years ago I had enjoyed the hospitality of an M.F.H. of the old school, and which I could see beyond the course, set in a typical English landscape, has now been converted into flats. As I pondered on these changes I was confronted by a portly figure.

"Good heavens!" said I, "I thought you were on business in South Africa!"

"I got back last night," said he. "Three nights ago I was dancing in Johannesburg."

For "period pieces" such as myself such statements come with something of a shock. That the world is spinning at a greatly accelerated pace "down the ringing grooves of change" few who inhabit it are in a position to deny ; not, to quote the late Mr. Hooker, that such change is lacking in convenience. Inconvenience, I suppose, has not been suffered to a greater extent by any generation other than mine. When we look back it is to a world so different from that which saw our advent that we might be on another planet. Then it was a smaller, or, if you like, a larger world, but one much pleasanter than that in which we live now. We could not, it is true, transport ourselves in the twinkling of an eye to lands far distant, but had such methods been possible we could have done so, because in those days we had, though we never gave the matter a thought—freedom. Scarcely was it necessary to possess a passport. Had we managed to accumulate a few golden sovereigns, these would take us anywhere. Scarcely was there a corner of the world that was closed to us. There was no iron curtain. Tibet and Nepal, it is true, failed to welcome the casual traveller with open arms. The Eastern fringes of the former country I have visited, though an intolerant priesthood made shooting impossible. But apart from such distant bournes we were free to go where we liked. Now the would-be traveller or sportsman, even if permitted, is limited in his choice of hunting grounds though he wishes to go no further afield than Europe.

The Duchess of Sermonetta wrote in *Sparkle Distant Worlds*:

" Our homes and our cities stood as safe as the ground under our feet. We could not conceive our relations with people of other nationalities being anything but polite and friendly. When we wished to travel we just bought our tickets, made our reservations and started for any part of the world we wished. Passports did not exist, and we changed our money unrestrictedly into any other currency we required. It now seems incredible.

With freedom, that priceless heritage, has gone much else —leisure, courtesy, good will, charity and a standard of manners now sadly lacking. Ministers of the Crown who should, presumably, set an example, did not then stigmatise those from whom they differed on political questions as "lower than vermin." Doubtless there were many wrongs to be righted, many evils to overcome, but incitement to envy, hatred, malice and all uncharitableness can scarcely be regarded from an unbiased point of view as a sound basis on which to build national unity.

Well, we period pieces knew the golden age and it is "better to have loved and lost than never to have loved at all," even though we could not then realise how lucky indeed we were. Whether our children will live to see anything approaching those spacious days which their fathers enjoyed no one can tell. I have always regretted that I did not take more pains to learn from my parents of the people and conditions which they had known. My mother was

acquainted with Jane Austen. The name of the author of
Pride and Prejudice, as a child, meant nothing to me. Now I
would give a good deal to have learned of her at first hand.
I have many other regrets. As we grow old we do not, it is
true, have the fun we did, but still we can get a good deal of
amusement out of life. One of our greatest pleasures is to
talk, with those similarly situated, of the past. This, strange
as it may seem to the young, grows ever more vivid. At
times, no doubt, we become very boring. Then the young
drift silently away and leave us to doze, or reminisce by
ourselves. The advantage of such recollections being set
down in print lies in the fact that they can be instantly
abandoned or shoved back on the shelf without any dis-
courtesy to the author. He, indeed, need never be patronised
at all. Some young men, however, as well as the older ones,
like to hear of a former way of life, for there still exist young
men who take an interest in things which were close to the
heart of an older generation. Sometimes they even take the
trouble to tell us so and then we feel that perhaps our time
has not been entirely wasted. Environment, no doubt, plays
a great part in deciding a young man's future, though the
young man of to-day has a far harder job in deciding on his
future than had we—even though his chances of ultimate
success may be greater. The man who becomes an artist or
a writer might under different conditions have developed
into an actor, an advocate, a preacher or an auctioneer.
Speculations as to his success in such varying rôles must be,
however, purely problematical. Perhaps I have not chosen
so badly. It is true that books on sport and travel usually
fail to provide their authors with large sums of money.
Pictures do not always sell. On the other hand I have been
my own master, which counts for a great deal. I have seen
much of the world. I have met a number of charming and
interesting people, many of whom I am proud to count
amongst my friends, I have been much in the open air and
have learned something of human nature.

It was while I was reading for the Bar that my chance

came. I was asked to go round the world. My father, quite rightly, said that I must first pass my final examination. I worked as I had never worked before. The anxiety with which I awaited the result is better imagined than described. At last the list appeared and my name was included. A week or so later I set out. It was two years before I returned.

For a young man it was a wonderful experience, and one which has coloured my whole life. Those who have never travelled have only one standard by which to measure their fortunes. To have seen strange countries and peoples, to have looked at things from the standpoint of others, to have mixed with all sorts and conditions of men, is to have gained knowledge which nothing else in the world can bestow.

I have always felt grateful to my father for allowing me to undertake a journey since he must have had grave doubts of its outcome. Many parents, confronted with such a problem, would unhesitatingly have vetoed the project from the start, and my life might have been entirely different. If, now, every lass is no longer a queen, and some of the swans have developed into geese, before the trees turned brown, I was away round the world, and it was thanks to him whom some still remember with affection and love, though he has been dead for forty years. Too busy to travel as he would have liked, he had acquired from books an extraordinary knowledge of foreign countries, being especially interested in Africa. It was he who first inspired me, and I like to think that some of my writings would have interested him. A man of enormous personality and charm with a wide outlook on men and affairs, he was loved by everyone who knew him.

After my father I suppose the man who had the greatest influence in forming the outcome of my life was Johnnie Millais. Though considerably older than myself he was for many years one of my greatest friends. I remember so well taking him some of my early attempts at depicting deer and asking him if he thought I could ever hope to achieve any

B

success as an artist. Johnnie scrutinised them carefully whilst I, trembling with anxiety, awaited his verdict. "Well," said he, "I don't think you'll ever become a really great artist." My heart sank. "But," he went on, "if you work hard I think you'll be able to get a bit of fun out of it and probably give many people a good deal of happiness." I like to think that, though fully aware of my failings, judging from some of the letters I receive I may claim in some degree to have fulfilled his prophecy. Of the first part of his forecast I have no doubt, coupled as it has been with moments of utter despair.

It was many years later that I met my old friend Lionel Edwards. I have already recorded my gratitude to him elsewhere; gratitude which I can never adequately repay and to him I am profoundly grateful. To these two fine artists I owe what knowledge of picture making I possess. Archibald Thorburn and Sidney Steel were others who advised and encouraged me, as did George Lodge who is still, well on in his eighties, painting with the charm, vigour and enthusiasm of a young man. From him I had a letter only last week. He wrote:

"I have much to be thankful for. Although I can no longer get about I still have good health and during the last six or seven years have done 370 full page plates in colour for a book on *British Birds*. I got them all done last year, just in time, before my eyes gave out. One of them is out of action altogether and the other is seeing double (not whisky!). I can still blunder along and do a bit with my brushes but it has been goodbye to my guns, rifles and hawks. I think a lot of the good old days when I used always to get away to Scotland after stags and grouse and to Norway on two occasions with dear old Johnnie. Do you remember when I stayed with you at Corriemony? I love reading about deer and seeing pictures of them."

A pretty gallant effort from a great gentleman and an artist, unsurpassed in his own field.

I am proud to have been able to count such men among my friends. Johnnie was never old and it was impossible to think of him as being old. He was sixty-six when he died, but carried with him wherever he went, and with whatever company, a hungry curiosity of the mind and the spirit of eternal youth. Life to him was a great adventure, full of romance, and he faced it with the zest and enthusiasm of a boy. He was never happy unless he was doing or planning something, and whatever his hand found to do, whether it was painting, writing, gardening, shooting or fishing, he did it with all his might. He was a great inspiration to the young, and the primary thought of many on returning to England from some trip after big game abroad was to go and see "Johnnie" and tell him their experiences.

Most of the men I met when young were enthusiasts about their own particular subjects, and a predominating passion is a sure magnet attracting those with similar tastes. Men whose interests lay in travel, natural history, art or the hunting of big game, whether with the rifle or, as later developed, the camera, have an inexhaustible storehouse on which to draw. They were always enthusiasts, as I have said, and enthusiasm is not too common. The traveller is usually a simple-minded person, and simplicity is the hallmark of truth.

No meetings of such a type can fail to provide a variety of subjects which it would be difficult to match in any company. The best kind of hunter, whatever his nationality, is not the brutalised savage depicted by the anti-sport brigade. He often, in fact usually, has a contemplative and poetic side to his character which, if he is an Englishman, he is at great pains to conceal. He rarely speaks of his own experiences, but will wax eloquent on those of another. His concomitant interests are surprising and varied. During an evening spent in such company you may learn not only how to grow rhododendrons, the history of the Church of Scotland, the birth of Icelandic poetry, or the exact method by which the early Egyptians embalmed mummies. You may also hear, to your considerable surprise, what the chief secretary said on receiving the news of his appointment as governor; why Her Excellency refused to allow the new governess to accompany them; what steps were taken when the ex-monarch, presented with his bill, airily remarked "Kings don't pay"; and a good many other stories which will not bear repetition.

In the following pages you will find something of the doings of men such as these. Perhaps they, and I who followed in their footsteps, may appear out of date and old-fashioned in the beliefs and interests in which we were brought up but, right or wrong, we followed them whole-heartedly. Looking back there are things which I regret, opportunities missed, things undone which might have been done and things done which might well have been left undone. On the whole I can say with Hazlitt, "Well, I've had a happy life." Possibly some incidents in it may be of interest to a succeeding generation.

II. NOTES ON BIG GAME COLLECTIONS

East of the Mahanadi and north of the Nicobar
You will come to Evening Island where the santomingoes are;
Their wings are sunrise-orange and their tails are starlight-blue;
You catch a santomingo and all your dreams come true.
SANTOMINGOES—Hilton Brown

I HAVE always been glad that when I was a young man I conceived the idea of asking all the prominent hunters I knew personally to write their names on a page in my game book. A reproduction of this page appears overleaf. Opportunities to secure the autographs of all I knew were lacking, but there can be but few places on the earth's surface which have not been visited at one time or another by those whose signatures were appended. Of these, some, among them my dearest friends, have already passed to the happy hunting grounds. Others still survive to enjoy, I hope, much good sport in the years to come. What great men they were, some of those whose names appear. F. C. Selous, the last of the great professional big game hunters,

23

F. C. Selous
Gerald Legge
A. F. R. Wollaston
George Fenwick-Owen
Douglas Carruthers
J. G. Millais
St George Littledale
Warburton Pike
P. B. Van der Byl
Jack Hornwall
Malcolm McNeill
Robert Page
Edmund Giles Loder
A Buxton
Charles Howard Bury
Norman B. Smith
R. L. Scott
Courtney Brocklehurst
Peter Haig Thomas
Gilbert Blaine
G. F. Archer
H. W. Hall
Dobrinskoy
P. P. Branch
A. A. Douglas
W. M. Bell
J. Alexander Barns
C. E. Radclyffe
A. Radclyffe Dugmore
Denys Finch Hatton
Elphinstone
W. Gordon Cumming
R. C. Cunninghame
G. S. Rowley
W. R. Baker

who was killed in the 1914–18 war by the bullet of a German sniper in the Africa he loved so well. Alexander Barnes, R. J. Cunninghame, J. Stevenson Hamilton (who wrote one of the best of all books on African game—*Animal Life in Africa*) and W. D. M. Bell, the author of *The Adventures of an Elephant Hunter*, have all left names famous in the Dark Continent. A. F. R. Woolaston, who was shot by an undergraduate at Cambridge, also was an African traveller. St. George Littledale, Cumberland, and Jack Miller, a great friend of mine, specialised in Asiatic travel and secured some wonderful trophies. Douglas Carruthers made a trip with the latter. The author of *Unknown Mongolia*, he also adventured in Arabia and killed the rare Arabian oryx. One could write a book on the adventures of these distinguished men. Gerald Legge, a brother of the present Lord Dartmouth, was killed in the first world war. A charming and delightful man, he had great knowledge of bird life. Of Lord Lonsdale I have written in *Happier Years*. It is unlikely that a future generation will produce so striking a personality. Denys Finch Hatton died as a young man in an accident, regretted by all who knew him. Archie Dunbar Brander wrote the best book of all on Indian game—*Wild Animals in Central India*. F. M. Bailey's adventures in the last war are unsurpassed even in fiction. Charles Howard Bury, who was in the same house with me at Eton, led the first Everest expedition. As I have said, the adventures and journeys undertaken for the love of the game by these men would fill a book, if not many books. I have mentioned but a few. They are all outstanding.

One of the most interesting experiences which a knowledge of natural history brought me was a visit to the late Duc d'Orleans, a year or two before his untimely death. Mr. Burlace, the late managing director of Rowland Ward's, who has befriended so many hunters of big game, accompanied me to the Manoir d'Anjou, near Brussels, where the Duke's collection was housed. Our object was to tabulate and classify the enormous number of trophies. The Duke

was a charming man, and lived for many years in England.
Being heir to the French throne, he was not permitted by
the Government to live in France, and made his home in
Belgium. A great traveller and sportsman, he was in appearance not unlike his ancestor, King Henry of Navarre.

The chief feature of the museum was the Arctic exhibit.
Going through a small door in the corner of the huge room,
you found yourself on board a replica of the yacht in which
the Duke visited the Arctic. Mounting the bridge, you were
surrounded by ice-floes on which were grouped representative specimens of many of the Arctic fauna and birds. This
idea was afterwards carried out in a similar manner with
groups of African animals. No description was allowed to
be published during the lifetime of the Duke, but the whole
collection was left to the French nation and housed near the
Jardin des Plantes. Whether it is still in existence and unharmed I do not know. The only collection constructed on
similar lines in this country is that formed by the late Major
Powell Cotton, at Quex Park.

Ever since the days of those early hunters Nimrod,
Tiglath Pileser, and others, men have been ready to under-
go hardships, discomforts, and great personal risk in order
to gratify their love for the chase. This passion, so deeply
implanted in the human heart, is no doubt a relic of the dim
red dawn of man, when the unskilled hunter went supper-
less to bed. Before the last war game was regarded in most
countries as a national asset to be preserved and encouraged.
It has endured many vicissitudes during the past few years
and the visiting sportsman has few countries to which he
can obtain free access. About the only one left in Europe
where he is made welcome is Spain. Here he can still obtain
magnificent sport with the Spanish ibex and chamois, while
the salmon fishing in the north is being carefully looked
after and the conditions improved.

It is curious that though we may claim in this country
to have some of the finest private collections of trophies
from all over the world, and indeed to have been pioneers

in this field, the ordinary public takes not the slightest interest in such matters. The attendance at the British exhibit, which was transferred to London after the close of the International Hunting Exhibition in Berlin in 1937, attracted but a few thousand spectators. On the Continent the annual exhibitions of trophies which were held in various cities were always well attended and visited by large numbers from all classes of the community. Half a million visited the Berlin Exhibition.

When I was a young man I visited nearly all the best collections in this country and many abroad. Generally speaking in variety and excellence of specimens the private museums in Great Britain were unsurpassed, though at the present day the collections in America would take a lot of beating. Now I am constantly receiving letters from friends of mine asking me what they can do with such collections. I wish I knew the answer. In America a famous collection would, as a matter of course, if the owner wished to leave it to any of the great institutions, be set up exactly as he wished, intact. Here, if sufficiently worthy of note, the best trophies might be displayed in the Natural History Museum in S. Kensington, but the majority would disappear. It is a pity that one of the great houses which have ceased to be homes could not be utilised for the housing of such collections. With the advance of "civilisation" these will never be seen again. They might at least serve to show youth what strange animals once peopled the earth.

Among the collections which I described was that of Major Cumberland, the first Englishman to undertake an expedition in pursuit of the great Asiatic sheep. He was followed a year or so later—in 1888, I fancy—by St. George Littledale. This delightful man was one of the limited few who ought to have written on sport. Gifted with a keen sense of humour, great powers of observation, and a capacity for clear and lucid description, the only contributions to the literature of sport from his pen are the three chapters in the Badminton Library.

As a young man I sat next to him at one of the dinners of the Shikar Club. Rather awed by my proximity to the famous hunter, I timidly asked him to what locality his next trip was planned. "To the cemetery, I expect," he answered abruptly; but the twinkle in his eye and the charming smile which accompanied his remark put me completely at my ease, and I spent a wonderful evening in his company. His next trip, I am glad to say, was not to the place specified, and he lived for many years, dying in 1930. May he rest in peace!

A very varied collection was that of Mr. P. B. Vander Byl, who with the Lord Elphinstone and Major C. E. Radclyffe, founded the Shikar Club. A handsome man, with his brown beard and blue eyes, he always reminded me of Sir Henry Curtis in *Allan Quatermain*. Lord Elphinstone's sheep and moose heads are famous and Major Radclyffe has some of the best heads of the latter in the collection of a private sportsman. Actually the finest collection, so far as records go, was owned by Sir Edmund Loder. Though he had travelled all over the world and was a very fine shot, many of the best heads in his museum had been obtained by purchase or exchange. He was an enthusiastic gardener and people came from great distances to see his plants and private zoo at Leonardslee. A taste for gardening seems to run with that for hunting, and many big game shots take to it as they grow older.

Sir Robert Harvey had some fine heads at Langley Park, having shot in North America, India, the Sudan, Kenya, Siam, Burma, Tibet, Newfoundland, Norway and Austria, to name his principal hunting trips.

F. C. Selous's museum, as I have said, was probably that best known to the general public, for his fame as an African hunter was world-wide. It was presented after his death to the Natural History Museum by Mrs. Selous, and one cannot but regret that it was not housed and maintained intact, for to no other collection attaches the same interest. Major Gilbert Blaine has one of the finest collections of African big game and another collection with some magnificent trophies is that at Swythanley Park. It was formed by Sir Philip Brocklehurst and his brother, my old friend "Brock", of whom I wrote in *Happier Years*. J. G. Millais's collection is still intact at his house near Horsham and is remarkable for the variety and excellence of its trophies. There are many others in different parts of England and Scotland, the very names of their owners, beyond their immediate circle of friends, being quite unknown to the majority of people.

It is curious, producing as we have so many famous hunters, that we have never brought forth a great painter of big game, one who would compare with the Germans Kuhnert and Friese. It is true that Joseph Wolf, perhaps the finest animal painter who ever lived, spent his life in England and did all his best work here, but he too was a German. Artists in this country seem, for some obscure reason, to despise subjects dealing with natural history and wild life. I heard of one artist whose pictures, usually dealing with leopards, tigers, peacocks and macaws in attractive colour compositions are obviously "made up." A big, blundering, beef-eating big game hunter, who knew nothing about art, but liked pictures of animals, conceived the idea of getting this painter to accompany him as his guest on a trip in order that he might study wild nature on the spot instead of in the Zoological Gardens. The suggestion was ill-received. "Animal life does not interest me from that point of view," was the cold answer he got. Perhaps the non-existence of a great English animal painter is scarcely to be wondered at.

In these days it is no easy matter to house a collection of big game trophies, apart altogether from the expense incidental in securing them. The only place where they look well in a private house is in a large hall, if the owner is fortunate enough to possess one. They completely overpower small rooms and never show to advantage. A pathetic spectacle is the bachelor who has decorated the house with specimens of his prowess! He decides to add to them a final and supreme trophy, and asks some charming young female to marry him. She assents, and after the honeymoon the first thing she does when she really gets going is to "scrap all that rubbish!" The visitor under the new regime, missing his old friends, tactlessly, perhaps, enquires as to their whereabouts. In reply, he is shown a poky little back room designated "Archie's den," in which his host sheepishly shows him a couple of heads of the smaller species of game which he has managed to secrete there. The bulk of the collection stare with glassy and dust-dimmed eyes at the walls of an outhouse or garage, where they slowly moulder into oblivion. The owner in his less sane moments may wonder if his final trophy outweighs the loss of the majority, and goes off for long walks by himself on spring evenings when "he has smelt wood smoke at twilight." It is then that his wife complains to her friends that "Archie is so difficult!" So, if you want to shoot big game, make quite sure first whom you want to marry.

I may add that such was not my own experience!

> "An' he pints wi' his pipe to the sophy,
> Whaur his wife sits infusin' the tea;
> An' he says: 'Yon's the bonniest trophy
> That ever was won by McPhee!' "

as my old friend the late Patrick Chalmers wrote.

If you want a thing very much and you get it, I have noticed that you very seldom get it in exactly the way you want. Fate or circumstance creates a snag. In the course of my life I have managed to collect a large number of heads of various kinds. It is the custom nowadays rather to belittle their acquisition, and to label their owner a butcher. Though the desire to kill decreases with advancing years, there is very little that I regret in my hunting career. Had I been born in the present century I dare say that I should have been content to photograph wild game instead of killing it. The former is certainly a more difficult undertaking, and to obtain a good photograph of a record head a more desirable achievement than the head itself. Which brings me back to the workings of fate.

My heads for many years were widely scattered. Some were stored and I had not seen them since I got them. The larger mounted trophies found a home in Scotland, where I saw them at intervals. My modest dining-room in a London flat held a few skulls. To house the collection as a whole was one of my great desires, but the expense of building a room large enough to contain them was prohibitive, and it seemed unlikely that my ambition would ever be achieved. Then fate decreed that I should find a home in the Midlands. The house was delightful, part of it built before the days of Elizabeth, but the atmosphere of the Midlands is not conducive to the proper maintenance of trophies. That was the snag. In the garden was a tithe barn, built in 1664, 90 feet long and just under 20 wide. A brick partition cut off a third of it, the floor was uneven; wooden hoardings converted one end into a dark lumber-room, one corner held an obsolete electric light plant, another a carpenter's shop. Wide doors broke the walls, through which in the old days wains laden with corn found entrance. The windows were in the wrong places. The roof leaked, though the old original oak beams, hard as steel, still lent dignity to the structure. It was an unpromising outlook, but my wife said: "This is the place for your heads."

The next step was the arrival of the representative of a big London firm. You could tell he was something very grand, because he was much better dressed than I, and wore a diamond pin. I felt inclined to call him "sir," and he treated me like a well-meaning child. He inspected the barn. At first he was very suave, and brushed aside any question of expense as being something too crude to mention in the circles in which he moved. Then he warmed up, and his aitches began to fly. I did not feel so inclined to call him "sir." He mentioned a thousand pounds as a good basis on which to start the work of restoration. Seeing that he had overshot the mark, he pulled out a notebook and inscribed a series of hieroglyphics which he studied thoughtfully in silence. He then announced that he might be able to do it,

without fireplaces, for £873 16s. 3d. The 16s. 3d. sounded
very convincing and I began to see my visions of a restored
barn fading away. Gauging my mental attitude, he dropped
his deferential manner and adopted what I believe is known
as a hectoring tone. He fancied he had got us! That was
because he thought he was dealing with me. My objections
he pooh-poohed, sweeping them aside with an air of
grandeur which I secretly envied. It was then that he discovered that he was dealing, not with me, but with my wife.
Women have much more courage than men. She turned on
him, and in less than five minutes he was in his car and on
the way back to London.

A local firm came and inspected the barn. They cleared
it out, knocked down the brick partition, filled up the doors,
repaired the walls, removed the carpenter's shop and the
electric light plant, took off the roof, put on a new one fitted
with skylights, installed two fireplaces, laid down a cement
floor, and charged me about half the original figure. So
much for the London representative!

They also introduced me to Frank. Frank was a professional football player until he dislocated his knee and took
to carpentering. He weighed 13 stone, and was as quick on
his feet as a cat. Then the heads began to arrive. I have
hung hundreds of heads and knew pretty well where each
was to go, but even so it was no mean feat to have hung
sixty-five in a day. Some of them were large, and the wall
had to be plugged for each one. Without Frank it would
have taken at least three days. He was the quickest worker
I have ever seen.

The barn is divided into sections by oak posts which
support the roof. This helped the arrangement of the heads
considerably.

At the north end are the North American specimens.
The two wapiti are very moderate compared with really
good wapiti heads, such as were to be obtained seventy or
eighty years ago. As trophies, secured twenty-five years
later, they are not bad. Hung next to the head which,

originally in the collection of Lord Powerscourt, is now in
the Millais' museum, they would show up very badly. This,
however, is the finest wapiti head I have ever seen. There
is a photograph of it in *The Gun at Home and Abroad*. Below
the wapiti are Rocky Mountain sheep, again moderate. I saw
a much better one, and cut a tuft of hair from his neck at
250 yards ere he went bounding down the hill in a flurry of
snow and was lost to me for ever! Next these are Rocky
Mountain goats, prong-horn antelopes, and mule deer.

These goats are weird animals, and I could never make
up my mind whether they are absolute idiots or extraordinarily well able to look after themselves. There are four, and
after many day's stalking, I got them all in one morning.
The best, an old male, is quite good, but unfortunately the
smoky atmosphere is not improving their condition. After
twenty years in Scotland they were as white as the day I got
them. Now their skins are a dingy grey. The best mule deer
is good, with sixteen points—nothing unusual, though the
normal head carries ten. The record has thirty-seven. My
best prong-horn is a nice head, though nothing great in the
way of length. Over 15 inches is the record in this country,
and mine is 12 inches. He is a most sporting little beast, and
I shall never forget the dry sage-covered plains, the clear
air, and my hunts with Yarnall. The old man must have
died many years ago, as he was no longer young when I
first met him. How I loved his tales of the Wild West and
his adventures as a boy!

On the east wall is a mixed collection: an Australian
fallow deer, a descendant of some imported from England;
two New Zealand red deer, a European lynx, a Russian
wolf, a roe from Dorset, chamois, two Polish elk and a
Spanish ibex, a German red deer and a mouflon. The best
New Zealand stag is a fourteen-pointer. When I killed him
in 1907 he was a nice second-class, typical South Island head
with good shape and points, but not to be compared with
really first-class trophies such as were obtained by Lord
Belper in 1925.

The wolf and the lynx I got in 1914, while on a visit to friends in Russia. A bear was my real quarry, but the weather conditions were unfavourable, and I never even saw one.

My first chamois was killed in 1930. When shooting at Karvendal with "the Diplomat" in 1938, I killed a much better one whose horns are in the gold medal class in an international show. The Polish elk I got, too, in '38. I gave something of their history in *Happier Years*. The Spanish ibex is a very pretty representative specimen.

The mouflon and the German stag I killed in the Harz Mountains and Schorfheide in 1937. My adventures there I have also related in *Happier Years*.

Opposite, on the west wall, are my five best Scottish red deer heads. Only one is first-class, a beautiful and almost perfect royal. I got him at Wyvis in 1926. The other four royals, I should describe as nice, second-class heads. They all measure about 32 inches in length, and unless it be something very exceptional, you cannot call a head first-class if it is much under 34 inches. These four, from Benula, Glenkingie, Dundreggan and Glomach, apart from length, fail, when judged strictly, in some respect. The Benula head has a fork on one top and four on the other; that from Glenkingie is very massive, with first-class brows but narrow. The Dundreggan head was a wood stag, and I killed him almost on the march. His points are good but again the span is narrow. He was the first really good stag I ever killed. The head from Glomach is beautiful in shape, of the hoop type, but the third point on each top is very short, which spoils him.

Next this group are six heads, three of them royals, shot by my wife. Nowadays it is nothing for a lady to stalk, but when we married it was very different, and the number of lady stalkers could be counted on the fingers of one hand. They did it for the love of the thing and not, as so many did in pre-war years, because they thought it was the smart thing to do.

Opposite these, on the east wall, is the only group of rare heads in the collection. They all came from China, with the exception of the chinkara gazelle and the blackbuck, which are Indian.

The Kansu stag hangs in the centre. Not so large as the wapiti and bigger than a red deer, he has some of the characteristics of each species. On one side hangs the head of a golden takin, that strange Semitic-looking animal which lives in the highlands of Shensi in Central China. On the other is a burhel or blue sheep, and a malformed roebuck, the only one I got. The Mongolian and Prezwalskis gazelles, both with the soft fur-like hair these animals grow in the highlands of Asia, were killed in the Gobi Desert.

There are a few skulls of the takin and one of a Chinese domestic sheep, which I bought for sixpence (the only head I ever bought!) from a Chinese butcher. Experts on sheep always get very excited over this skull, as it is one of the few known breeds of sheep growing the horns at right angles to the axial line of the skull. The Moldavian or Wallachian breed, which I believe is now extinct, had a similar characteristic, and sheep of this description are common on the Gold Coast of West Africa.

These heads are all I have to show for a journey which occupied nearly a year, but they are all rare, and very few specimens of any of these species have been killed by English sportsmen.

The whole of the south end of the barn contains African heads, most of them killed in Kenya, or, as it then was, British East Africa, in 1908. There is nothing particularly worthy of note, and none of the heads are records, though all are good representative specimens of adult males.

My dear old friend Colonel H. C. Brocklehurst was game warden in the Sudan for eight or nine years. Not a year passed when he did not say: "Why don't you come out?" At last I went. The group on the west wall is the result. There is a good buffalo, very good for the Sudan, with a

c

span of 37 inches; a beautiful Defassa waterbuck, 32 inches by 32 when he fell; a good ariel, or Soemmerings gazelle; a fair roan, reedbuck and ibex from the Red Sea hills; poor tiang and oribi, though I might have got better if I had killed my limit; and last, but not least, what I really went for—a lion and a lioness. It is true that the lions in the Sudan have no manes, or very poor ones, but a lion is a lion, though he be as bald as a coot. It was one of the nicest trips I have ever done, and I enjoyed every moment of it.

Tucked away by the door is a fox's mask, of which I ought really to be very much ashamed. I was once at a crammer's, and the crammer kept a pack of beagles. We were supposed to hunt hares, but our beagles would hunt anything that ran. This was what the fox did. So did the beagles, and so did we. Eventually he went to earth. One youth, more venturesome than intelligent, put his hand down the hole and got it nearly bitten off for his pains. Our quarry's mask should by rights, surrounded by whips, spurs, sporting prints and an edition *de luxe* of Surtees, adorn the den of some member of the very exclusive hunt from which we poached him; though I doubt if the latter would have got so much fun out of him as we did.

The old-fashioned sportsman is in danger of becoming an anachronism, though crowds of "sportsmen" attend race meetings, dog tracks and fill in football coupons. Many still fail to realise that the old type of sportsman was the best friend of the wild life of the countryside. If sport goes there will go too much of the wild life which to many of us is its greatest joy. So when I go into my barn and wander round it, looking at the heads which hang there, it is not just a collection of glass-eyed trophies that I see. Memories are evoked which no money can buy. Dim red dawns and sunsets and the old chant of the sea; lonely hillsides swathed in mist; hot, baking plains from which the sun struck fiercely; dense jungles and park-like vistas with pools of water shadowed by trees. Strange faces peer at me. Wild-looking

Tibetans, clad in fluttering, stained robes; a Masai warrior, slender and erect, half naked, with his lion skin headdress and long spear; a laughing girl in the shadow of a Belgian wood; bearded Russians amid snow-clad firs; a lean figure galloping through the Australian bush; and with them the friends I have loved. Brock, Johnnie and Hugh, the three with whom I shared most intimately reflections such as these; Charles, being chased by an elephant; Tom and Hubert; and all those with whom I have trodden the hills of Scotland for so long; all my Spanish friends—in fact memories of half a century. As Hilton Brown who, with Kipling, almost alone has expressed in verse the unspoken dreams of the big game hunter, writes:

> "In every one of them is locked away
> Some golden memory, some happy day.
> And one has need of such."

For in truth they do indeed take me back to the Land of Heart's Desire, "East from the Mahanadi . . . to Evening Island where the santomingoes are."

Perhaps no one has ever *really* caught one but I, at any rate, have plucked a few of their feathers, sunrise-orange and starlight-blue and even for a few moments seen their crests of flaming scarlet, their purple-golden breasts, and heard their voices which are "like all the music that ever you liked the best." It is not given to everyone to have known that.

III. A RED LETTER DAY

"Set thy face toward the mountains."—EZEK. vi. 2.

IT chanced to fall on September 20th—in a stalker's calendar "The Day of the Roaring"—when I was staying in a far-off Inverness-shire glen a few miles distant from the lovely shores of Loch Ness. The ground was new to me, but motoring up from Inverfarigaig I had passed a fir plantation which looked suspiciously like roe, and my host had very kindly given me leave to go out for a buck when I liked. So, as I started on my two-mile walk to the wood a couple of mornings later, I did not even ask myself whether I was a fool to leave my warm bed at so unseasonable an hour as 4 a.m. Nature herself set any doubts I might have had on that score at rest.

The first faint flush of dawn had not yet quivered in the eastern sky as I walked down the drive, and the only light came from the stars and a bright moon which flooded the sleeping valley. Indeed, it was still dark as I finished my climb, and looked down into the deep and rocky ravine which lay at the back of the plantation; but, dimly, noiseless forms stirred below me, and the first rays of the sun over the hilltops revealed a doe and her kid occupied on their morning meal. I had been told to shoot anything, but not wishing to disturb the whole of the ground at the start, I went quietly back out of sight and continued my way. A few minutes later, as I crossed up out of the plantation there came a rush from a small hollow on my left, and I was just in time to see the hind-quarters of a buck disappearing over the crest. That he was a good beast I could see, and so, sitting down, I pulled out my glass. He obligingly stopped about three hundred yards off, and for some moments stared back. Then he dashed off again, barking and making a great commotion, though I knew that he had not really seen me. Accordingly, for ten minutes or so I lay quiet, for I thought I knew what he would do next, and then rose to follow. I had not gone twenty yards when, across the ravine, I saw something, and putting the glass on him found to my joy that it was the buck. Between us there lay an open flat, where once a saw-mill had stood, and though I started to cross it, I found at once that he must inevitably spot me if I continued. There was nothing for it but to crawl back. This I did, and before going down into the wood took a last look at him. He was lying, almost entirely hidden from view, beneath an old birch tree which overhung the ravine. It stood in a line with three solitary firs, and by these I easily marked the rock, within forty yards of it, which was the most convenient spot for a shot. The greater part of my stalk was simply a walk, but two hundred yards from the birch I had to go very gingerly to avoid striking one of the many boulders which were strewn all over the ground. At last I reached my rock, and peered cautiously over. There was the buck, still lying on the little plateau which the gnarled roots of the birch had formed, fifty yards below me, and utterly unsuspicious of danger. For a moment I watched him, the central figure of the glorious view before me. Below us the ravine dropped steeply away. At its foot were piled the huge grey rocks, lying as they had fallen when the mother cliff first cast them off. Beyond them rose the grey lichen-clad face of the opposite wall of the narrow gorge, full of rifts and crannies, in which adventurous seeds of the birch and mountain ash had fallen, to take firm root. On its summit lay a purple carpet of heather, from which rose the red-stemmed pines. Up the strath, and beyond it, a sea of peaks caught the eye; and over all was the atmosphere of a Highland glen in mid-September, to describe which one would want the pen of a greater even than Walter Scott. As I looked something rose in my throat, and I almost crept back the way I had come, with the "safety" still showing on my rifle and the buck lying beneath the overhanging birch. It would have been the finer thing to do. But then, well— the mood passed, the hunter in me awoke, and you can guess the rest; it is a moment on which I will not dwell. At any rate, he felt no pain, and as I walked back to the lodge I congratulated myself on a good beginning to my day's sport.

Two hours later I started for the "hull" with Duncan and Scott. The former was stalker, and he, as he went, unfolded his plans to me. The wind was going round to the north— the right airt for us—and we all felt optimistic.

"A' thunk, Muster Fraank, we'll be having luck the dee," remarked Duncan as we walked; but for some three hours we kept going up through the deep course of a burn, with frequent stops for spying as a fresh bit of hill opened out from behind the corner of a knoll, yet with never the sign of a beast.

Our optimism began to evaporate. Then, as we spied some distant mosses and peat hags, of which the greater part of the ground was composed, Duncan spotted two stags. They carried nothing very wonderful in the way of heads, but one he thought sufficiently good to kill. They were lying a good four miles off, nor had they moved twenty minutes later, as we again reconnoitred their position from behind some peats. Duncan suggested lunch, in the hope that before that function was completed they would have enabled us to settle our future movements by rising. So we lay there; I, on my back, thinking that it was much better than the grimy Temple, where in another fortnight's time I should be trying to concentrate my thoughts on that fascinating trinity, "Procedure, Pleadings, and Practice," whilst the two men, a little distance apart, watched the deer.

A dark speck came floating up out of the blue beyond Coignafearn, which, as it grew larger, resolved itself into an eagle. When just over our heads he swept round into the wind, the widespread feathers of his mighty wings bending sharply beneath the sudden strain. Slowly he sailed round, his bright eyes turned fiercely down on us; and then in ever-widening sweeps disappeared into the wild fastnesses from which he had come.

Time was getting on and, though the heat haze rendered spying a matter of great difficulty, we could see that the stags had not risen. I proposed a move.

"Weel, sir," said Duncan, "I just think we'd better. I hearrd a shot over the mairch, and I was hoping it would ha' put some deer over; but likely they'll no come so far." So we prepared to leave. It was then that Scott, who had the most wonderful sight, suddenly flopped down, with the remark, "Mon, there's deer!" Over the old sheep fence, which indicated the march, a line of black dots were stringing. The shot which Duncan had heard had done its work—well enough for us at any rate; and when we got the glasses on them I saw that my luck had not changed. No one spoke at first save Scott, who, as each head was thrown into relief against the sky-line, exclaimed in heartfelt accents, "Gude Lord! Taalk about staags!"

They certainly were a good lot. There was a very dark, heavy-looking switch, a nice eight-pointer, a dozen or so other stags, but the pick of the whole lot was an eleven-pointer; he was one of the finest-looking stags I have ever seen when in motion. They came slowly down the hill, every now and then looking back. We followed the direction of their gaze, and saw another lot of deer, all small stags with one exception, standing by the fence, irresolutely watching their companions. At last they made up their minds what to do, and fed quietly along just over the march, while the first lot still came on down the hill. They were only about a quarter of a mile off, and we had to crawl very carefully into the bed of the old burn, from which coign of vantage we could watch their movements with greater safety.

"Waatch them when they get the scent of our tracks," said Duncan; "I hope the brutes wull gang awa' doon the hull!" Almost as he spoke the leading stag, a small six-pointer, stopped dead and threw his head up. The other deer followed suit, and a grand picture they made. I have seldom witnessed a more striking example of the wonderful power of scent which red deer possess, for it was fully an hour and a half since we had passed that way. For some awful minutes it was a toss-up whether they would turn back or not; then we uttered a prayer of thankfulness as the six-pointer continued his way down the hollow. Waiting until the last stag had disappeared, we doubled on in time to see a number of deer slowly moving away from us into the burn. Through the glass I made out a switch, and so jumped to the conclusion that they were our beasts, when Scott, who saw no reason for uselessly varying his conversation, again ejaculated, "Mon! there's deer!" Sure enough, lying on a hilltop a mile or so off were twenty to thirty smallish beasts; whilst over a knoll, within four hundred yards of us, were the tops of some other stag's horns. On Scott's excited mutterings becoming intelligible we understood him to say that he saw the head of the one and original switch among them.

I was sure he had gone down the burn with the other deer, but, on looking through the glass, my convictions wavered, and were finally dispelled, for there, never to be mistaken, was the eleven-pointer! A rapid glance over the other heads assured us that they were indeed the first lot of deer we had seen, and the others which had moved down the burn a fresh herd entirely.

We were very much exposed, but a wet and careful slither brought us into the concealment of some peat hags, and, leaving Scott there, Duncan and I, by dint of pulling ourselves along a few yards at a time on tussocks of deer grass, got within a hundred and twenty yards of them. They were all lying down, their horns and one or two heads just showing above the hollows in which they lay. On the left some small beasts, well to the fore, of course, whilst the switch, with two other stags, was in the middle. Between the two several good beasts were lying together, it being almost impossible to pick out the horns of any individual stag from the cluster which they formed. One of these stags, Duncan declared, was the eleven-pointer. From the moment when we first saw them until our last spy, he and the switch had kept side by side, never separating; then he had moved away to the left all by himself, and in the cluster of horns before us I could detect no well-defined cup, such as he carried on his left horn. So taking the glass from Duncan, I carefully slid it round a tussock. There, framed in the circle, just where we had last seen him, were the well-known horns showing above the waving deer grass, and I was happy. It might be cold; I might have to wait two hours for a shot; all the qualifications necessary for a chill might be there ready; yet within a hundred and twenty yards of me was a herd of deer and by my side was a rifle!

Duncan, as we lay there in the peat bog, reopened a question which had been discussed earlier. He was very anxious for me to take the switch first if he gave a good chance; but Scott, at this suggestion, had been shocked into loquaciousness. "Maan!" said he, "you'll never tak' yon brute furrst, wi' thaat graand eleven-pinter before ye. Whaat an aaful sin! But, O maan! A' wush he'd another pint!"

Anyhow, Duncan and I argued it out, and settled that I should take whichever of the two rose first, and trust to luck for obtaining a second chance. From 3.30 until 5.15 did we lie there. Once an old cock grouse, unconscious of the tremors he brought with him, settled on a hummock just behind us. A prolonged investigation apparently satisfied him as to our harmlessness, and he presently departed, his warning "Go back! go back! go back!" unuttered. Occasionally one of the smaller stags would rise, stretch himself, and then lie down again. Once the switch got up—a three-quarters view—and I had the rifle levelled, waiting till he should turn his side to me. Then, as my finger curled round the trigger, down he went again. To Duncan's muttered anathema I returned, I must confess, a prayer of thankfulness, for the eleven-pointer had not yet moved; I knew his position to an inch. Every little stone, every little tuft of heather, every burnt patch on the opposite hill which had any bearing on his position, I had noted, so that the opportunity should not find me wanting when it did occur.

I could not see him at all, save the tops of his horns, and those but faintly, for they were very black. Then the chance came! A dark cloud rolled slowly from before the face of the sun, whilst a ray of light fell directly on the deer. It lit up each stag in turn, like the beam of a passing searchlight, throwing their heads into strong relief against the dark background of the hill beyond. It was one of the finest natural pictures I have ever seen, and for a moment my thoughts wandered. Then, with something like a shock, I turned again to my bearings; but they had vanished as the stag rose! Even as I looked, he moved, and I raised myself above the tussock.

Duncan said never a word, but with the tail of my eye I saw him biting his lip. For a second or so the eleven-pointer stood there, and I felt a brute. Then, at the crack, he turned a complete somersault and fell back among the peats, stone dead. The other deer had all risen, and were standing in a bunch; but the dark coat of the switch rendered him easily recognisable; and as he moved forward I fired. He fell at once, but, regaining his feet, struggled a few yards. Then as another bullet struck him he too passed into that shadowy forest where marches are not, and was at rest. My luck had held!

IV. BIG GAME IN EUROPE AND CHAMOIS IN PARTICULAR

"For all good hills I give my thanks as through this world I go."
FRIENDLY MOUNTAIN—Hilton Brown

DISTRICTS in which big game, or such of it as still exists in Europe, can now be found are for the most part barred to the visiting sportsman. There are, in any case, few uncontrolled areas left where animals can wander unchecked or where the adventurous hunter can roam without coming up against existing and established rights. Every year the world grows smaller and the numbers of game decrease. There are but few areas privately owned; and game in a democratic age has but little chance of survival. Some democracies, it is true, prior to 1939, realised the value of their native fauna as a national asset and, as a means of attracting money to their country, gave it all the support they could. It was the right outlook though in many cases it came too late. Before the last war I had hopes of writing a book on European big game but I, also,

45

am too late and such brief notes as I have been able to collect on game which I have myself hunted must suffice.

Big stags were still to be got on the eastern borders of Europe and in the forests of Austria, Hungary, and Germany before the recent war. They had suffered much in the first war, and the conditions under which they existed approximated more closely to the democratic state prevailing in other parts of Europe. Sport in Austria prior to 1914 was conducted on very much the same lines as in feudal times. In most places where the control of game laws is in the hands of the people, the game itself has but little likelihood of continued existence. The best chance it then has is when it is realised that in its preservation lies a probable source of income.

The European bison, if it still exists, cannot be far from the point of extinction. In the forest of Bielovieza in Poland the last specimens were preserved by the Tsar. Some, prior to 1939, still lingered in a wild state in the Caucasus, where they were much harried by poachers. Poaching, of course, on the Continent is a very different thing from what it is in this country. There the poacher is almost invariably a man who poaches from a love of sport and not as a financial proposition. They are always armed, as are the guardians of the game, and when they encounter each other they both shoot to kill. Many stories are told of homeric encounters which did not always end in a victory for the keeper.

Elk still linger, I presume, in Poland, Siberia and Norway, the best heads coming from the former country. They cannot of course compare with those of the Alaskan moose. These, the red deer, the roe and the reindeer where they did survive, owed their existence to sportsmen without whose protection, save in very remote districts, they would have completely vanished. Bears and wolves are yet to be found though the former are rare. The latter, if anything, increased during the war years. They are numerous in parts of Russia; a good many are killed normally in France, and they are also found in Spain. In England these animals survived until the reign of Henry VII, and in Scotland until the beginning of the last century. It is claimed that the last wolf in the latter country perished in Glen Urquhart, though there are as many pretensions to this honour as there are beds in which Queen Elizabeth slept, or caves in which Prince Charlie sought refuge.

In Northern Piedmont, the National Park of the Gran Paradiso, once the hunting ground of the Dukes of Savoy, is now controlled by an independent body, subsidised by the Italian Government, together with local authorities of Aosta and Turin. Here is the last home of the Alpine ibex, with the exception of the Swiss National Park. The mouflon is still found in Sardinia and was successfully established in various parts of Germany. The wild sheep of Cyprus is preserved in this island; and in some of the Ægean islands and the Caucasus, the pasang, or wild goat, is to be found.

Spain is particularly well off for big game which is now strictly preserved. A friend of mine there wrote to me not long ago to say that he was one of the few Spaniards to have killed specimens of every variety. These included bear, ibex, chamois, red deer, stag, roe, wild boar, wolf and lynx.

Count Pali Palffy, that versatile and entertaining hunter, known throughout Central Europe, was kind enough to invite me to the Carpathians in 1939 but the war put an end to that with many other things. That any British sportsman will be in a position to undertake the pursuit of such game for a very long period seems highly improbable. The European bison I saw in Bielovieza in 1938. An article on the present state of these animals appeared in July, 1949, in the Journal of the "Fauna" Society.

Some magnificent roe heads were shown in Berlin in 1937 from Rumania and Poland which, I fancy I am right in saying, holds the record for a European head of this species.

Fallow deer are found in many parts of Europe, but probably the finest examples are not superior to the best heads from Petworth or Drummond Hill. The latter place is now owned by the Forestry Commission and where the Forestry Commission is there will the eagles most certainly not be gathered together. They would have a job to get a meal. Fallow deer on the Continent were normally, as in this country, extremely capable of looking after their own safety.

Before the Second World War, the bachelor sportsman could get very much more for his outlay by renting some stalking on the Continent than by going to Scotland. Such was often based on a graduated scale. A big stag with over twelve points might cost him £40, a smaller one £30, and so on. A miss was charged so much; for a wounded beast he was mulcted more heavily. Prices, of course, varied with localities and a really big stag or a fine elk might cost the foreign sportsman £100. Advertisements appeared in the best sporting papers though it was always advisable for the intending lessee to make careful enquiries from some friend who really knew local conditions or he might find that these did not come up to his expectations. Whether such holidays will again be possible remains to be seen. The outlook at the moment is far from rosy.

In many places wild boars are plentiful, though they are not any too popular with agriculturalists, as they do a great deal of damage. I shall refer to these animals later when talking about sport in Belgium, where I served my novitiate though I have also shot them in Spain. Like any game animal a boar can present a very difficult target. The last one I fired at in Belgium was at one of those little intimate shoots with a few friends and one or two hounds, which I much prefer to a large "set piece." I knew a boar was in the covert, for I heard the hounds giving tongue. Presently something flickered through the trees and scrub in front of the vide where I stood. Then I heard a crackle in the undergrowth. A shadow came to rest ten yards from me on the edge of the bushes. It was cold and I had on various borrowed coats and woollies. These I used as an excuse subsequently when explaining why I had missed. The boar, for it was a boar, having quickly reconnoitred the position, shot across the noe with the celerity of a rabbit and into the bush on the bank beyond. The two bullets from my (borrowed) over-and-under gun did some damage to the bank and some saplings. Otherwise everything was as before except that Françoise took the opportunity to make some caustic remarks about elderly Scotsmen who couldn't see.

A friend of mine went wild boar shooting in France. The host explained that no stags were to be shot as the district was hunted by a ducal pack whose owner lived near by. The rifles were lined up. The drive started. Almost at once a very fine fourteen-pointer emerged close to my friend, moved slowly along the covert until aware that he was being watched, when he moved in again among the trees and out of sight. Almost at once there came the sound of two shots. The rifles assembling at the end of the beat, it was discovered that the host himself had fired both barrels of his shot-gun into the unfortunate animal, thereby spoiling any chance the ducal hunt had of any sport. My friend and another Englishman were not slow in expressing their views of such conduct, views shared by a V.I.P. of royal birth who was one of the other rifles.

Such were considerably strengthened by subsequent events.

The next morning the V.I.P. was requested to take a telephone call. His former host apologised for disturbing him. His reason was that the duke had heard about the fourteen-pointer and had expressed his views pretty forcibly. What the host wanted to know was, would the V.I.P. whose word would carry so much weight, be so very kind as to, in his turn, ring up the duke and say that one of his English friends, Englishmen being notoriously bad linguists, had failed to understand the instructions given before the shoot as to killing deer and, thinking no harm, had slain the unfortunate stag. That was all.

For sheer, unadulterated nerve this request takes a lot of

beating. So thought the V.I.P. He told the gentleman on the telephone that had he been the host there would have been a car by his side within five minutes and that the culprit would have left then and there, nor would he ever again have had the opportunity of shooting wild boar, let alone stags, in his company.

The chamois probably provides about the best sport to be found in Europe today; though with him I would bracket the Spanish ibex, that fine mountain goat which is unique and found nowhere save in the Peninsula. The pursuit of both these animals entails great exertion, a cool head, and good marksmanship on the part of his pursuer. The ground on which they live is steep and difficult, becoming really dangerous in wet weather. To enjoy the pursuit of mountain game of this description one should be young, in good condition, and accustomed to the sport.

I never for one moment dreamt that the "Lonely Lady," for so we dubbed her, who daily walked along the Nile bank would lead me to my first chamois. Being of a shy disposition, I never ventured to address her. Her tall, erect figure passed each evening through the hotel lounge without a head-turn or a gesture to show that she was aware of the existence of other mortals. Slowly she would pace out of sight, while we speculated as to who she might be. That she was a foreigner was obvious. Obvious, too, that she was "hochgeboren." Whether she could talk English or not was uncertain, for she never addressed a word to anyone. The hotel proprietor said she was Hungarian. Though she looked so lonely, though I had always wanted to meet a Hungarian as well as shoot a chamois, to advance and address her in English and to be ignored or answered in a foreign tongue was more than I could face. Several times I was on the point of screwing up my courage, but when it came to the point and that tall, aloof figure appeared, I collapsed. Then I really did collapse with an attack of dysentery, and Charles, the debonair Charles, who visited me daily, stepped into the breach. He reported that she was charming, that she spoke English, and that she had made enquiries as to my health. Dysentery is an unpleasant complaint, but if it had not been for that, I told Charles, he would have been snubbed. Then my wife joined me in Khartoum, and presently we left for Luxor. On the platform was the "Lonely Lady," lonely no longer, for accompanying her was her husband. She came up and spoke to us, and we discovered that we were travelling home on the same boat. It was an Italian boat, and I very soon discovered that her husband was one of the best "raggers" I had met for some time.

At Naples we visited a small restaurant where an Italian football team, decked with large rosettes, were partaking of a meal. It was quite obvious that, as foreigners, we aroused a certain amount of interest. Every head was turned in our direction. The husband of the "Lonely Lady" grasped the situation in a second. He marched in, stood stock still, and flung up his hand in the Fascist salute. There was a roar of applause, under cover of which we slunk to our table. It was a most uncomfortable meal, as enthusiastic members of the football team would keep jumping up and drinking our healths. To these cordial gestures we could do no less than respond. They finished their meal before us, stood in a line, saluted, and walked out, full of smiles and friendly hand-wavings. But all that happened over twenty years ago.

We left the "Lonely Lady" in Naples with her husband, but not before we had received a cordial invitation to visit them in Switzerland that autumn.

It was late August when we met again.

After the gloom of the Midlands it was very pleasant to sit on a sun-bathed terrace looking across the fields to where the Rhine slid past the towers of Gottlieben, dreaming, bowered in trees of past glories. Here you may see in one of the towers the wooden cage which held John Huss for six long, weary weeks before he went to his death at the stake five hundred years ago. Beyond the chateau, on the south bank, is the house which Eugene de Beauharnais built

D

and in which Queen Hortense lived long after her great stepfather had ended his stormy life on that bare rock so far away in the Atlantic.

Very pleasant it was, too, to stroll through the woods when the evening shadows lay far athwart the lush green meadows. It was then that the roe showed red and clear in the sunlight, and here I have seen so many as ten together, and more than twenty in an evening. It would be possible to develop really first-class roe stalking in this part of Switzerland. Under the existing laws, however, by which the shooting is put up to auction every few years, it would be very difficult to arrange and a very expensive proceeding. Anything more infuriating than to own ground of this nature and to be compelled to listen to the local butcher and his syndicate of fellow "sportsmen," warmed with wine, slaughtering the poor little deer with shot-guns I cannot imagine. My poor host suffered tortures, and I am quite sure that in his place I could not have stood it.

Golden was the weather, and those are days which I shall never forget. Not least the voyage down the lake in the little white steamer, past smiling country dotted with cheerful red-roofed houses gay with flowers, spired churches, and old grey castle walls. At times I fancied that I was back in the old days on Loch Ness. There was the same important clanging of bells as we arrived at a pier, the same mild, leisurely bustle, the same influx of "touries," only here each tourist, male or female, however strangely, to our eyes, garbed, was burdened with that most useful of all travelling contrivances, the rucksack.

At the far end of the lake rose mountains, blue and silver, towering into golden clouds which shredded about their tops. Below them was Austria.

From the steamer we changed into a little mountain train, which puffed importantly into each diminutive wayside station. Not that we minded the delays, for each was full of new charm: country women, soberly dressed in black, with flat black hats, typical black pleated skirts with a narrow blue line, and black aprons; men in leather shorts, with Tyrolean hats decorated with chamois "barts"—all of a type which, apart from dress, you might have seen years ago at any Highland railway station.

All mountain scenery has points of similarity, and comparisons, to a Scotsman, were inevitable. There were, of course, obvious differences, but many and pleasing likenesses, mainly among the people themselves. The tanned faces were the same; the gait was the same; the expressions were the same; and one bearded old gentleman might have walked, just as he stood, out of any of a hundred whiteharled cottages which I have known all my life.

At the terminus, a village set in the heart of the hills, we left the train and embarked on a nine-mile motor drive. A clear blue mountain stream bore us company all the way, laughing, twisting, and winding below the road, here contracted in a narrow gorge, there swelling into a placid pool.

It was late in the evening when we arrived at the shooting lodge, and never did I feel on more familiar ground than when I saw, seated on a low knoll, armed with long sticks and glasses, three stalkers. They were spying for deer, as I have no doubt many a stalker was spying outside many a lodge in my own country. Deer, too, we saw. Young stags, all of them, but each must have weighed some 20 stones.

The dawn had not yet broken, when at 4.30 the following morning there came a knock at my door. It was still dark as we went up the glen. With me were Brugger, the head stalker, well known to many English sportsmen in the past, and Hamerle, for whose beat we were bound. The former was a great character, and I much regretted the fact that I was unable to talk to him in his own language. The ex-Crown Prince of Germany had rented the forest for ten years or so prior to 1914, and was very fond of the old man. He insisted that Brugger should visit him in Berlin, and after a good deal of persuasion the latter consented to go. During his stay his host sent him one night to the opera and gave him a box close to that in which was seated the Kaiser. Subsequently he asked him what he thought of the war lord.

"Oh," said the old stalker, "he looks healthy enough!" Which was certainly not the answer expected.

On the last day of his visit the Crown Prince said to him: "Well, Brugger, now tell me, which part of your visit have you enjoyed the most?" To which without any hesitation he replied: "To be going back to the mountains."

I have met many Highland stalkers whose outlook on life and whose mentality were exactly on a par with this dear old Austrian. Nearly every Austrian I have encountered has been perfectly charming, and of them and of the little I saw of their beautiful country I cherish the most delightful memories.

Both these stalkers wore, stuck in the back of their green felt hats, the curving feather of a blackcock, Brugger's being fastened with a gilt W surmounted by a crown, given him by the Crown Prince.

The road on which we travelled had been constructed by Russian prisoners of war, and a very good job they had made of it. I fancy the local inhabitants would have raised no objections if they had been kept where they were sufficiently long to have completed it. Beneath a white-walled, thin-spired church in the centre of a small mountain village it petered out into a narrow track. Up this we climbed. Cow-bells were beginning to tinkle and signs of life to become apparent as we rose higher.

It was a couple of hours from our start that I spied my first chamois, four in number, feeding unconcernedly above us, but they were females with kids. Past a small croft we followed the track, and then the two jaegers settled down for a spy. The place which claimed their attention was a rock-face stretching for half a mile and more beyond the river above which we lay. For fully half an hour they examined every corner of it, and then decided to advance. We crossed the river, and it was at this moment that the inhabitants of the croft decided to get busy. An active young thing of some forty summers, armed with the inevitable umbrella, suddenly skipped into view with a herd of cows. Not unduly incommoded by her activities, they proceeded leisurely on their way. Then two men with a drove of pigs made their appearance. Several youths with another large herd of cows came to life from behind the farm buildings. From whence they all materialised I have to this moment never been able to discover. We were nearly half-way to the rock-face by this time. The pigs grunted, the cows mooed, the bells tinkled (some of the bells are as big as a large cooking-pot, so they "tinkled" at a considerable distance), the lady waved her umbrella and yelled, the men yodelled, and in the middle of it all Brugger suddenly sat down. He sat down so suddenly that I knew something was up. It was. Almost immediately I saw two chamois about 400 yards off. One never really appreciates anything until one has lost it, but I did appreciate the bigger of those two chamois. They were both bucks, and good ones. I am not an expert on chamois, but I could tell that, and also that one was considerably better than the other. If the pigs had not at that particular moment grunted, the cows mooed, the lady yelled, and the men yodelled (there was a horse, too, which I had forgotten; it did not, it is true, make a noise, but galloped madly about and added to the general air of excitement!)— if, I say, all this had not taken place, I might possibly have got that buck; but I didn't. He was about a quarter of a mile away, and apparently flew up an absolutely perpendicular wall of rock. I fail to see how else he got there! I had my glass on him. At one moment he was at the bottom, the next with a slight momentary hitch in the middle, he was at the top. There he stayed for some minutes in a typical chamois attitude with all his feet bunched below him on a space the size of a threepenny-piece, while he surveyed the pigs grunting, etc., and I fancy we three, trying to make ourselves invisible in the middle distance.

It was very tantalising, and after some little time we tried to get in, failed, and saw the chamois mount steadily higher and higher until at last we lost sight of them. After a long climb of an hour and a half Hamerle, who was leading, jumped them again, and though the good buck stood for a second at 180 yards I did not have a chance to fire.

Inability to talk the language of one's hunter is the greatest drawback with which the stalker in strange country has to contend, and though during this particular incident the result, had I spoken German, would probably have been the same, I was at a great disadvantage throughout the day.

Later on we found a herd of about thirty chamois, and with them a buck, but carrying nothing like as good a head as the one I had first seen. When confronted with a herd of animals, the females of which all carry horns varying only very slightly from those of the males, it is extremely difficult to pick out the latter. Moving across a snowfield at a range of 300 yards I at last made out the buck, and in a very cramped and uncomfortable position not unnaturally missed him.

In September the best bucks are always alone, or with another male. They do not join the females until November, which is the best time to stalk them, as they then carry the much-prized "gemse bard," or beard. This consists of the long white-tipped hairs growing along the spinal ridge. For a really good specimen large sums are paid, £8 or £9 being nothing unusual.

Chamois are much blacker in winter than in summer, when they appear to be a yellowish-grey, which against certain backgrounds looks almost red. The horns of the bucks are stronger and more "pinched" at the curve than are those of the females, though the latter attain greater length at times.

The Continental method of measuring I may say, (1930) was to add three times the greatest beam at the base of the horn to the length of horn in a straight line, plus the length on the curve, plus half the width between the two horns from centre to centre at the top.

The walking is extremely hard at times, for the steep

grassy slopes offer but little foothold, the danger being much greater after rain. Muddy patches on the hillside are very difficult to negotiate, but the worst going of all is on steep, loose shale, which slides beneath one's tread, and on which it is impossible to hold firm even with the aid of a stout Alpine stock. A slip is nothing when stalking in Scotland, though it is as easy to break your neck mountaineering there as in Switzerland, if you want to; but when a slip involves a fall and a slither down a steep face, which may or may not end in a sheer drop of several thousand feet, great care and a cool head are required. The ordinary brogues one wears when shooting in Scotland are useless, and strong boots, well studded with proper Alpine nails, are an absolute necessity. One's life may hang on them.

After my miss we had a long and tiring walk over steep, rocky country, rather of the type which one finds on the "tops" in Scotland. There was one really difficult bit of ground, very steep and covered with loose damp shale, which descended almost perpendicularly to a nasty drop. I was glad when we had passed it. At the foot a wide snow-ringed corrie opened out. Into its centre jutted a rugged bastion of steep rock with practically sheer sides. Round this the mist swirled, for the day had become overcast, and at times completely hid it. As it drove clear, clinging to its topmost crags, silhouetted against the wreathing vapour, we could see dim forms of the chamois we had moved. They were quite unapproachable, as were a dozen or so others which fed or lay on the steep slope of shale beyond this crag.

Over the edge of the corrie shot a waterfall, dropping a thousand feet or more ere it reached the swiftly-flowing river below. Skirting its edge, we crossed the foot of the snowfield to where beyond a smaller corrie climbed steeply to a height of nearly 7,000 feet. It was then that I sympathised with those novices at stalking in Scotland who complain that they know not whither their stalker is leading them nor what are his plans. I was in a precisely similar predicament. I knew not to what heights we were going nor to what goal we were bound. The spirit was willing, but I must confess that the flesh was beginning to flag, and the last 100 yards of the climb tried me severely. It was when, close to the crest of the ridge, I saw Hamerle take off his rucksack and peer over the edge that hope began to revive. He made a remark to Brugger, and though I could not translate it, the tone of his voice made me realise that he meant that there was a buck somewhere close by. I crawled up the last few yards and looked over.

We hung on a spur looking sheer down into a narrow gully which cleft the side of the mountain as though with a knife. It was very rocky, and 3,000 feet below I could see the little church which we had passed so early that morning. As my eye began to focus its surroundings I made out a chamois feeding at the foot of a rocky cliff. Close to him lay another, almost red in colour against the rock, a well-defined black line running down his back. He moved his head alertly, but never looked up. On the better of the two I could have dropped a stone, for he was directly beneath me. Feeling all the while as if it would fall out of my hand, I aimed the rifle. Seeing the motion, Hamerle signed to me to wait till he rose. Knowing that it was my last chance and that he would, clearly, rise before long, I waited. Five minutes later he got to his feet. I was not excited, but I missed! I knew exactly what I had done, and aiming this time well below him, he fell.

A few minutes later the gully was a cauldron of mist in which it was impossible to distinguish anything. Hamerle gave me to understand that I was to go round the back of the corrie with Brugger whilst he retrieved my beast.

I still have the fir twig which he, on the crown of his hat, presented to me when we met two hours later by the road-side, the chamois slung on his back.

The ceremony of presenting the "bruch" used to be a matter of much greater formality than it is now. The fir twig was broken, not cut from the tree, and on the death of a stag or chamois a certain form of words was used on presenting it. Its object was to show those whom the sportsman met on his return that he had been successful, as they might see by a glance at his cap.

The following is the correct form of presentation and the appropriate reply:

ALTDEUTSCHER SPRUCH BEIM DARREICHEN DES BRUCHES

"Vor meinem Herrn hin ich tritt
Mit Waidmansgruss und mit der Bitt',
Es hatein gerecht' Schuss gethan,
Drum soll er den Bruch auch nehmen an,
Und tragen wohl in Freude,
Dem edlen Wild zu Leide.
Braucht Eure gute Wehr'
Allzeit zu Gottes Ehr!"

ANTWORT DES HERRN

"Hab Dank, mein lieber Jager frei,
Trag' alle Weil der Dinge drei:
Wehr' ohne Schart' und Fehl,
Gerarden Sinn ohne Hehl,
Treues Herz ohne Wank,
Habe Dank uberall, habe Dank."

In the event of a stag being killed, the successful sportsman, in addition to the "bruch," was presented with the two single teeth in the upper jaw, which were cut out by the keeper. These were made into pins or buttons.

A novice who had not previously killed a stag, unless he wished to be looked down upon by Austrian sportsmen, was well advised to submit to the ceremony of being "blooded." In Scotland the stalker usually dabs a spot of blood on each cheek. In Austria the performance was more elaborate. The party formed in front of the house where the stag was laid out. The successful stalker was then led up to the spot in solemn procession accompanied by the keepers. He had to kneel down over the stag's body, and round him a ring was formed. He was then struck over the shoulder three times by the leading personage present, or by his hostess, who pronounced the following words: "Der Este Streich für Kaiser und Reich, Der Zweite Streich für Ritter und Knecht, Der Dritte Streich für Waidmannsrecht" (The first stroke for Emperor and Empire, the second stroke for Knight and Serf, the third stroke for the Sportsman's privilege). The novice was thus made free of the forest.

Another rite to which great importance was attached was the gralloch. This, as everyone who has stalked deer in Scotland knows, can be made quite revolting. To see it cleanly and expeditiously performed is one thing, to watch an inexperienced ghillie attack a dead beast as if he meant to tear it asunder by main brute strength is another. A Scottish stalker or ghillie always takes off his coat. A self-respecting Austrian jaeger would never do so. One such, asked the reason for this, replied: "That would be very unsportsman-like. I am not a butcher; butchers do that!"

A properly executed gralloch on the Continent should not leave a spot of blood on the coat-sleeves.

I still hear Hamerle's voice saying, "Waidmannsheil," as he presented me with the "bruch." I hear other voices saying it, too, for it came to my ears many times during my short stay in the mountains of Austria. To these voices, which, alas! I hear only in my dreams, I answer, as I should, "Waidmannsdanks," and though now I am far away, I hope perhaps that they will hear.

V. SPORT IN BELGIUM

"From the earliest times . . . the boar has been one of the favourite beasts of the chase."

ENCYCLOPÆDIA BRITANNICA

IN 1932 I was asked to act as the British judge at an Exhibition of Sporting Trophies which was being held in Belgium. There is a fellowship of sport which overcomes the difficulties created by the Tower of Babel, and my intercourse with foreign sportsmen during the progress of the exhibition was pleasant and friendly. The exhibits included a large number of red and roe-deer heads and to those who, like myself, had not hitherto regarded Belgium as a sporting country, these came in the nature of a surprise, many of the roe in particular showing very high quality.

The judging itself was not easy, the other three judges and myself not holding precisely similar views on the points to be awarded for each characteristic. Length and thickness seem the greatest attributes a head can possess to Continental sportsmen, and though no head can be first-class without these qualities, a finely-formed symmetrical head with long, even points should, in my opinion, take precedence over a longer and badly-formed trophy with short and ugly points. It is noteworthy in this connection that both the late H. J. Elwes and Johnnie Millais considered that in the great Vienna Show of 1910 not nearly enough value was given to beauty and the symmetry of heads when they were being judged. On this question, however, it is unlikely that British and Continental sportsmen will ever agree, their standards being dissimilar.

Unfortunately no catalogue nor measurements were published, and the photographs of the best heads which were promised never materialised. Consequently I have to rely largely on memory for their details. Certain charges, too, in connection with the loan and freight of some of the British exhibits were left for me to pay. These expenses had been guaranteed by the secretary of the exhibition prior to my consenting to act as judge, and failure to make them good has marred the recollection of an otherwise pleasant experience.

A large number of the thousand roe heads exhibited, it may be admitted at once, might very well not have been shown at all. In an exhibition of this sort it is far better to concentrate on the best heads from each individual collection. Numbers are of no value save as an indication of the energy of the stalker, and the observer derives no benefit from the spectacle of a large number of mediocre skulls and horns. The display of all the heads from the collection of an individual has one advantage. It is possible to tell whether the sportsman is "out for blood" or whether he has stalked and picked old bucks in preference to indiscriminate massacre. To the credit of exhibitors it may be stated at once that by far the greater proportion of heads shown were those of old bucks. Very few mounted heads were shown, Continental sportsmen, as a rule, preferring only the skull and horns. Generally speaking, compared with British roe, those from Belgium are heavier, thicker, more roughly pearled, and, I think, longer, though the best heads from both countries would vary but slightly in this respect. On the other hand, British heads as a rule are better shaped and more symmetrical. The same, again speaking generally, may be said of Belgian red deer. The Scottish heads exhibited could not compare in·beam with the Belgian, but in shape they were much more graceful and with greater span. The Belgian heads, as a rule, were narrow, owing probably to the nature of their habitat, thick, but with a greater average of points. The skulls are slightly larger than those of Scottish stags and the weight greater. The majority of Belgian red deer and roe come from the Ardennes, about 2,500 roe and 400 to 500 stags being killed annually. It may, perhaps, come as a surprise to British sportsmen to realise that something like a million roe were shot, annually, on the Continent prior to 1939. Most of the roe in Belgium are shot in drives, which seems a pity. At Jannee, the estate of Baron de Woot, about 180 roe are considered the right amount of stock for 500 hectares of wood (1 hectare = 2 acres). At Waillet, the home of Baron Van der Stratan, the proportion is rather less. If the stock becomes too large for the acreage the roe become diseased. They are in bad condition when the winter starts, and fall a prey to a species of maggot, which infests the passages of the nose and throat and works its way to the brain. The only cure is to kill off about two-thirds of the stock.

The season for roe opens on November 1 and ends on January 1, bucks being shot to the end of the month. This seems an unnecessarily arbitrary arrangement, as the finest sport with roe is to be obtained by stalking. The season for buck should at any rate open on June 1 and end in November, by which time their horns are shed. Efforts to have the season altered have, since the Second World War, met with no success.

Some of the best roe ground in the Ardennes and surrounding districts is held by private owners, but a large number of sporting properties are in the hands of syndicates, who only regard the roe as an animal to shoot in the drives which are held in the winter for wild boar. The bucks at this time of the year having in most cases shed their horns, many possible good heads are sacrificed to no purpose.

Syndicate shoots are leased for nine years. In some an arrangement is made by which a rifle is allowed to shoot two bucks by stalking, but as the majority are reserved for driving, this in practice means that if there are eighteen members of the syndicate (about the average number), the individual only stalks two bucks during the whole of the lease.

During the First World War most of the best collections of roe heads were looted by the Germans and all the best heads taken, the horns in many instances being sawn off.

It is interesting to note in this connection that, so sure were the Germans of retaining the occupied territory, that they carefully picked out stags with bad heads and shot them, anticipating an improvement in the stock when they were subsequently free to take advantage of the sport. Similar procedure was followed after the occupation of Belgium in the last war. Very few stags were shot though a good many roe were killed. In the exhibition of post-war heads held in Brussels, December 1946, there were very few recently killed roe heads exhibited for this reason. In 1932 only one collection of roe heads in the exhibition was pre-1914, and that contained a head (killed in 1863) which, as in the exhibition of 1946, was held unanimously to be the best shown.

Of those shown in 1932, it was decided to award marks to the six best heads in each individual collection, points being given for length, beam, shape, and pearling. The head which I have already mentioned was taken as the standard, with 20 marks. The length of this head was $10\frac{5}{8}$ inches; round both coronets the measurement was $10\frac{5}{8}$ inches. The longest head shown measured 12 inches, and the widest $8\frac{1}{4}$ inches tip to tip.

The collection of Baron Hubert de Woot de Trixhe was

awarded 98 marks; that of Baron Jose Van der Stratan Waillet 97 marks. Personally I considered that the latter represented a better normal average than the former, but the 12-inch head to which I have already alluded gained Baron de Woot the extra mark.

The only other measurements of heads I have been able to trace are:

Length.	Tip to Tip.	Round both Coronets.	Killed.
$10\frac{1}{8}$	$6\frac{3}{4}$	$9\frac{1}{2}$	1929
$10\frac{1}{4}$	5	9	—
$9\frac{1}{2}$	6	$10\frac{1}{4}$	1931

The second of these heads was certainly the best-shaped head in the exhibition, and I awarded it the special prize allotted to each judge to dispose of as he wished. A remarkable head killed in 1933 at Dave had the following measurements: Length, $13\frac{1}{2}$; beam, $3\frac{3}{4}$; brows, $4\frac{3}{8}$; tops, $4\frac{3}{4}$; back points, $3\frac{3}{8}$; round coronets, $11\frac{1}{8}$. Horns straight, thick, and narrow. It was figured by me in the *Field*, February 3, 1934. The following were the best red deer heads:

No.	Points.	Length.	Beam.	Span.	
1	6 + 5	39	$8\frac{1}{2}$	29	} 1st Prize
2	9 + 8	38	$7\frac{1}{4}$	29	
3	7 + 7	35	$6\frac{1}{4}$	24	17-inch brows. 2nd Prize
4	7 + 8	$37\frac{1}{4}$	$6\frac{1}{4}$	25	
5	5 + 5	37	$5\frac{3}{4}$	29	} 3rd Prize
6	5 + 5	34	5	29	

An attempt was made at the International Hunting Exhibition at Leipzig in 1930 to record with a certain precision the relative merits of the different heads exhibited by what was known as the Nadler formula.

I will not weary the reader with the discussions and recommendations employed by various distinguished Continental students of horns during the years preceding the International Hunting Exhibition held in Berlin in 1937. After various meetings the Conseil International de la Chasse (of which I have the honour to be a member), finally agreed on a formula which was employed in Berlin and is now used at Continental exhibitions such as that in which I was the British judge in Brussels in 1946.

This is the formula for the antlers of red deer (unless subsequent modifications have been made). Others which are not at present relevant are employed for judging the trophies of fallow deer, roe, chamois, mouflon, bison, wild boar, bear, wolves, lynxes and wild cats.

1. The average length of both horns including the coronet (1 centimetre = 1 mark). Curve on the outside is taken, the tape (steel 5 mm. in width is recommended) following the curve of the horn to the longest point of the top.

   The average length of both horns is multiplied by 0·5 (i.e. a quarter of the sum of the two horns).

2. Circumference of horns between the brow and bay, or tray if the former is absent, measured at the thinnest point (1 cm. = 1 mark).

3. Circumference of both coronets (1 cm. = 1 mark).

4. Average length of both horns divided by 4 (1 cm. = 1 mark).

5.   ,,   ,, ,, ,, trays   ,,   ,, (1 cm. = 1 mark).

6. Weight with small skull in kilograms multiplied by 4 (1 kg. = 2 marks).

   (Small skull means that the lower part has been sawn off as if for mounting on a shield. The majority of Continental trophies are treated in this way. According to the amount of skull left points may be added or deducted.)

7. Spread. Maximum inside span between tops.

   This is expressed as a percentage to the average length of the sum of length of both horns.
   Less than 60% of average length   = 0 points
   From 60% to 70% of average length = 1 point
   More than 70% of average length   = 2 points

8. Points. Artificial tops, or points, and completely broken points are not counted.
   Each point = 1 mark.
   A point must have a length of 2 centimetres to be counted. Two or three small points may be counted as one.

9. General appearance left to individual appreciation of judges.

To the points found by measurements may be added "points of beauty" or marks may be deducted for "faults":

1. Top, crown, cup or "hand"
    (a) Simple top, short, weak points, in all 5–7 points including both tops = 1 mark
    (b) Simple top, with points longer and stronger in all 5–7 = 2–3 marks
    (c) Simple top, with long, strong points in all 6–7 points; a double crown or one with ramifications and shorter and weaker points, in all 8–9 points = 4–5 marks
    (d) a double crown or one with ramifications and long, strong points, in all 8–9 points = 6–7 marks
    (e) strong top in shape of chandelier (scoop, cup or hand) with strong, long points and at least 10 points = 8–10 marks
    When appreciating merit of top, short points are those with points of 5–10 cm.; average length 10–15 cm.; more than 15 cm. —long (at the curvature).

2. Very small points can be given 0–2 marks, i.e. 2 marks for small, normal, regular points on each antler.

3. *Colour*

					Marks.
Light yellow ⎫					
Yellow ⎬ colour ..	..	..	..	0
Artificial ⎭					
Light brown—or grey ..	..	..	..	0–5
Brown	..	..	..	..	1
Dark brown ..	..	..	..	..	1–5
Black ..	..	..	..	..	2

4. *Pearling*

Beam or top—smooth ..	..	..	..	0
Lightly pearled ..	..	..	..	1
Good rough pearling ..	..	..	..	2

5. *Points of tops and crown*

Tops dark or splintered	..	..	..	0
Good white points	..	..	..	1

Faults may be deducted: For irregularities, malformations, exaggerated width in proportion to main beams.

To obtain a gold medal in international competition a head must be awarded over 210 marks:

A silver medal ..	..	..	..	200–210 marks
A bronze „ ..	..	..	..	190–200 „

E

Central European sportsmen speak of a head in weight and not in number of points, arguing that the heavier the head, the better the stag irrespective of appearance.

Example (of a fourteen-pointer)

Length of two antlers 85 + 87, av. 86 × 0·5 = 43
Circumference of antlers below trays
                    13·5 + 13·5 × 1 = 27
    „   of antlers above trays   = 25
                    12·5 + 12·5 × 1 = 25
Length of brows 28·5 + 27 ÷ 2 × 0·5   = 13·9
  „   „ trays 26·8 + 25 ÷ 2 × 0·25   = 6·6
Span between main beams 65·5 = 76%   = 1
Weight 4·5 kg. × 2   = 9
Number of points 6 + 8 = 14   = 14
Cup (point of beauty) 4–7   = 7
Outer points   = 0·5
Colour—dark brown   = 1·5
Pearling   = 2·0
Colour of tips of cup   = 1

                              151·5
    Penalty—points small and splintered   − 1

                              150·5

We, in Great Britain, have not so great a wealth of wild life. We have only the roe and the red deer, for wild fallow deer are rare. Nor do we indulge in annual horn exhibitions. Our red deer, compared with those to be found on the Continent, are small, both in numbers and horn. Consequently the same standards do not apply. British sportsmen are a conservative race and it is unlikely that they will employ standards for judging trophies other than those to which they have, though comparatively recently, become accustomed.

Messrs. Rowland Ward—to be exact in 1892—laid down certain standards of measurement which have become established in this country. Nor, with a limited field in every sense of the word, are others necessary.

These formulæ employed by sportsmen on the Continent arriving at a standardised system of measurements have one ultimate aim in view. That is to enable the sportsman (for it is on his behalf that these learned gentlemen sit up all night with hot towels around their throbbing brows evolving formulæ which leave me, personally, often in a state of bewilderment, for I have always been an atrocious mathematician) to estimate the value of his trophies in comparison with those of a rival. For long I held that all such attempts were bound to fail.

We take the greatest length of horn, we take the measurement of the beam between the brow and tray or between the bay and tray, we take the span, we take the spread, we take the number of points, the colour of the horns, their roughness and any other particulars we like. We put them all down on paper. We compare them with the measurements of some rival head, and where are we? Probably firmly fixed in our original opinion that our head is as good as, if not better than, the other!

We may scrutinise as closely as we can the data concerning any particular woman. We may put down her height, her weight, the length of her hands, the colour of her eyes, her hair, the sum total of her charms. The study of these will enable no student to name with any certainty, except that in the opinion of other students he will certainly be regarded as an ignorant and self-opinionated fool, the most beautiful woman in the world.

Such measurements and such data do not and cannot take into account the infinitesimal curves, the subtle gradations of form, which compel us to say that one woman is more beautiful than another.

When I was in Spain I held great arguments with Conde Eduardo Yebes, a very well-known sportsman and artist in that country, on this point. We each drew up a list of lady's attributes which we considered should be awarded marks totalling up to 300. Our maximum for each of these varied, as those of experts on the horns of the cervidæ vary. I will not go into details, merely remarking that a certain lady being taken as an example I allotted her 273 out of the total. My formulæ card having been basely betrayed to her I was overwhelmed with confusion.

Similarly a list of measurements and weights fails to enable the sportsman to say with any certainty which is the better of two heads. One may be a little longer, the other a little thicker. One may have more points, the other may have tines which are longer and more finely shaped. Even at exhibitions of trophies the verdict of judges is seldom, save in very rare instances, unanimous, for each has his own standards, and some quality which may appeal to one is overshadowed by some other characteristic in the opinion of another.

It is well that this should be so. Imagine the chaos if there was but one standard of beauty for woman! We may estimate from measurements and formulæ the class to which a head belongs, but unless we can actually see two or more heads hanging side by side, it is impossible to say which is the better. The final judgment is bound to rest on personal opinion. The whole object of formulæ, however, is to eliminate personal opinion. Having taken part as a judge in many exhibitions of trophies on the Continent I have come to the conclusion that some kind of formula, especially for the judging of stags' heads, is necessary. The choice of the best head must remain a matter of personal taste, irrespective of the total number of marks awarded.

During the course of the 1932 Exhibition which was held at Spa, and which has led to the above dissertation, I met two Belgian sportsmen, ardent roe-stalkers, whom I will call T. and H. That was fifteen years ago and they are still two of my dearest friends. T. insisted that I should return to his home, which I very willingly did. It was slightly bewildering at first. A succession of young men, nearly all of whom were over 6 feet in height, alternated with a bevy of young ladies, varying in age from slightly over twenty to somewhere about seven, in greeting me. Never in my life did I so regret that I had not learned to speak French, though my regret was modified by the fact that they all spoke excellent English. They were my host's brothers and sisters, though, when meeting their mother, you would never have suspected it. Vying with each other as they did in making me feel at home, I recall these days as full of fun, laughter, and happiness. When I visited Brussels in 1946 I, again, stayed with this charming family whose home for the second time in a generation had been occupied by the German hordes. Perhaps at a later date I shall be able to enlarge on this visit. Suffice it to say here that all the daughters, some of whom I knew as children, are all married, save one. My particular friend is now the mother of five children though her charm has, if anything, increased and she is still the darling she was when I first met her. So is advancing age brought home to elderly gentlemen like myself.

T. and I spent several early mornings after roe. The undergrowth was very thick and the food in the woods abundant. There was consequently very little inducement for the bucks to emerge from their thickets in search of sustenance. I saw only two good ones, and these both eluded me. One evening I spent stalking with H. Just as it was getting dark we found a nice buck feeding in a ride. It was very hot, I was dripping with perspiration, my glasses were covered with steam, and I had a borrowed rifle! Creeping down the ride as far as I could, I had a shot, which, not altogether to my surprise, I missed.

My visit was followed by an invitation to return in November for the annual drives for roe and wild boar. My wife accompanied me, and though on this occasion I did not get a boar, I was much interested in watching this, to me, new form of sport.

The procedure is as follows: The rifles, to the number of twenty or so, are lined in accordance with their numbers along a ride facing a wood. At each end of the wood are fifteen or twenty beaters. At a blast on a horn the two lines advance to meet in the middle, and continue their progress to the opposite end of the wood. This "combing" is an excellent method, for a beast that has squatted (I am speaking chiefly of roe) is almost always moved by the second line advancing. The beaters, who struck me as a cheery crowd, know their work well and keep an excellent line. They then got about 25 francs a day, with beer.

The shoots in Belgium at which I have been present as a guest have always been very well run and excellently organised. All the Belgian sportsmen I have met have been very careful, and in most cases good shots. It takes skill to hit a galloping roe crossing a ride, the majority of such shots being snaps after the animal has passed.

Boar roam about a great deal, and on this particular occasion we saw none. When moved they go in single file, and if the leader is killed the others go on. The average weight of a good boar on the fringe of the Ardennes is about 80 kilos (roughly 160 lbs.). The record at T.'s shoot is 186 kilos, and, so far as I know, that for Belgium 210 kilos. A wounded boar is a tough animal to tackle, and inflicts a nasty wound with its sharp tusks. The sows bite. On a subsequent occasion one of the rifles wounded a boar, which charged him. He not unwisely ran away, when his hat fell off. This the boar charged, and amid a good deal of chaff he reappeared at the end of the beat with his hat covered with blood-stains. In three days' shooting we killed sixty-five roe, nine of the bucks carrying horns, one being a good head. I have seen a buck with horns, another which had just shed, and a third which had shed one horn, killed in the same drive. The first day resulted in thirty-one, the second in sixteen, and the third in eighteen. On the second day seventy-seven shots were fired, and on the third seventy-nine. This represents an average of between four and five shots per kill, which on the whole is not at all bad shooting. I consider an average of three shots to one stag in Scotland very fair, taking into account *every* shot fired. One may perhaps kill a succession of stags with one shot each, but a couple of wounded animals will lower your average alarmingly, and a good many of those shots in the neck "just to finish him off" are not included. Anyway, to shoot for an average is a bad system.

A great deal depends, of course, on the ammunition. Prior to the First World War, with copper-tipped, pointed bullets, using a ·275 Rigby Mauser, my average of shots to stags was very much better than now, when reliable copper-tipped bullets seem unprocurable and gunmakers recommend soft-nosed bullets. With the pointed bullet I seldom had to fire twice at a stag. A beast, when hit, seemed anchored to the spot, all his nerve centres were paralysed, and he was unable to move. My experience with the soft-nosed bullet is that, though hit apparently in the right place, a beast will carry on for a considerable distance. On more than one occasion I have put three bullets within a few inches of each other before the stag dropped, and on going up to him found that the first shot was all that was really necessary.

Shooting at a stationary stag is very different to firing at a galloping roe. A magazine rifle, too, is unsuitable, and a double-barrelled weapon almost essential. I used a double ·275, which Belgian sportsmen considered too heavy to handle, but a beautiful weapon. Many of them use an under-and-over rifle or a double rifle with a shot-gun underneath.

The following year I was again asked to shoot in Belgium, this time actually in the Ardennes at Orval, which Baron d'Otreppe has rented for many years. Long before 1914 I had corresponded with him on the subject of roe heads, and it was a great pleasure to discuss with him our favourite sport. Hearing that I was staying with him, Baron Brugmann very kindly asked me to shoot at Mohimont, one of the best boar shoots in Belgium. At Orval on the first day we killed seven boars and seven roe; on the second day three boars and twenty-one roe; and at Mohimont, in the three days, nineteen boars, thirty-five roe, and four stags.

It was bright, frosty weather, bitterly cold, with snow in patches, and rising at 5.30 a.m. every morning was no joke.

One wanted all the warm clothes one could get, and I was none too warm in two "woollies" and my Loden cape, those light, green Austrian shooting coats which are so good for this kind of work.

Many of the Belgian sportsmen wore brooches in their hats made of stags' teeth, or else the "stag of St. Hubert," which held in place the long hairs from the boar's back, similar to those taken from chamois.

At the meeting-place the first thing the sportsmen do is to form a circle. The host stands in the middle, and pointing at one of the guns asks a guest, who has turned his back, to name a number. The host then numbers backwards to one, and starts again, completing the circle. The guest retains his number for the two or three days of the shoot. Both at Orval and Mohimont I drew number thirteen, usually considered lucky. It was not so in my case. The rifles on each side of me killed good boars with fine heads. At T.'s shoot in the same week I drew number twelve; H. drew thirteen and killed three boars in one drive.

It is interesting, when taking part in a new kind of sport, to analyse the elements of success. The wind, for instance, which blew from the north-east, not only chilled one, but rendered it much more difficult to hear the approach of game. The relief when it fell! I also found it much more of a strain being stationed close up against thick cover than in a comparatively open space.

The country was very varied. Thick fir plantations in one drive would give place to a ridge covered with oaks; again, broom and oak scrub—a great favourite with boars—would alternate with large pines or beeches. Much of it at times reminded me of the woods in which I had loved to stalk roe at Milton in Dorsetshire.

The stands for each rifle were often marked with red and white circles painted on trees, with other marks to indicate where it was unsafe to shoot. At some shoots the keepers are very smartly dressed in green or grey, the head keeper being distinguished by a badge. Either he or the under-

keeper comes armed with a plan of the shoot and places the
rifles, telling them where to assemble after the drive is
over. Though not to be compared with stalking, this moving of game is interesting and exciting. The braying of the
horn indicates the position of the beaters, which changes to
a sharp toot! toot! toot! if a boar is seen. Dogs are often
used, and their shrill yapping shows the direction in which
the boar is heading. It may go right outside the beat, circle
round, and re-enter from behind the rifles. On the dead
leaves of the frozen ground the dainty little feet of the roe
patter, stop, and as you peer into the shadows to distinguish
their grey forms, which blend so exactly with the background, there will come a sudden rush, and almost before
you have time to get your rifle to your shoulder they have
crossed the ride and crashed into the thicket beyond. To
make up your mind exactly where you are going to shoot
is essential, and a larger foresight than one usually adopts
when stalking is an advantage. It is more easily picked up.
If you do not make up your mind as to the exact spot at
which you are going to take your shot you are likely, in
swinging, to shoot down a young fir tree. I have seen this
done more than once.

On December 6 I saw a big buck with newly-grown
horns showing well above the brow. It was shot by Baron
d'Otreppe, who told me he had seen a buck which had not
shed on February 18. In entirely new country and in a new
form of sport one has much to learn. I, for instance, did not
know whether the position I occupied in any drive was a
good one or not. Many of my fellow guests did, and would
tell me so. Their politeness, courtesy, and kindness to a
stranger have left me with many pleasant memories. At one
drive, just before lunch I was posted halfway down a steep
hillside with a fir wood on my right, a scrub-covered hill
before me, a steeply rising bank behind, with two rides cut
through the fringe of low firs adjoining it.

"This is a good stand; you will be lucky," I heard, and
took my place. T. I could see on the top of the hill above me.

The other rifles walked on to their positions, a horn blew, and everything became still. Far off I heard a jay. They often follow boars, and also stags, as they move before the beaters. It is always wise to keep an eye on their movements. This bird I could not see, for it was beyond the ridge. I strained my ears, for I thought I heard a faint sound, but it was only snow falling off the branches with a soft thud. The jay screamed again. Far away at the end of the line I heard two shots, then a third; after that silence. I glanced up the hill and saw T. suddenly galvanised into activity. He stood peering before him, suddenly swung round and fired. From somewhere beyond him came three more shots. Silence again. I was certain I heard a sound, but could not locate it. It was not the snow falling, but something crisper and sharper. T. heard something, too, for he pointed. Then came a definite crunching. I lifted my rifle and glared at the firs before me to my right. It came again, and then quite definitely a grunt. I was going to be lucky! Then pandemonium, or so it seemed to me. Pigs burst from the firs like a covey of partridges over a hedge. They tore, grunting and squealing, into the next strip of firs, and as they did so I grew cool, for I knew that they must cross the second ride. I picked what looked the biggest and fired. It held on and I fired again. Into the gloom of the firs they vanished, to reappear high up above me as I fumbled to reload. How, on this occasion, did I long for my stalking rifle! I could have easily fired again. Fumbling and harassed, at last I slipped the second cartridge into the breech while I kept my eye on the game. One pig, a big one, seemed to be going much more slowly than the others. It was stopping. It was sitting down. It gave a loud grunt and disappeared.

In the next ten minutes, till, in fact, three loud blasts on the horn indicated that the drive was over, T. derived a good deal of amusement from my antics. I knew the pig was there, but I could not see clearly on account of the undergrowth. I peered and stooped, sideways and forwards, and not until I climbed up through the snow and the bushes did

I find it. A fair-sized sow of about fifty kilos, neither big nor small, but at any rate I had killed my first wild boar.

A man may kill fifty or sixty boars before he gets a really good one. It is very largely a matter of luck, though knowledge of the habits of game will enable an experienced hunter to get a shot where a novice would not. So many trifling details decide where the game may go, or whether you may get your chance. The wind, a movement, a sound, may bring luck or disappointment.

At one stand I had a large pine wood in front of me; round the corner at right angles on my left was Baron d'Otreppe. I saw and heard nothing until he fired three shots in succession. After the beat I went through the wood and found a very large boar had walked slowly out of the wood towards him. He had missed it, reloaded, and killed it behind him with his third shot. It might easily have come to me.

These, with the one I killed, were the only living pigs I saw, which was my chief disappointment, as an old full-grown boar must be a fine sight.

On private estates very good sport is had with wild boar during the late winter months. They are located in the woods in the morning and moved to two or three rifles. Great care has to be taken with regard to the wind and the method of driving employed. This varies with the nature of the ground. An old boar is nearly always alone, except during the rut, which is irregular. The young are born at any time, March and April being the most common. An old boar which has been disturbed may break anywhere from a wood. When the undergrowth is covered with snow they are very reluctant to move, and often neither men nor dogs will shift them more than a hundred yards or so. The beaters sometimes have to seek safety in trees, and dogs are frequently killed.

The sows have one litter a year. A year-old sow rarely has more than two, three, or four young ones; an old one may have as many as twelve. The young, when three or four months old, lose their yellow stripes. An old boar becomes black with age, the tips of the hairs on the head and shoulders being grey. When caught young they are easily tamed, and I have heard of one that would run half a mile and swim across a pond 100 yards in width to reach his mistress. These tame ones are not safe with strangers.

Baron de Woot, a well-known Belgian shot, killed a very large boar which, when wounded, treed a man, stood on his hind-legs, and proceeded to bite his foot.

When fighting, I am told that they will stand up with their fore-legs touching and slash at each other with their tusks. Another Belgian I knew was knocked down in the snow by a boar which tried to bite his knee. It tore a hole in his knickerbockers before he managed to shoot it.

Though not to be compared with stalking, this form of sport was to me very novel and entertaining, and I look forward to the time when luck is with me, and a large and accommodating boar walks slowly out of a wood into a nice open space in front of my stand.

VI. THE TALE OF A ROYAL

"My thoughts are ever on the hills."
LAMENT OF THE DEER—A. Mackenzie

MR. DAVID MACBRAYNE'S "swift mail steamer" *Glengarry* had conveyed me with its accustomed celerity across Loch Ness. From the little pier, whence one could see the white house which had formerly harboured many a Jacobite conspirator, a motor drive of six miles landed me at my destination. On the way up through one of the finest gorges I knew, my host (long dead, but the memory of whose kindness I shall always cherish) had pointed out a thick young fir plantation as the abode of a royal. Several attempts had been made on his life, but, like much-enduring Ulysses, he was possessed of considerable guile. He had sustained the assault of a great legal luminary (the late Lord Alverstone) and prevailed; he had, driving being resorted to, swept aside a stalker who was sufficiently misguided to endeavour to stem his headlong charge up a ride; but, as the season advanced, refusing to appear in the open, he hugged his fir plantation, where he knew his position was impregnable, and lay low. Altogether he was something of a celebrity.

This was to have been the story of a failure. Duncan, Diana and a damp spot in a turnip-field converted it into a success. For the first few days we stuck to the open forest. The approach is one which I always enjoyed. It lies across a river flat beside the course of a burn which comes brawling down from the tops in a litter of grey stones between great grassy banks. On one side lies the sanctuary about a gnarled old birch wood, among whose stems the sun falls in patches and gleams here and there on a red hide. For some miles the road continues thus, ever ascending; then the burn narrows, its sides become less precipitous, the green banks on either hand less prominent, until, finally, they merge in a wild tumult of peat hags, which stretch away to the stony tops crowning the sky-line. Such country is extraordinarily hard to spy. There is nothing on which to focus; the eye becomes bewildered and you find with surprise that the sky-line, apparently a few hundreds of yards off, is in reality distant two or three miles. A hundred deer might lie hidden in the channels and fissures with which the trickling burns have seared the peat; and should one indeed appear, he shows in the distance as a tiny speck, almost invisible, until the glass reveals him as a flickering blur amid the heat haze which pours along the crest of each ridge.

Such was the ground on which many years ago Duncan, I and Scott the ex-policeman had compassed the death of a great eleven-pointer, something of whose history has appeared in these pages. That, too, was in September, when a stag, surrounded by his bachelor friends, all on the alert, and with no watchful hinds to rely on, is a very different animal from the beast he is in October, his senses dulled by passion and his attention occupied by the flirtations of a flighty harem. The weather was superb; but how I prayed for a change! In bands of varying size the stags lay contentedly about the tops and basked in the warm sun, while the approach of an enemy, if not advertised by the hurried scrambles of a swarm of mountain hares or the hoarse chuckle of an old grouse, was betrayed by the crackling rustle of the dry heather. The views were magnificent, and one gazed upon a blue sea of peaks from the Boar of Badenoch and the Atholl Sow to the Cairngorms, Wyvis, the hills beyond Braulen and Kintail, Glenquoich and even Nevis himself; but no stags came into the larder. On the 13th, it is true, I might have had one. A small party of deer, among them a fair six-pointer and a beast with a crumpled horn, evaded us all day. The wind veered, grouse were abundant, and the deer themselves subject, as at times they are, to sudden, apparently causeless dashes. We made, I think, three distinct stalks after them. The first time we got to within four hundred yards before they were off, headed by an old yellow hind, whom I eventually grew to loathe. They moved across a wide flat and into the course of a deep burn, which lay hidden in the grey and brown mass of peats. Directly the last had vanished we dashed across the flat in an endeavour to intercept them, but were just too late, for as we reached cover that horrible yellow hind appeared. The deer all filed past her while she lay and looked superciliously at the spot where we cowered. Duncan and I were hidden, but Curly, the son of that "handsome John MacDonald" spoken of by Crealock, with whom I too have enjoyed many a good stalk, was in full view and detailed her movements in a muttered whisper. "She's lo-o-king this way—She's watching a smaal staag—She's after turning her heid. The auld deevil" (this in a venomous aside), "she's up." Then followed a subdued growl, interspersed with hoarse expletives. Late in the evening we did get in a shot at the beast with the crumpled horn. Apparently he was hit, and disappeared with a lurch into the burn. We crept to the edge, hoping for a shot at the six-pointer. The deer finally emerged in a bunch on the opposite bank, he of the crumpled horn conducting the retreat. He can only have been wounded very slightly, and I do not know to this day where I hit him.

It is most difficult on an occasion of this kind to pick the right stag. It is equally hard for the stalker to explain his position. "Yon's him!" he exclaims. "The second frae the richt." You find the second from the right is a panic-smitten knobber, who returns your murderous glance with a look of horror-struck amazement. The deer are moving all the while, and by the time the glass is readjusted and your prospective victim identified are out of shot. On the whole, perhaps, it is best to keep one's own glass out. Later in the season such a quandary is unlikely, the black neck and horns of the stag being easily picked out in a bunch of hinds and young beasts.

On the 14th we spent most of the day over a misleading animal who beguiled us as he lay in a peat hag. On the 15th I was up early, tried for a buck and missed him. After breakfast we turned our attention to a narrow strip of wood running parallel to the river on the other side of a rush-covered flat. The net result was the expenditure, with great rapidity, of four cartridges at a galloping roebuck which I certainly ought to have got, as the first shot was comparatively close. The river flat was, perhaps, eight hundred yards in length. Starting below the lodge, it was bordered for half its extent by a fringe of firs and spruces. Beyond these and above them lay the drive. On the left beyond the drive gates stood the plantation where dwelt the royal. The drive continued some ten or fifteen feet above the flat, until it met and joined the high-road which wandered down the strath. The flat was swallowed in a bed of rushes and luscious grasses, which in turn gave place to a turnip-field, distant some three or four hundred yards from the drive gates. On the far side of the river which ran through the flat stood a deer fence separating some tame hinds from the farm land.

To this turnip-field we repaired in gloomy silence. Around the edge the roots were thin, and though for the most part dry and hard, an occasional damp patch gave us hope. "We'll just have a look to see has he been working here," said Duncan, and I knew he meant the royal. Curly went nosing across the rills, and presently gave a cry. Duncan and I joined him. There on a dark patch of soil was the mark of a cloven hoof, broad and damp with long, pointed slots, which showed their maker did not love the open hill. "A beeg brrute," said Duncan, and followed the tracks. They were there in plenty, and left no doubt that a heavy wood stag had been enjoying an illicit meal. The marks were fresh, and I began to feel slightly more cheerful. "We'll just go above yon plantation," said Duncan, "till we see will he come late this evening, or, maybe, another stag."

There was not a breath of wind and the plantation lay below spread like a map, calm and motionless. Not a twig stirred, and the movements of even a rabbit, did he show in the open, were clearly revealed. As the sun sank behind us it grew cold. A few does appeared and moved cautiously around the young fir stems where the last rays shone, but never the sign of a stag.

"There's just only one chance," said Duncan. "We must try before it's light, for I know well he's into the wood for the day with the first streak."

Other attempts had been made on him, I knew, but he had never been seen, though fresh tracks betrayed his presence. The inference was obvious. I determined to run no risks, and took the precaution of borrowing an alarm clock, a truly fearsome-looking piece of mechanism. At 3.30 a.m. I woke for the third time, and, realising that the appointed hour was at hand, got up and dressed. The infernal machine was set for 3.45 a.m., so I took the precaution of muffling it with the bedclothes. As I crept gingerly from the room, taking great care to close the door, it suddenly exploded, and I feared that its strangled but irritatingly persistent endeavours would wake the entire household. I flung open the door, rushed back, lay on it till its energies were exhausted, and then stole silently from the house. Outside, in the clear, frosty night, I found Duncan and the two gillies. Curly, who lived some distance away,

F

was not present, a fact which I have reason to believe embittered his existence for some days. We walked noiselessly down the border of the drive while Duncan unfolded his plan. Forty yards beyond the drive gates stood a couple of stunted birch trees; any deer moved from the flat below invariably crossed into the plantation close to them. Here I was to wait. Duncan himself was to go for a quarter of a mile down the road, and there remain to turn any beast that tried to cross up to me. The two boys were to make a detour, come in the far end of the turnip-field and walk up the flat until they reached us. It was too dark to see anything ten yards off, but as Duncan and the boys moved away, leaving me at my post, the first faint glimmering of the coming day broke down the strath.

I raised my rifle against the black shadows below me. A faint pin-head of light pricked the gloom. Down the glen an old cock pheasant rose with his harsh Eastern cry, while the grouse still called their warning across the valley. Duncan's final words floated idly into my mind: "If I see anything I'll whistle." My glance wandered up the road, whose pale glimmer stopped at the dark gates which stood in the shadow of the trees, then back across the flat and down over the burn. The bushes clustered thick on the far slope of the hill, broken here and there by little glades, grassy and set about with rushes. Even as my look rested on them, swiftly and silently a dark mass shot across one. I looked again, thinking that my eyes had deceived me. Nothing could I see, and all was silent. Then, thin and clear up the glen came a shrill whistle. I will not attempt to describe such a moment, for to all save those who know and love the sport it is indescribable. There followed a crash, and I gripped the rifle in a fever of expectation. From the burn came a splashing and terrific clatter, then a steady thud, thud. From the bank below me grew a silver birch, and through the tremulous whispering of its leaves I saw an animal's back. It moved, and I became conscious of a pair of antlers. So hidden was he by the tree that I hesitated to fire. Still he stood there, but at the shot moved slowly forward. Behind a dip I could see the line of his back and neck. As he turned, crossed the burn and walked across the flat, I felt a sudden sickening sense of disappointment. Then he wavered, swayed and turned his side. In vain I tried to steady the rifle. My hands trembled, and I even lowered it in disgust. At length I fired, and he dropped like a stone behind a tuft of rushes. Then Duncan appeared. "Did ye get him?" he cried. I nodded. The patch behind the rush clump caught his eye, and he scrambled down the bank. "I wonder what he'll be?" he continued. "Yon eicht-pinter, perhaps!"

"He's very light coloured," I said.

Duncan's reserve suddenly vanished, and he rushed forward, "Maan!" he cried, "it's him. You've got the roy-al!"

So I had, and he weighed twenty stone!

VII. THE DREAM THAT FAILED

"Women!" said Callaghan. "You know just what they want you to know at any particular moment. All the rest is guessing."
SORRY YOU'VE BEEN TROUBLED—Peter Cheyney

CAPTAIN JOHN SORREL (pronounced "Sawl," more because its owner thought this sounded rather grander than for any other reason—"Old Huguenot stock, you know," he explained—) was one of those hard-bitten he-men with black eyes who liked having his own way. Not that he by any means always got it. His sister, Miss Janet Sorrel, who kept house for him, was actuated by a demon of possessive jealousy which caused her to keep a very strict eye on his doings and effectively did away with any chance of calling his soul, or anything else, his own. She was not above opening his letters and he had not a nook or corner which was not liable to be searched at any moment. This feature of their daily life not unnaturally embittered a disposition which could hardly have been described as sweet at the beginning. Her great fear was that he would get married, which accounted for the constant surveillance to which he was subjected. She could very nearly, but not quite, read his thoughts.

As is not uncommon with unimaginative men, once he had got an idea into his head he so dwelt on it to the exclusion of everything else that it became an obsession. He had one possession which his sister could not get at and this was what, in the privacy of his own thoughts, he called his "dream lady." A married woman, who was certainly no better than she should have been, had once, many years before, told him that he was good looking, and he had never forgotten it. His "dream lady" frequently told him so, but then she had never set eyes on him. Captain Sorrel's idea was "catch 'em young and treat 'em rough," which may perhaps have accounted for his singular lack of success in finding a mate, such an attitude being scarcely the best to adopt as a prelude to adventure.

His "dream lady," it should perhaps be mentioned, had grey eyes, a wide and tender mouth, golden russet hair and long and slender hands.

It was just after breakfast and Captain Sorrel turned to his wardress. "Well," he remarked, "I must be hitting the trail."

He was one of that type who are always "hitting the trail." After "a quick one" with his pals he "hit the trail." Where he hit it did not much seem to matter. A few moments later he emerged from the house, a rifle slung on his shoulder, a glass on his back and a stick in his hand. His sister poked her head out of the window.

"Where are you going?" she queried.

"On the hill," replied her brother. "Dugald told me last night he saw a very good royal close to the march beyond the little loch. I'm going to try for him before those people over the march hear he's there."

He went up through a small birchwood, gold and yellow

in the blaze of autumn, to where the bracken made great splashes of red and bronze against the dead heather. Presently a little loch came into view below him, making a picture which would have delighted the heart of a lover of nature or of colour, but nature and colour hardly entered into the scheme of things so far as Captain Sorrel was concerned. He was out for a stag, or rather *the* stag; for stags of any size were rather rare.

He ran his black eyes over the scene, then stiffened, for only rather over a quarter of a mile away he saw a movement. He was well screened from view—he had taken care of that—so, putting his rifle on the ground, he drew out his glass and steadied on his stick. Several hinds were at once magnified into life. For some moments he watched them, but could see no stag. Then a flicker of light brought his glass to rest on a small ridge of rock. The grey object which might have been a dead branch moved, and a still more careful examination revealed it as a stag's horn with three good points on the top. Returning his glass to its case the stalker picked up his rifle and disappeared.

Meanwhile, from beyond the burn which twisted and turned between little meadows, yellow now with autumn grass, dells still green with ferns and mosses above which the golden sequins of the dying birch-leaves made a carpet, another stalker, this time a lady, was making her way. As she came to the edge of a knoll she, too, stopped and, taking out a glass, proceeded to subject the vicinity to a close scrutiny. Presently, too, her glass remained motionless, focused on the same area, though from her point of view it presented rather a different aspect than had been Captain Sorrel's. She, then, after a short pause repeated exactly his actions and disappeared.

For a considerable period nothing happened. Then from behind a knoll about four hundred yards from where the deer were feeding a small grey object showed. Five hundred yards distant another small brown spot with a hint of gold in it appeared. Behind it was the little loch and to the left the burn sang and laughed between steep banks to where some duck swam lazily in the reeds.

Just as these separate movements took place a great grey stag on a sudden stood above the hinds. Giving a loud roar he paced slowly towards them. As he drew near one of them raised her head. The stag stopped and looked at her. She took a few steps away from him. The stag advanced. She took a few more steps. The stag followed. She broke into a trot. The stag into a gallop. Straight away from the watchers the chase continued, the hind keeping well ahead. As she turned the stag turned, like a collie with sheep. In and out among the peat hags they went until at last the hind, having got well away from her pursuer, trotted sedately back to her companions. Then occurred one of those things which stalkers always hope for but which so seldom happen. The stag with raised head watched her, then lowering his head made straight for the burn which defined the march. He was well over a quarter of a mile from his hinds when he suddenly stopped, then gave a spring, dashed madly forward and collapsed in the burn. A loud crack at almost the same moment came to the ears of the male watcher. The hinds at the same moment bolted past him, scattering wildly as he rose to his feet almost in their path. Muttering expletives he cautiously made his way to the march. He reached the bank of the burn and peered over. Just below him lay the stag and bending over it with a knife in her hand was a slim, girlish figure. As he watched she gave an ineffective jab at the animal's neck.

Captain Sorrel's expression, though still pretty grim, relaxed. "You seem to be having trouble," he said.

The girl whipped round, presenting a startled face to the onlooker as the knife dropped from her hand. "Oh! What a fright you gave me!" she gasped.

Captain Sorrel's expression again changed. Not to put too fine a point on it, he goggled. His jaw dropped and for an appreciable pause he just gaped. For here she was, his "dream lady." She certainly presented an attractive, spectacle. Her face was flushed, her golden russet hair was in delightful disorder, her mouth was parted to show a row of little white teeth and her long and slender hands destitute of any adornment were clasped in front of her breast.

"Oh!" she repeated, noting the onlooker's expression, an expression to which, it may be added, she was not entirely unaccustomed, "what a fright you gave me. I didn't know there was anyone there."

There was no doubt whatever that Betty (for that was the name of the young lady) was, at times, an absolute little devil. She was, to start with, small, which always tends to bring to the fore that " poor little woman " feeling in the heart of the protective male. "Poor little woman," they say, blowing out their cheeks and puffing at their moustaches. "They don't understand her!"—"they" being anyone, male or female, with whom the object of their solicitude is brought in contact, from a husband to her "in-laws."

Captain Sorrel's heart sang, if so entirely an unmusical organ could be so described. Anyway, red in the face he plunged forward, picked up the knife and muttering, "Allow me," proceeded to bleed and gralloch the stag.

"Oh! how clever you are," exclaimed Betty, gazing down at him, "and so clean. I mean," she added hastily, "you've done it so cleanly. Hardly any of it happened when I tried."

"Gad!" thought the gallant captain, "I'm making an impression. By gad, I am."

He tucked the stag up comfortably, displaying his undoubtedly good figure to the best advantage during the operation.

"Strike while the iron's hot," he thought.

"Your people can get him in all right now," he said awkwardly. "A jolly good head. I wonder if you'd mind if I came over and measured it. Rather interested in heads."

"Oh! do," said Betty. "When'll you come? To-morrow's Saturday. Come on Sunday. We're sure to be in in the afternoon."

"Damn," thought Captain Sorrel, "I wonder who 'we' is?

She might have asked me to lunch." Aloud, still goggling at her, he said, "Thanks awfully. Love to." "Like any lovesick boy!" as he thought to himself angrily after they had parted. He turned to watch her growing smaller in the distance. She had got a good figure!

To say that Captain Sorrel thought of nothing else during the next two days is no under-statement. He grumpily told his sister on his return that he had had no luck. "No luck!" sang his unmusical heart. He did not tell her where he was going when he set out on Sunday afternoon, having announced in no uncertain manner that he was not going to accompany her to church. Time enough to tell her anything when it was all fixed up. For that he might fail to fix it never entered his head for a moment. He had found her at last! When he reached Kinravoch he suddenly realised that so stunned had he been he had never even enquired his divinity's name. He rang the bell, and when the maid appeared stammered out, "Is anyone in?"

"Captain Sorrel?" said the maid.

"That's me," he gulped. It was all right. She'd told them he was coming. She must be looking forward to seeing him. He was shown into a pleasant room, bright with flowers. The door opened and he whipped round. Only a man.

The latter came forward, holding out his hand. "My name's Gratton," he said. "How are you?"

The door opened again before he could say any more and *she* came in.

"I think you've already met my wife," said Gratton.

VIII. THE ETERNAL FEMININE

"What a lass to go a-gipseying through the world with."
THE JOVIAL CREW, *The Examiner*, July 1819—Charles Lamb

IN these days when women do everything that men can do—with a few trifling exceptions—it is not surprising that they have taken up stalking. That their prowess is looked on with unqualified approval by the male sex is perhaps open to doubt. Said one embittered stalker to me as he departed in an endeavour to procure an October grouse for the larder: "These damned women take up a whole beat a man might be stalking!"

That some ladies can walk and shoot as well as a man needs no emphasising when, as, say, in 1930, most of the good heads were killed by women. But that there are many other forms of sport more suited to them is, I think, equally true. Fly fishing is a sport well adapted to the fair sex and a good line thrown by a girl a very attractive sight. She may hunt and at the end of a good run, despite or even because of her appearance, capture the heart of every susceptible male within range. But no woman who has played the game without shirking during a hard day stalking can hope to look otherwise than bedraggled, powder she never so wisely.

The Exception it was who nearly converted me. It was in

those far-off golden days when the ladies who stalked could be counted on the fingers of one hand, and did it because they loved it, and not because they thought it was the right thing to do. Their names never figured in the papers nor did one see pictures of them carefully posed beside dead stags. I had known the Exception ever since she was a black-legged flapper, the terror of every governess who came to the house, and from the days of our earliest intimacy it had been her ambition to kill a stag. At the death of her first I was not, alas! present, being on the other side of the globe; but that we were to have a day's stalking together as soon as I returned had been an understood thing from the first. One July we lunched together—a pretty dashing thing to do in those far-off days—the Exception wonderfully arrayed in a Merry Widow hat and a little frilly thing round her neck, which will enable my older readers approximately to fix the year. We talked stags all lunch and settled when we were to have our day down to the very date. Then I called for the bill.

"What's my share?" inquired the Exception in a lordly tone. "I'll pay. I've just made a bit!"

To my query she revealed a complicated transaction in which figured a dress, a match, and an insurance company, the latter a bad last!

It was on a glorious October morning that we next forgathered. To his bitter and loudly expressed grief, Archie, who was to have accompanied us, had been sent out on the home beat with another rifle. Of Archie I have written much and now, alas! can write no more. Deer were his passion. Many a time and oft when shooting grouse have I looked round to see where he might be. The dogs roamed half a mile off at their own sweet will, and over the sky-line went the grouse, while Archie submerged in heather lay on his back, his dangling leg supporting a spyglass, the while he gazed with an intensity of devotion on those "whose skins gleamed red in the sunshine." There he lay and crooned to himself in a high sing-song falsetto.

"A graand heid! Eicht, nine, ten he has. A ten-pinter. Whaat torps he has. Mphm. A graand beast. Whaat a bordy. Eichteen stanes, I would think."

Here I would mildly suggest that we were supposed to be shooting grouse.

"Oh! Is it the grouse?" in a tone of deep disgust. "Weel, I suppose we may go on a bittie, but well I know that it is Muster Fraank who should be after yon beast."

"You're fond of stalking, Archie?" he was asked.

"Aye! Aal my faamily are grand at the staalking. There was my grandmither. Eichty-three she was and on her deithbed. But it was herself that went oot of the hoose and killed three staags before she deed." Thus Archie, though in what manner his aged relative achieved this remarkable feat, or in what forest, he never specified.

In his stead came the head stalker, James, and "Andra," a young and unsophisticated gillie. We had a long walk. Up through the wood where the roe glinted among the bracken and cunning old blackcock rose in the distance or hung, black specks amid the bronzing birches. Then out by the loch side where a grey heron fished at his ease, and so to the open hill and the grey rocks and the heather. From the spying stone we could see but little of our beat, which lay beyond the distant sky-line. There was one narrow glen which might have held deer, but it proved empty. On Archie's beat, which stretched on our left, we could see a herd of about thirty hinds held together by a black stag whose distant roars came to us across the burn, but they were on forbidden ground. So by the rough track we went for another mile and then struck off across the heather. Arrived at a spot from which a view of the ground could be obtained, James stopped and began to spy. I watched him until out of the corner of my eye an irregularity on the hitherto tenantless sky-line attracted me. The stalker had seen it too, for with one watchful glance back he rolled sidelong into the heather. Over the ridge a quarter of a mile away came a stag, a traveller.

"Get the rifle!" I whispered. The Exception shook her head violently. "Go on!" I hissed. By means of an intricate wriggle she turned her back and murmured "You!" over her shoulder.

From Andra's convulsively working face I was assured that no time was to be lost. I made one more useless effort and turned to James. Stifling a semi-audible volley of imprecations at this ill-timed hesitation on the part of the Exception, he thrust the rifle into my hands; the stag pranced up in all unconsciousness to within twenty yards of us when, with not a little compunction, I shot him through the neck.

The Exception weakly apologised to James, who received her excuses in stony silence; the usual rites were performed, the pony signalled and we proceeded on our way.

James, of course, went first; we followed, and Andra brought up the rear. That at least was the order in which we started.

I have, I think, already mentioned that I have known the Exception since early flapperhood. She was then, as she phrased it, "getting on"—though twenty did not strike me as a very advanced age and our relationship was purely platonic.

Nothing was to be seen in front; there were no hidden dips which could conceal a wandering beast; the Exception and I were amicably conversing when, as we crossed a piece of rough ground, she put her hand on my arm. I glanced back, and to my astonishment noticed Andra exhibiting marked signs of discomfort. On catching my eye he suddenly ducked his head. My companion's hand was still resting on my arm. She had noticed nothing. I took another glance back. Andra was blushing violently. I gave the Exception's hand a gentle squeeze. Looking slightly surprised she remarked, "Don't be an idiot!" I gazed hungrily into her eyes and was rewarded by seeing that Andra was threatened, apparently, with an attack of apoplexy. He evidently regarded himself as the unwilling witness of an impassioned love scene. The Exception turned. She is fortunate in possessing a keen sense of humour, took in the situation at a glance and went off into peals of silent laughter. Whilst she lay and shook convulsively, Andra ducked and doubled behind us, rejoining the stalker with an obvious sigh of relief; nor did he quit the latter's elbow during the remainder of the day.

As I spied I felt a tug at my arm, and following an out-stretched finger discovered a roebuck feeding in some long grass, and with him, revealed by the glass, a doe.

They fed quietly, nor did they move as we slithered over to where James lay beside a rock.

"Shall we try him?" I asked.

"Let's!" said the Exception.

James regarded the roe dispassionately for some moments.

"He's no a vera gude head," he announced. It was his way of intimating that in his opinion (an opinion unreason-ably shared by nearly every stalker) such a beast was un-worthy of notice.

It would take too long to describe all the incidents which befell us on that day so long ago. A stalk after a switch with a very wide span resulted in a long shot and the escape of the switch. Various excuses presented themselves to account for this, to the switch, satisfactory *dénouement*, the real one being, as is the case with many a miss, a too great haste.

Then as we had lunch a hind suddenly showed on the flat below, and a moment later another. I had not noticed them until they rose, nor for that matter had anyone else; yet there they were, a dozen or so in number with their calves. So wonderfully did they blend in with their sur-roundings that even a trained eye might be forgiven for having passed them over. The two which had risen stood with cocked ears, facing a rocky slope some distance to our left. There came from behind it a subdued roar, and presently a stag stepped into view with more hinds but a few yards distant from the march.

"We may try him if he stays there!" said James; and we started, the Exception, as is her custom, chewing a bunch of rushes. Soon crawling became necessary. Her skirt—for ladies wore skirts in those days on the hill—apparently offered no impediment, and she progressed swiftly and with ease. I lumbered heavily behind.

James peered through a clump of heather and sank back into himself.

"Eichty yards!" he whispered.

Two hinds feeding with their backs to us turned and moved a step or two in our direction. After a few uneasy snatches at especially succulent tufts they fed over the brow. Some distance in front the stag roared and grunted. I looked back over my shoulder. The dozen or so hinds whom we had first seen were all up staring in our direction. One started at her graceful, swinging trot and I knew that the chance was a small one.

James whipped out the rifle. The Exception seized it and made a bolt for the top of the knoll. Three hundred yards off a string of deer were crossing the march. The Exception said nothing. James, looking pained but resigned, took the rifle.

"No chance at aal," said he; "I doubt we'll get a shot the nicht."

Then we turned back.

Down the glen, almost within sight of the little loch in which the heron had fished so quietly in the morning, ran a narrow ridge which separated the forest from its neighbours. Over it as we tramped down the bridle path some hinds sedately moved. In their midst a small stag, emboldened by the gathering dusk, gave forth emulative roars. Four or five hundred yards ahead of us he was answered. Then above the hilltop on our right appeared the challenger.

James's glass was on him in an instant.

"He'll do," said he briefly.

Then he turned to the Exception. "Two hundred yairds, on the sky-line, and ye'll hae him richt eneuch!" he remarked encouragingly. The Exception murmured a protest, but the stalker was off, for there was no time to be lost, the small stag and his harem being in full view. The light was fading rapidly and soon it would be too dark for a shot.

"You take him; I can't see," said the Exception, but I was firm.

A huge rock lay in a hollow by the burn, and as we gained its shelter another roar rang out above me.

"You'll hae a good chance directly," said James.

The Exception hung back.

"It's absurd," she cried, "I couldn't hit the thing at that distance in a good light."

Then it was that James showed himself to be a man of resolution. No more feminine vagaries for him. Turning sharply he addressed her.

"You'll just come along and do what I tell you," he hissed.

I have often, since then, admired his resolution.

The Exception collapsed and crawled up beside him like a lamb. The light was atrocious, but a good hundred and eighty yards off I could see the form of a stag clearly silhouetted against the sky; in the heather beside the rock, two dim figures. I heard a gasp.

"Canny, noo, canny!" from James.

Then a thin spurt of flame. My eyes were on the stag. He stood quite still, thought about it for a second, lurched slowly sideways, and lay kicking in the heather.

It was nearly dark; she had just killed a nice stag at something under two hundred yards; James, I and the gillie were the only people within miles, yet what do you think was the Exception's first exclamation? She seized me by the arm and cried, "I'm sure my hair's awful!"

It was the triumph of the Eternal Feminine.

WHAT ABOUT IT?

IX. THE END OF AN ERA

"Most of their discourse was about hunting in a dialect I understand very little."

DIARY, 22 Nov. 1663—Samuel Pepys

IN those far-off days before our world was shattered in pieces, I was asked to shoot in Russia in the hope of getting a bear. Never having seen one of these animals in a wild state, I was keen to go, so my wife and I set out and eventually found ourselves in St. Petersburg, as it was then called.

Quite apart from shooting, there was much to see that was interesting. The wonderful collection of pictures at the Hermitage was, alone, worth a visit. Dating from the second half of the eighteenth century, it contained many priceless works of art. A number of these, I believe, have now been dispersed. At least forty examples of Rembrandt, including some of his finest paintings, were among them. I could have spent weeks looking at them.

Though not a beautiful city (St. Petersburg cannot compare with Moscow), the view across the Neva to the Fortress of Peter and Paul, with its thin spire rising against the sky, is one which no visitor can fail to remember.

To see new surroundings is always an interesting experience, and to have known Russia before 1914, even casually, as we did, is one which can never be repeated. Many of the Russians—indeed, the majority of the aristocracy—were magnificent-looking men, and in their gay uniforms presented a splendid sight.

To gauge correctly internal conditions during a brief visit is difficult, more particularly if one is ignorant of the language, but the state of Russia immediately prior to 1914 could not fail to strike the most casual observer. In modern slang the upper classes "asked for it." They were charming to meet, but one thing impressed me very much. "Who is that?" I would ask, as some pretty and attractive woman drew my attention.

"Oh! she is So-and-so," would come the reply. "That's her husband over there, but she is engaged to the fair man she is talking to."

This sort of thing was quite common and was discussed without any attempt at concealment; an extraordinary arrangement whichever way it was regarded.

At a circus one evening we saw the poor little Tsarevitch with his faithful sailor in attendance. Mutterings of the coming storm, though it did not break in full force until three years later, were heard even then, and at times threw our host into deep depression.

Two years previously I had travelled across the great continent from east to west on my return from a hunting trip in China and passed many nights in the homes of Russian peasants. The majority of those I met possessed the simplicity and charm of Scots country folk and treated the casual foreigner with a courtesy and kindness which has left me with many pleasant memories. What they could do for me they did, and hospitality can go no further. On that occasion my one anxiety was to travel as quickly as possible, and under such conditions existence was comparatively simple.

Life in St. Petersburg was much more complicated. It

seemed to me that no one woke up until about midnight, and as I have no fondness for late hours our ideas needed a little adjustment. Our host and hostess never appeared until lunch time, when we were rushed off sight-seeing, always a tiring performance. I remember the first morning well. I was making preparations to shave in a dressing-room which was not very well lit, there being only one small window. A slight noise behind me attracted my attention, and, turning, I was confronted by a gigantic figure in Cossack uniform with a large dagger slung diagonally across his waist. Bald as a coot, with long drooping black moustaches, he vaguely called to mind pictures of Genghis Khan and Asiatic freebooters. Fixing me with what appeared a menacing glare, he moved stealthily forward and seized my shaving-glass. He then planted himself firmly in the window, effectively blocking what little light there was. It took me some minutes to realise that he was endeavouring to the best of his ability to assist my shave. Not without some difficulty did I eventually persuade him to leave.

One of the most interesting places we visited was Gatchina, where the Tsar kept his wolf and bear hounds, the latter gigantic animals. Here we met Prince Galitzin, the Master of the Hunt, a most charming old gentleman, who might easily have been mistaken for an English country squire of a type which is dying out. Talking perfect English, like all those of the best type fortunate enough to have been born in a high position, he was as simple and natural as one of his own keepers. A natural simplicity and freedom from pose are qualities too often lacking. In itself, the acquisition of money seems to destroy the very qualities which are most to be envied in those who have inherited it. Possibly those who have made money, knowing how hard a job it is, value it more than those who have never felt its absence, and measure everything by a monetary standard which is entirely false. My own experience has been that those born in great positions are nearly always simple, natural and unassertive.

The kennels at Gatchina were very well kept, the hounds

well looked after and in excellent condition. Those used for
bear were not unlike huge St. Bernard dogs. I have never
seen hounds like them, and I fancy they were specially bred
for the purpose. Borzois are, of course, well known in this
country. In Russia, in addition to the kennel maintained by
the Tsar, was another famous hunting establishment at
Pershino, in the province of Tula, belonging to the Grand
Duke Nicholas. Originally designed for M. Lazarev, a
banker well known in the days of Catherine the Great, the
house was one of the few perfect examples of the handsome
country seats which were at one time numerous. The estate
was presented to him by the Empress in exchange for a
wonderful diamond which up to 1917 adorned the Tsar's
crown.

Wolf-hunting, as carried on by the Grand Duke, was an
exciting sport. The wolves were forced out of cover by
hounds of the English foxhound type. Great care had to be
taken in locating the wolf's lair without letting the animal
know that he was the object of pursuit. It was necessary
without giving any warning to enclose his retreat on all
sides either by nets or a chain of beaters. This having been
done, it was the object of the hounds to force him into the
open. Many of the peasants were experienced in woodcraft,
and by imitating the cry of a wolf at night-time at some little
distance from their supposed locality could tell by the
answer to their call not only the number of wolves, but their
approximate ages.

The mounted hunters, each holding their borzois in leash,
and the borziatniki (huntsmen) having taken up their
allotted stations, the hounds were loosed in the covert. An
hour or more might pass before the wolf appeared. Time
had to be given him, before unleashing the borzois, to get
well into the open, so that he could not break back into the
covert before the hounds could get up with him. When they
succeeded in doing this their object was to seize the wolf by
the throat and roll him over. While in this position, and held
down by the hounds, the huntsmen would get astride of the

recumbent body of the wolf and endeavour to force the "strunka" between his jaws. The "strunka" was a stout stick to which was attached a thong, by means of which the jaws could be firmly bound. A grown wolf not infrequently escaped; indeed, in twenty-five years the Pershino Hunt only took 56 as against over 600 yearlings. The borzois in pursuit of a wolf of this type suffered severely, as one snap from the jaws would rip open their sides. The Grand Duke used to improve the pace and mettle of the borzois by running them against English greyhounds. The latter animals at times have been known to attack a full-grown wolf, a great tribute to their courage.

Hares and foxes were also coursed, though this form of sport was not nearly so exciting as the pursuit of wolves.

Another favourite sport in Russia was capercailzie stalking, though we could not indulge in it, as it did not start until April. The Tsar was particularly fond of it. Known as the *tok*, this term was applicable both to the sound made by the cock bird when uttering his spring love-call and to the place where the birds assembled. They come back every spring to call almost from the same tree.

The sport required great patience, as the slightest noise made by the hunter, save during the few seconds when the concluding notes of the call change to a hissing sound, was sufficient to give him away. During those few seconds the bird is entirely deaf.

Blackcock were shot in a rather similar manner on their spring tournament grounds. Care had to be taken not to shoot the first bird to arrive, as he was the one whose call usually caused the others to assemble. Eight or ten was considered a good bag, while seven caper have been killed in a morning.

Interested as I was in hearing of these different forms of sport, news of bears was what I really wanted, and though bulletins with regard to them, to which I listened with ill-concealed eagerness, kept arriving, these were not of a sufficiently optimistic character to lure my host into the

country. I began to think that we should never get there!
City life, starting at an hour when we should normally have
sought our beds and lasting until the small hours, did not
agree with me, and grew slightly monotonous.

One incident I recall which amused us at the time. I
became the innocent cause of an acrimonious correspondence in one of the English papers between no less a person
than H. G. Wells and Walter Winans. The latter's father
had been the contractor for the St. Petersburg-Moscow railway. Having been born in Russia, he knew the country well,
often revisiting it for the sake of sport. He was a magnificent
shot with both rifle and revolver. Trotting matches were
one of his hobbies, and in the last in which he took part he
had just flashed past the winning-post when he fell back
dead. There are worse ways of dying. A similar tragedy
occurred at Fannich in Ross-shire, owned for many years by
Mr. Vernon Watney. He had just killed a stag and was about
to take the second. On this animal the stalker held his glass,
when, hearing a deep sigh and surprised at the delay, he
turned his head to glance at his master. To his surprise and
horror he found that the latter was already dead. We pray in
the Litany to be delivered from sudden death, but such pass-
ings as these seem to me merciful and not so dreadful for
those who are thus released as for those suddenly separated
from their loved ones.

This, however, is by the way. To return to St. Petersburg.
One morning shortly after our arrival the telephone bell
rang and a voice enquired if "Mr Vellice" was there. After
a certain amount of argument the voice rang off. A few
minutes later the bell again rang and another voice, female
this time, asked if "the master was at home." Following a
still more prolonged argument, she also rang off. Whilst we
were discussing these mysterious calls a further ring at the
front door heralded the advent of a very spick-and-span
gentleman who wanted to know if he could have a chat
with me. We chatted. His English was not very good and
my French was worse. The talk turned on books. Had I ever

written any? One or two. What were they about? Travel
and shooting. This seemed to intrigue my visitor, and he
began to press me. I answered as well as I could, though I
had an uneasy suspicion that the conversation was not
running quite so smoothly as he had anticipated. This I
attributed to the confusion consequent to the erection of the
Tower of Babel. Subsequently a friend sent me a bundle of
newspaper cuttings from England. In one was a letter from
Mr. Wells denying that he had been the subject of an
interview in St. Petersburg. He never allowed himself to be
interviewed. It had been Mr. Winans. Mr. Winans, it
appeared, had been interviewed, but not in mistake for Mr.
Wells, of whose books and tastes he knew nothing. This was
followed by another rather acid letter from Mr. Wells accus-
ing Mr. Winans of " unsportsmanlike repudiation." Mr.
Winans countered that Mr. Wells could romance as he liked
about planets, but that he did not allow any romancing
about himself! At the time Bombardier Wells was in training for a fight with a gentleman called "Bandsman Blake."
A correspondent of the paper facetiously suggested that it
was the Bombardier who had been interviewed! Mr. de
Schelking, my spick-and-span visitor, then stepped into the
breach. He stated that he had interviewed me under the mistaken idea that he was interrogating Mr. Wells. I was
pleased to find that while talking to me—"still young, virile,
and tall in stature"—he had been much struck by my excessive modesty!

I have said that Walter Winans was a magnificent shot.
I once watched him practising with a heavy revolver, and
enquired if he did not find that his wrist got very tired. His
answer was dramatic. Unfastening a large gold watch from
his chain, and remarking, "I'll soon stop it getting tired!"
he hung it just below the playing-card at which he was
shooting. Stepping back, he then proceeded to obliterate
the ace with a bullet, a performance which he repeated
several times.

At length, after nearly a fortnight in St. Petersburg, it was

decided that we should go to a place in the province of
Vitebsk, owned by my host, and see if our presence would
galvanise the bears into activity.

Bears usually lie up in November and remain in their
winter quarters until March or April. While they are choosing their holes they are tracked by hunters, who locate the
"den" by the absence of further tracks. In the event of the
animal being found on land which was not held in private
ownership, the hunter proceeded to sell his bear at so much
per "pood" (32 lbs.), the price varying with the accessibility
of the locality. In the old days the ordinary price was five
or six roubles per pood (10s. or 12s.), but with the demand
for this kind of sport and the consequent decrease in the
number of bears the price increased to twelve or fifteen
roubles, it being often stipulated that if the weight of the
bear exceeded a certain figure the price rose in proportion.
Thus an animal weighing, say, 200 lbs. might be sold at
eight roubles per pood, but if it turned out to be much
heavier when shot, the additional weight might be charged
at twelve roubles per pood.

These hunters were up to all sorts of tricks and might sell
the same animal to two different persons. If so, the bear was
moved the night before the drive and the sportsman told
that it had broken back through the beaters. He was
mulcted of a sum agreed upon in the case of failure, the
same bear "circled"—that is, tracked—again the next day,
and a second sportsman allowed to kill him. Such consideration, however, did not apply to us, as we were shooting on
a private estate. On arriving at the place where we meant to
hunt we were told that no bears had been located, and the
factor suggested that in lieu of anything better we should
try for lynx.

It is interesting to compare the estimation in which the
same animal is held in different countries. In Rumania the
lynx is classed as vermin; in Hungary he is regarded as
the premier game animal. Count Szechenyi, writing before
1914, stated: "A sportsman has indeed to regard himself

as extraordinarily lucky should he bag two or three in a life-time—so difficult is he to obtain." In the last sentence lies the crux of the matter, for any animal that is difficult to obtain always holds a high place in the estimation of sportsmen. In parts of Austria the killing of an eagle with the rifle was looked on in the old days as the highest mark of sportsmanship.

In my brief acquaintance with the lynx I should think he must always be hard to secure. In a beat he often climbs up a tree and remains motionless until the beat has passed. They are savage brutes and will kill for the sake of killing. In Europe they prey on birds and small mammals, young roe being often taken. The tail is very short, the throat has a tuft of long hairs, the skin being a beautiful rufus fawn with spots. They usually stand about 16 to 18 inches at the shoulders, the long hairs descending from the tip of each ear giving the animal its characteristic appearance.

We heard that a lynx had been "ringed," and the following morning drove out in sleighs to the wood where the animal had been located. I was posted in an opening, though my range of vision was very limited, the ground and trees being covered with snow. Here and there were open spaces. Fallen trunks showed through their thin white covering, partially submerged wrecks of what they once had been. The deadening silence of winter enveloped the whole atmosphere, broken only by the cry of the distant beaters. Gradually these drew nearer, and I began to wonder, as one always does at such a time, if, after all, our efforts were to end in vain. Then from the tail of my eye I caught a flicker of movement. I saw nothing, but was conscious that a shadow had passed for a brief moment among the tree trunks and undergrowth. Motionless I waited, but nothing stirred, and I began to doubt the evidence of my sight, for the wood was noiseless as before. Then the shadow stirred again behind the interlacing branches. What it was I could not tell, but that there had been movement of some sort I was certain. Very slowly I turned. Suddenly, with the swift,

apparent ease which nearly all wild animals possess, something large, silent, and ghost-like floated, rather than sprang,
across a small opening behind me and landed on a fallen
tree trunk. Automatically I swung towards it and fired.
There was a flurry of snow and the shadow vanished, but
not before I had had time to fire a second shot. Something
tore and ripped at the fallen snow and then lay still. When
I reached the spot where it lay I found a fine female lynx
quite dead. Very glad I was, for in but few private collections
have I seen its counterpart. Every bear having apparently
vacated this particular part of Russia, we decided to try
elsewhere, and moved to another locality some distance
away.

Here the news was no better and it appeared that, so far
as bears were concerned, our journey had been in vain.
The weather was glorious, which was some consolation,
and to occupy the time my host instituted a hare drive. A
long line was formed, about a dozen guns being interspersed
between the beaters. We had a good deal of walking, but
not much sport. Once a terrific outburst of yells and barking
heralded the advent of game, though what it was I could not
at first tell. Presently a solitary hare, hotly pursued by two
or three mongrels, appeared in the distance. It was greeted
with a volley by the nearest sportsmen, tore frantically
down the line in a smother of snow, and finally vanished into
the distance, unharmed, the mongrel pack still in pursuit.

Our visit was drawing to an end when, one evening, news
was brought that some wolves had been seen. Enthusiasm
revived, and next morning saw us setting out in sleighs for
a distant wood.

Our hostess—may her shadow never grow less!—had
armed herself with an automatic repeating shot-gun con-
taining ten cartridges loaded with buckshot. I must confess
that as we plodded through the snow in thick leather sheep-
skin coats, for it was very cold, I suffered many qualms. The
owner of this dreadful weapon, which she resolutely refused
to relinquish, plodded gamely on, stopping for breath at

intervals, when the muzzle described an arc which seemed invariably to end at a point directly opposite and level with the middle of my body. I remonstrated in vain, so directly she stopped I manœuvred as quickly as the loose snow would allow for a position immediately behind her. She was a dear, but ought never to have been allowed to handle firearms!

Arrived at the rendezvous, we found about twenty convicts from the local jail assembled in charge of two warders armed with revolvers. They greeted us with smiles and, as soon as we were posted, trudged off to the far end of the wood, talking amicably to their keepers.

My hostess was at the end of the line of fire, my own position being next to her. I had a small screen of undergrowth and saplings in front of me and could see for 30 or 40 yards comparatively clearly. As before, not a sound broke the stillness, and I meditated on what would happen if the monstrous piece of artillery I had so far managed successfully to avoid should be turned in my direction. Presently loud yells from the neighbourhood of the convict beaters announced that something was happening. Almost at once two large animals galloped past me in the direction of my hostess. I could not see clearly on account of the intervening stems, nor could I shoot, for they had passed too quickly.

Hardly had they gone when a terrific fusillade opened on my right. My feelings sank, for it seemed unlikely that any living thing could come unscathed through such a barrage. However, I was unduly pessimistic, for as the firing ceased a large wolf, looking very scared, appeared just opposite me, giving a splendid chance. He turned out to be a big male in full winter coat, and weighed just 100 lbs. Standing 31 inches at the shoulders, he measured 58 inches from his nose to the tip of his tail. The other escaped without giving any opportunity for a shot.

I was lucky to have got such an easy chance, for had the wolf not broken back, after having been turned at the end of the line, I should never have got him. Drives, at the best of times, are always full of uncertainty, as a very trifling incident may ruin them completely.

So ended our short visit to Russia. It is true that in its main object, bear, we had been unsuccessful, but success lies not altogether in accomplishment, but in what has been attempted. Our experiences had provided an interesting contrast to other forms of sport in which I had taken part, and the bag, though small, a welcome addition to my collection. The European wolf and lynx are not rare, but specimens are not commonly found in private museums in this country. As I look at them hanging on my wall I confess to a feeling of sadness when I think of the fate which has overtaken so many of those whom I met during the course of our visit. Brutally murdered or forced to live in exile, their homes plundered and destroyed, the fate of many of those dear to them unknown, those who survive are fortunate if they possess a pittance of their former wealth or means to continue an existence which to some is almost insupportable.

In spite of that, I feel that I was lucky to have seen a phase of life which has passed for ever, and which none of those now living will ever see again.

X. THE SPANISH IBEX

"Spain," said the Padre, "is a wonderful country, rich, beautiful, with a climate like none in Europe . . . for a traveller for pleasure I think this country is second to none."

IN KEDAR'S TENTS—Henry Seton Merriman

A FRIEND with whom I have spent many happy hours, overcome at times by the stagnation of daily life, relieves her feelings in the heartfelt exclamation "Oh! I wish something nice would happen." Not too frequently is this aspiration fulfilled. At times, however, something nice does happen which may even exceed our untold dreams. One such occasion materialised in my own case in the autumn of 1943. I received a letter bearing a Spanish stamp, a matter alone for speculation. Opening it with some eagerness I found that it was an invitation to visit Spain in order that I might offer what advice lay in my power for the preservation of the game in that country. The season was too far advanced to render practicable a visit before the shooting season ended. There were many formalities to be observed, passports, visas and a variety of matters to be attended to and it was not until 1944 that, thanks to the help of the Diplomat and the good offices of the British Council, I was ready to start.

The preliminaries to a journey of this description are, to me, always exciting, and anticipation lends enchantment to the unknown. In this instance the prospect of flying rendered it even more of an adventure, on realising that what I had been accustomed to regard as a voyage of several days could be accomplished in as many hours. On a dull, grey, drizzly morning I embarked on a Dutch aircraft. We took off at 9.30 and at 2 o'clock I was sitting in the sunshine of Lisbon enjoying a glass of sherry. So rapid a transformation still savours to me of magic. I feel that rightfully I should be a participator in one of Mr. Walt Disney's fairy stories. The following morning I set out in a Spanish 'plane *en route* for Madrid.

It was fascinating to watch the estuary of the Tagus opening below, to see the lines of Torres Vedras, to trace the course of the river past Abrantes, from which the fascinating Laura's husband took his title; to fly on over the brown landscape dotted here and there with olive yards and vineyards between the mountains of Toledo and the Sierra de Gredos, and to note names which later I got to know so well, Oropesa, Talavera de la Reina, and others.

So in time Madrid itself came into view, the trees and lakes of its lovely parks making bright splashes of colour amid buildings shining in the morning sun. At the aerodrome I was greeted by Professor Walter Starkie, that genial, Irish bohemian, head of the British Institute in Madrid, whom I always likened to Diego Valdez. The kindness and hospitality shown me by him and Mrs. Starkie have left me with many grateful memories. At lunch I was introduced to Luis Bolin, the Director-General of Tourism in Spain, to whom my visit was due. There are some nationalities who instinctively sympathise with each other's outlook. In my experience those with whom we most naturally fraternise are the Austrians and the Spaniards.

Prior to my present visit, though my wife and I had paid fleeting visits to the south of Spain when staying with our old friend Admiral Burges Watson at Gibraltar, I had not met many Spaniards. Now I count some of them among my dearest friends. Before leaving England I had been told by one who knew the country well that I would find much with which I was in sympathy, both in the country and its people. The reality by far exceeded my expectations. Spain is a country of great contrasts as well as great traditions. You may pass, in the space of a few hours, from grey rocks, firs and high hills so like those of my own country, the home of bear, lynx, chamois and deer, to a land of oranges, roses, blue seas and bright sunshine. The plains of La Mancha and Don Quixote you may exchange for the mountains of the Pyrenees and the Picos de Europa.

Everywhere names will fall on your ear like echoes of "music when soft voices die," Valladolid, Ciudad Real, Mequinenza, Guadalajara, Avila, Miranda, Calzado de Cala-trava, and, loveliest of all, the two Madrigals, Madrigal de la Atlas Torres and Madrigal de la Vera. Everywhere, too, and always exactly in the right place, you will see castles, palaces or fortresses. Some are derelict. Some are private dwellings, though these, as in our own country, are becoming increasingly rare. Some have been adapted as paradors to thrill the imagination of the visitor with their ancient walls, spacious courtyards, and sunlit corridors. All are fascinating and intriguing.

The Spaniard, highborn or lowly, is a great gentleman, of a charming courtesy and manner. He is also a great sportsman with a sense of humour closely akin to our own. The Spanish lady, in addition to these qualities, is also extremely easy to look at, equally keen on sport and even more charming.

Arriving as I did in Spain, an elderly and completely

unknown Scotsman, my welcome filled me with wonder. Reading memoirs of Regency times we come across records of foreigners arriving in England with a few introductions, and their appearance at parties and routs. Acquitting themselves tolerably well, with their behaviour up to a certain standard of manners and address, they are passed on by their hosts and hostesses to their friends, and the accounts they have left of their entertainment leaves no doubt of the impressions they enjoyed. So it was in my own case. When I landed in Madrid I knew, as I have said, no one. When I left, after a visit of four months, I like to think I left a large circle of friends. For all the kindness, hospitality, and the generous welcome I received, I find it difficult adequately to express my gratitude. To enumerate the names of all those who entertained me so lavishly would occupy too much space, but to the Duke of Algeciras, the Duke and Duchess of Montellano, who entertained me at Rincon, one of the best shoots in Spain, to Conde Eduardo Yebes, one of the most gifted of Spanish sportsmen, and to Don Luis Bolin my most grateful thanks are especially due. They have left me with many memories which will never be effaced.

Spain is very well off for big game, though the fact is not generally known. In addition to bears, wolf, lynx, and roe, there is excellent chamois shooting in the Pyrenees and the Picos de Europa. Red deer abound (though in numbers reduced since the civil war) in the mountains in Montes de Toledo and the Sierra Morena, and some very fine heads, even judging by Continental standards, have been killed. But the chief game animal in Spain is, without doubt, the Spanish ibex (*Capra Hispanica*), which is found nowhere else. This grand little goat, which stands about 32 inches at the shoulders, is stockily built and handsomely marked. The general colour is dark, greyish brown with a dark line down the middle of the back, a band on the chest and flanks and the greater portion of the limbs black. The inside of the thighs and the stomach are lighter in tone. The chin has a small beard. The horns are triangular with a sharp twist

A CASTLE IN
SPAIN.
ARCOS DE LA
FRONTERA

and the front irregularly knobbed and ridged at the base. Lydekker describes their form as "an open semi-spiral, the direction being at first upwards and outwards, but afterwards backwards and inwards with an upward and slightly outward terminal flexure, although the tips are generally turned inwards."

The character and form of the horns is intermediate between the Caucasian tur and the true ibex though nearer to the West Caucasian tur than to the latter. Lydekker also states that "it may best be called a goat rather than an ibex," though it is generally known as the Spanish ibex. Later in this chapter I give measurements of some of the best heads of recent years.

The most difficult European trophy of which to secure a really fine specimen was, prior to 1939, without any doubt the Carpathian stag. However much youth, experience, hard work and energy was brought to his pursuit a large element of luck was also needed; and luck was not always there. Many experienced and ardent stalkers endeavoured to circumvent a first-class head for years and never succeeded.

The finest Continental sport I always considered—though my experience is limited—the pursuit of the chamois. Since my visit to Spain I would now, from the point of view of the stalker, with the chamois, class the Spanish ibex.

Its stronghold is the Sierra de Gredos, within an area of about thirty miles by fifteen, though they are also found in the Sierra Nevada, the Serrania de Ronda, the Sierra Cazorla in the south, the Sierra Madrona, and the Montes de Tortosa in the east. Their existence in the Pyrenees is rather hypothetical. Over a hundred head have also been counted in another "coto" in the Sierra de Ronda between Malaga and Marbella, which has just been established.

In 1905, the number of ibex at Gredos was down to two males and five females, though these figures may not be absolutely accurate, as Abel Chapman makes them slightly larger. The credit for their preservation belongs above all others to Sr. Don Manuel de Amezua. It was through his

H

representations that the Marques de Villaviciosa persuaded the late King Alfonso XIII to declare Gredos a royal reserve. In 1914 the numbers of ibex were reckoned at 400 head. In this range there are at the date of writing probably 2,000 or more. To kill an adult buck a Spaniard has to pay a sum of 600 pesetas, a fee which, for a foreigner, quite rightly is doubled. A certain number are poached, but far fewer of recent years. Owing to the grazing of domestic stock and the consequent reduction of their feeding grounds their development was threatened, but the Government have now made new regulations; the crofters being compensated and other grazings substituted. About 23 per cent only of the land in Spain is suitable for agriculture and Spaniards are beginning to realise that game is a valuable national asset.

Don Luis Bolin, the Director-General of Tourism, the Department which deals with such matters, is an extremely far-sighted and hard-working man, and to him is largely due the interest now taken in the maintenance and preservation of Spanish game. There is still much to be done but he has made a very good start. The paradors and albergues (country inns and hostels) have been raised to a very high pitch of efficiency: in them it is always possible to get excellent food and wine, served by attentive and capable staffs, clean and comfortable bedrooms, and every attention that a traveller may require. The latter is also made to feel that he is a welcome guest and not a nuisance to be disposed of as quickly as possible.

It was from the parador at Gredos that I set out on my first hunt after ibex. Luis had snatched a day or two from his multifarious duties to accompany me, which made all the difference. The view from our headquarters, looking across a pine-clad valley through which murmured a clear-running mountain stream towards the Gredos range, topped by Almanzor, was magnificent. I was in high hopes, for the weather was clear on the night of our arrival, but before morning snow had fallen. We made an attempt, but conditions were too severe, and though I did, in fact, see ibex, they were immature and we had to abandon the effort.

It was later in November that I returned, passing through Avila, one of the loveliest towns in Spain. Rivalling, and in the opinion of many, surpassing Carcasonne, its walls date back nearly a thousand years. The sight of these, bathed in the sun, is an unforgettable memory for those who have been privileged to see it. I was accompanied this time by Max, whose friendship I had formed through a book of mine written thirty years earlier. What I should have done without his help I do not know. He was intimate with the country; Spanish was his native language and I owe him a debt which has, so far, remained unpaid. I could go on writing about Max and his adventurous life—he once dined with a party of tough he-men who had each killed their man, except Max!—and his charming wife "Mrs. Chips," but this is about ibex. All the same Max ought to write a book.

There was still much snow on the north side of the Gredos range and this made stalking difficult, though one could have managed with skis; but I am no skier. We did, indeed, see ibex. Late in the afternoon two bucks appeared a mile or more away, running amid the rocks and snow. It was then too late to pursue them and subsequent chances of success seemed slight.

"If we were on the south side," said Julio, the chief guide, "we should have a much better chance. But it is not easy. The climbing is much more difficult. You will have to sleep on broom in a shepherd's hut in the mountains and the fare is rough." So we decided to move and, on the following morning, set out for the south side of the range, through the Puerto del Pico. Felipe, the chauffeur whom Luis had placed at my disposal, was not too happy as the road was far from good. I got very fond of Felipe. He could not talk a word of English and I spoke no word of Spanish, but we became great friends. He always met me when I returned to Madrid from a shooting party and always overwhelmed me with a torrent of questions. I could not understand a word of what he said but I knew what he meant. "What had I shot? And had I done well?" Dear Felipe! He was mad on sugar beet. He came from a sugar-beet country and spotted any by the side of the road at once. When I left Madrid for the last time he came to see me off at the aerodrome and wrung my hand and slapped me on the back, as is the custom in Spain, with an emotion I knew was genuine. He was a superb driver and I cherish his memory. He negotiated the pass all right and about lunchtime reached a small place with the lovely and enchanting name I have already mentioned—Madrigal de la Vera. I found in a French guide-book that the great Isabella had been born here. I was told this was incorrect, but anyway it is a place I shall always remember. Roses were blooming, and oranges grew on the lower slopes of the foothills. We had a meal in a primitive local inn, half open to the sky with a peripatetic local population dropping in at intervals. There was a charming and attractive little child whose name was, of all things, Egypt, and a lot of cats and dogs. Egypt played a very popular game in the open, hopping about in squares marked on the dusty ground.

All the male inhabitants of Madrigal de la Vera (which I like writing again) had disappeared on a local wolf hunt. I remember walking about the village, met with the most courteous greetings "Go with God, Senor—Buenos Dias" and on these occasions to become impatient, difficult though it may be to control one's emotions, is fatal. Eventually, having run the Alcalde to earth, Max managed to secure some horses and equipment. Late that evening, after a three hours' walk, we found ourselves in a partially built house, at a height of 3,500 feet in a gully in the mountains. The following day—it was November 11—we started at 9 a.m. after a cup of coffee and a biscuit. That is the only quarrel I have with Max. For some obscure reason which I had not fathomed he thought it was a bad thing to start climbing after a good meal. I anticipated a proper breakfast of sorts subsequent to our light repast. No food materialised until about 4.30! Other drawbacks to my full enjoyment of the day were the facts that I was wearing nailed brogues and that I had no stalking stick. The latter is to me an essential for a day on the hill in any country. As regards footwear I should have done much better with crepe soles.

Not long after we had started Jose Nuñez, the stalker, made out far above us, on the other side of a deep gorge, an ibex which he decided to pursue. After a good deal of rough climbing we reached a spot, past which he thought the ibex would pass, if moved. To make a long story short, he disappeared and never again did we see him. But within half an hour Max came back to me after a reconnaissance and said, "Will you take a shot at an eighty-centimetre head at three hundred and fifty yards? We can't get any closer."

Here I must say a word about the Spanish countryman. Of all those I have encountered in many parts of the world, the Spaniard is as good as any. All the stalkers and keepers I met in the Peninsula were, without exception, delightful, real Nature's gentlemen, and those at Gredos the best. They were tough, hardy (most of them lived on goat's milk until they were about eighteen years of age), grand walkers, with but few comforts. These they do not seem to miss. They are generally small in stature, but excellent hill men, with great powers of endurance, keen on sport, generously helpful and unsparing of themselves, while they seem to expect no reward for their labours. I class them with the old type of Highland stalker and I can bestow no greater praise. In addition to their other qualities the Spanish stalkers I met were quite uncannily correct when "judging" a head. The length of any type of big game head with twisted, "curling" horns is very difficult to estimate in the field, whether in Africa, Asia, or Europe. If a Gredos stalker tells you that an ibex head, seen in the distance, is 75 centimetres, or 73 centimetres, you can be pretty certain that its length will not vary much in either direction. The particular head in question was not 80 centimetres; but it was 77—which is the difference of an inch, at three hundred and fifty yards!

In answer to Max's query I told him I would take the shot if it would create no undue disturbance and we could not get any closer. I was a little doubtful, using a strange rifle which I had been lent by the Diplomat. However, I crawled up under cover and saw the ibex, clearly silhouetted between two outcroppings of rock. Though small, seen at that distance, he was a good mark, but before I could come into action he settled my qualms by disappearing. Moving off for half a mile, though not much disturbed, we watched him settle beneath some jagged peaks of rock. So we lay in the sun and waited, watching him. His position was unapproachable, but one of the gillies, Domingo, said that he could move him to a better place. So off went Domingo. By this time, it was past five : I was feeling pretty exhausted though I had had some food. After a certain amount of cross-chat from one peak to another, we located the ibex in a fairly accessible position. Suffering as I was from lack of food, exhaustion, poor physical condition and no stick, after a good deal of climbing, descents, more climbing and various detours, I, at length, found myself perched on a rock between Domingo and Jose Nuñez, with the buck immediately below me in a rocky gully. Domingo was pressed against my left elbow, Jose Nuñez on my right. Mauricio, another gillie and brother of the former, was breathing hard down the back of my neck. Julio was craning over my shoulder and Max hovered somewhere in the rear. The ibex was quite unconscious of our presence.

To apprehend distance correctly in unknown country and alien atmospheric conditions is always a difficulty. I turned to Jose and held up one finger. "A hundred metres— cien metros?" I asked.

"Si, si," exclaimed Jose eagerly.

"Doscientos metros," I enquired, holding up two fingers.

"Si, si, si," assented Jose in a passion of enthusiasm.

"Dash it," I thought, "if I hold up five fingers, he'll agree."

"It's about one hundred and fifty yards," said Max, behind me. Dear Max, he was always there when wanted. I had the whole back to aim at. The ibex was feeding away directly below me. At the shot he dashed off and I have never seen an animal move faster. As he rounded a spur of rock I had another shot—through the telescopic sight—an inch behind him. There was no splintering of rock as there is in the event of a miss and talk broke out in a spate.

"Something has happened," said Max, as Mauricio dashed to a neighbouring peak on our left. Then he started yelling.

"Muerto!" shouted Julio, and seized my hand.

"Maestro!" howled Jose, clutching the other.

"You've got him," said Max.

It took me an hour and a half to stagger to the shepherd's hut where we spent the night. I have never in my life suffered so much from exhaustion, and felt very ill. I was very ill! However, after a good night before a blazing fire on branches of broom—there were eight of us in a space 15 feet by 10 feet—I felt myself again. Never could any have been kinder or more considerate to me that were those Spanish peasants. We had left the ibex where it had fallen and after breakfast Mauricio walked down the hillside with it on his shoulders, and joined us on the track, carrying it as though it had been a feather. Its horns measured, as I have said, 77 centimetres ($30\frac{1}{2}$"), which is a good length though nothing under 80 centimetres can be considered quite first-class. It was, however, so my friend Eduardo Yebes told me, as pretty a head as he had ever seen and as good a representative ibex as any foreign sportsman could wish for. The table overleaf shows some of the best heads killed in the Sierra de Gredos. The Sierra de Gredos will remain the chief stronghold of the ibex in Spain. Luis Bolin has, however, wisely determined to establish them in other sierras. A tract of hill country between Malaga and Gibraltar is particularly suitable, and foreigners at Gibraltar will, no doubt, later on reap the reward of his foresight. An attempt was made in King Alfonso's reign to start a new herd, but it failed and the ibex died. With increased facilities and air travel there seems no reason now why such an experiment should not prove a success and this splendid little animal firmly established on new ground.

Shot by.	Length.	Tip to Tip.	Circumference.
Edmond Blanc ..	$35\frac{3}{8}$	$31\frac{1}{2}$	$10\frac{1}{4}$
Keeper (for Museum)	$34\frac{1}{2}$	$21\frac{3}{4}$	$9\frac{1}{2}$
Luis Bolin	$34\frac{1}{4}$	$20\frac{1}{2}$	9
Duke of Arion ..	$34\frac{1}{4}$	$27\frac{1}{2}$	10
Michael Creswell ..	$34\frac{1}{8}$	$26\frac{3}{4}$	$9\frac{1}{2}$
Marques de Valduesa	$34\frac{1}{8}$	$17\frac{7}{8}$	$8\frac{3}{4}$
J. Munoz Aguila ..	$32\frac{5}{8}$	$33\frac{1}{2}$	$9\frac{7}{8}$
Infante Alfonso de Bourbon	$32\frac{5}{8}$	$19\frac{3}{8}$	$8\frac{3}{4}$

XI. THE CHASE OF A GOAT

"The rocks of the wild goats."—I SAM. xxiv. 2

I FIRST heard of him at a London dinner-party (this was forty years ago), and when F., who told me his history, finished by saying, "Come up to me in September, and have a go at him!" I felt that, even in the midst of the depression caused by a London fog, life had still some attractions to offer.

I heard much of him that summer, but until September 6 he remained shrouded in the mists of imagination. Then, as we were doing the last stages of my forty-seven-mile drive from Lairg, Mackenzie said, "There's the gorts!" There they were indeed, on the top of a rocky sky-line, and in the midst of them, the ewes and kids playing beneath him, was my old billy. He was standing with his head up, every inch of his splendid horns thrown into strong relief against the pale lilac of an evening sky, and as I watched him that attack of goat fever began, which in the end nearly made me lose him, and for the best part of three days rendered me the most unhappy man in Sutherlandshire.

The Highland wild goat is usually descended from domestic stock, but often carries a finer head. The late Walter Jones who, for so long was tenant of Meoble, there obtained one with a spread of 37 inches. Roualeyn Gordon Cumming's "Mascot," now at Altyre, is slightly bigger. Though their powers of scent are nothing wonderful, they have very good sight, better than that of either the roe or the red deer. Such, at least, was my experience. This is not to be wondered at, for all animals which live naturally in wide, open, and hilly country rely for safety chiefly on their powers of sight; whilst those which live in flat or wooded ground trust almost entirely to their nasal organs. A good billy will weigh about eight stone. I killed mine late in the season, when he was in very poor condition, or he would have scaled fully eight and a half stone.

There are two types of horn: one curves back over the animal's neck, like that of an ibex; whilst the other takes an outward sweep a foot or more from the base of the horn. The goat I was after carried a head of the latter type, and when, on September 7, I saw him in his home within half a mile of me, I longed for it with a great longing. It may have been wrong, it may have been a spark of the same spirit which filled the breast of some rude ancestor in the dim prehistoric ages when he saw an unusually fine specimen of *Cervus megaceros*, but there it was; and though I think that no one, unless he be altogether a brute, can kill a living sentient animal without having a certain tinge of pity mingled with his satisfaction, the instinct of the hunter predominates until his end is achieved.

They had certainly chosen their home well. Up from the shores of a little hill loch rose a steep and rocky face. Amid the grey, lichen-clad boulders, picked out sharply here and there, were green grassy slopes and cool dark hollows. In one of these hollows he was lying half hidden by a huge stone, looking out across the loch to where a mountain burn came brawling down from the mists around Arkle. There were about a dozen of them altogether: four or five kids standing on their hind legs and playfully sparring and butting, five or six ewes, and one or two young billys. As I watched, a black-and-white billy invaded the sacred circle, and with a rush the old fellow was on him. His long, dark hair, shading off at the flanks, almost touched the ground, and very savage and truculent he looked as he dashed at his rival. Doubtless the latter thought so too, for he did not await the charge, but fled to a friendly rock. It was apparently outside the danger zone, for the old billy did not pursue, and went back to his hollow. We were in full view of them, and to get near enough for a shot had to make a detour of at least three miles. However, we did it under an hour, and presently reached the hill in the shadow of which they were lying. We left F. where we had first spied them, and through the glass could see him signalling that they were still below us. We crept a little nearer; Ross, the stalker, first, and I close behind. A gust of wind came eddying among the rocks, and as it did so a horrid stench of goat took me in the throat. With his hand Ross motioned me to peep over the rock; forty yards distant, and below me, was one of the ewes quietly feeding with her kid beside her. Ross cautiously withdrew his head, and as he did so a pair of widespread horns came into view. I reached for the rifle, and saw the ewe, with her head up, watching me. The old billy raised his, as he caught her attitude, and faced me.

"Keep cool! Keep cool!" I heard Ross murmur. "Tak' your time." But the sight of those horns was too much for me, and I fired hurriedly as he stood there. At the shot he shook his head and then, turning, bolted over the rocks. I had a snap at his vanishing form, but he dashed on without any sign of a hit save an occasional angry toss of his head. At the time I did not know it, but found afterwards that my first shot had gone clean through his horn. Well, there it was. I had had my shot and lost him, and for the next half-hour I was pretty wretched, as we all feared he might leave the ground. So we had lunch, and then started off again.

I might go on to tell you of our long walk: of the beautifully graduated grey, pink, and white mosaics which we passed lying in little pools among the rocks; of the dimpling sharp-toed tracks we found leading across the tops; of how we lost them among the rocks and re-found them again further on, though we did not again see the little band who had made them; of how we continued the chase, hoping against hope, until the gathering gloom compelled us to turn our weary steps homewards; of the drive home, past long-armed sea-lochs looking out to where the Western Isles showed faint and grey on the broad bosom of the Atlantic; of Foinaven and rocky Arkle; of Ben Stack, Quinaig, Sugar Loaf, and many other landmarks with sweet-sounding names; but will ask you to start again with me on the Saturday, the whole of another day before us, and our hopes centred on the goat.

Before we had driven the five miles which had to be traversed before we could start stalking, the sky had become overcast, and we made our way to the spying-place in a thin drizzle. From there we could see nothing, and I suspected from my companions' faces that they feared the goat family had removed their Lares and Penates to a safer district. However, on we went, the grey, heavy-looking masses of dark clouds banking up in the west. Amongst the rocks a dull booming re-echoed, and as we crept under an overhanging rock the storm broke. The rain came down in buckets, while the wind tore and lashed itself into a fury. A curious cheeping noise from somewhere behind us caught my ear and I asked Ross what it was. "Just an eagle," he replied, and though at the time I could hardly credit him, I have since had his answer confirmed. It sounded just like a young grouse. Under our sheltering rock were some comparatively fresh grey droppings, and also a strong smell of goat. This revived our hopes, for it showed they must have been on the ground since Thursday. As we were discussing what to do, Campbell, who was carrying my rifle, came creeping to us with a look of portentous solemnity on his face. "The gorts are close by; within eichty yards!" he announced, so Ross and I at once went up to some rocks where we could spy. From there only the black-and-white billy and one ewe were visible, so we crawled back to another boulder. Ross slowly raised his head.

"I see them aal," he muttered; then, in a hissing whisper, "I see him; I see the big one!" We noiselessly retreated, and crawled up to a rock about one hundred yards from the goats. There he was, just about one hundred yards off; his horns, it seemed to me, longer, and even more desirable than ever.

"Tak' your time," whispered Ross. "Keep canny; he'll no move." I took time, and I was, as I thought, fairly canny. (Ross told me afterwards I was puffing like a steam-engine!) He was broadside on, and the light fair. After what seemed to me about three minutes I pressed the trigger. The old billy turned, and went scrambling off among the rocks at a gallop. This soon relapsed into the irritating half trot, half canter, which he could keep up for miles, and which I had grown to loathe.

"There they go!" said Ross, and we saw them straggling over a rocky top. Their pace is most deceptive; they will keep it up for any length of time, and though it looks slow, in reality it is pretty fast. They were nearly a mile and a half off, and, as we watched, the leading kid swung to the left. "I think they'll keep just the same traack they did on Thurrsday," he continued. "If they do, we can cut them off!" Accordingly we got up, and started for a distant knoll from which we could follow their movements.

My period of blank despair had gradually thawed, and after we had covered a mile or so, in spite of the pouring rain, I even began to take an intelligent interest in life. At length we reached the knoll, and lay among the rocks with our glasses ready. For a long time we rested there, hopes and fears alternately predominating as a grey rock deluded us with the momentary belief that it was a goat, and the spyglass revealed the brutal truth in a manner there could be no questioning. It is very hard country to spy. Indeed, it is a wild country altogether, this Sutherland, and unlike any other part of Scotland I have seen. The shaggy birch woods and melting hills of heather are gone, and in their place are the hard grey rocks lying in fantastic shapes on every side. They crop up in scarred ridges, like the healed blisters on a man's hand, or form gigantic monstrosities which loom largely at you from every sky-line. Here you see the presentment of a cottage loaf, there a whale leers dumbly at you, his half-submerged bulk rising from a sea of deer grass.

At last, very quietly, Campbell said, "I see them," and there they really were, still travelling in the same order—first three kids, then the old billy, then the ewes, and last the two young male goats. They were moving steadily onwards, as if knowing the road, and we stayed but to make sure of their direction, then tore for the next top. I thought that they had given us the slip after all, so long did we wait without a sign of them, when the leading kid, now only about six hundred yards off, proved me wrong by obligingly making her appearance from behind a hill. Ross and I dashed off again, leaving F. and Campbell to follow at their leisure. For five or six hundred yards we had a real hard run at top speed, parallel with the goats; a narrow ravine divided us from them, on the other side of which rose a rocky ridge. The goats were moving along behind this ridge out of our sight, but even as we stopped they came into view over the top, and began to descend into the ravine. As soon as they were out of sight at the bottom and began to ascend our side, we made a dash for the head of the pass. We reached it, and were crawling to the top of the knoll, when over some rocks I saw the head of the black-and-white billy, his progress arrested, watching us. The warning bleat which we were dreading never came, and as I sank behind Ross the leading kid passed an opening in the rock twenty yards off. Then came the other two, and after them I had a vision of a broad back covered with long shaggy

hair, and of curving, widespread horns. The sight steadied
me, for I knew it was my last chance. I saw the ivory foresight gleaming white against his dark side. Then I fired.
At the crack there was a rush and the clatter of falling
stones. But the old goat lay very quiet and still, an inert
mass among the rocks; whilst the black-and-white billy
who had failed him in his hour of need drove the ewes
before him down the pass.

XII. SOME CHANGES IN THE ART OF DEER STALKING

"And not to know the hills is like never having been in love."
                                    MARGARET OGILVIE—J. M. Barrie

IT is fifty years since I killed my first stag, and 1947 was the first year since then, unless absent abroad, that I did not stalk or fire a rifle. The reasons for this were bound up in the changed conditions under which we at present labour. Several of my friends were good enough to send me invitations. All I felt compelled to refuse. The middle-aged couple who were kind enough to oblige at five pounds a week, and had been left in undisputed possession for six months, suddenly decided, unknown to me, that they were being overworked. Surreptitiously packing their belongings into their car, they asked if it would be quite convenient for them to go out for the day. Receiving assent, they disappeared, and I have never set eyes on them from that day to this. Any feelings of decency or consideration one has long ago ceased to expect, but that such behaviour causes certain inconveniences is undeniable. I felt that I could not go off and attempt to enjoy myself, even if any petrol were available, leaving my wife to cope with the domestic difficulties. The weather, too, was far from attractive and I had not been in the best of health. Thirty, twenty or even ten years ago I could have selected a day, conditions being favourable, on which I could have gone over our tiny bit of ground with reasonable prospects of getting a stag. In 1917, having secured a fortnight's leave, my wife and I had stalked for twelve days on Corriemony and killed forty stags between us. Corriemony lies between Balmacaan and Guisachan. In the former forest the birchwoods, which then extended through the length of Glen Urquhart, provided good cover. Now they have ceased to exist and the Forestry Commission's fenced plantations deny any protection to deer. To the west the natural woods which rendered Guisachan an ideal forest for an elderly stalker have suffered a similar fate. Corriemony, a narrow strip of 10,000 acres between these two, though never a forest in the proper sense of the word, owing to the absence of really high ground, was always full of deer during the latter part of the season. Under present conditions, constantly disturbed by shepherds and dogs, the woods which held deer laid low, a couple of rabbits and an odd pigeon is about the extent of the game population to be expected. In addition, supposing that I had been able to stalk there and was lucky enough to find and kill a stag, the difficulties attendant on getting it down from the hill were such as to make one pause before taking a shot. Formerly such considerations were of no moment. One could tell the stalkers to send out a pony and bring it in or leave word at what point a gillie and pony should be in attendance. When there is no stalker, no gillie and no pony to drag a dead stag single-handed over rough heather and hill for a mile or more is not a task which I envy anyone, particularly in October when days are short and weather uncertain. So 1947 was a blank year for me as far as stalking was concerned.

Conditions have indeed changed. In the palmy days sport was a conduit through which flowed a golden stream into the Highlands. Now, in all the many schemes and activities designed to revive Highland life and to render the north of Scotland a place fit for tourists to live in, shooting is entirely disregarded. The sportsman is, as I have said, an anachronism. Committees, commissions, boards and controls regulate the life of the Highlands. Writes Dr. Fraser Darling:

Deer forests and deer have been the subject of an extraordinary amount of misunderstanding and bad thinking. Our approach need not be political and coloured by sectional bias. It is unfortunate that the use of the deer forests in the middle years of last century has been debited with the clearances which to a very much greater extent were conducted half a century earlier, when the sheep farmers came. It is quite wrong historically to saddle the deer forests with the depopulation of the Highlands. It is equally unscientific to work up a personal animus against a very beautiful and useful animal because its hunting has been confined to a certain class of society.

That there were abuses is undeniable. Ground which was unsuited and could have been put to better use was labelled "deer forest" and these "frontier zones" were responsible for much of the criticism and abuse subsequently directed at deer forests proper. "It is doubtful," writes the authority already quoted, "whether the rabid anti-deer-forest section of society realises how little Highland ground is devoted absolutely and exclusively to deer, or how little of it could be better used than it is." I quote from *Natural History in the Highlands and Islands*. In those far-off days when I first stalked, such considerations troubled us but little. There was a large area of ground abounding with deer and here were we, young and active, with nothing to hinder us from enjoying ourselves, and enjoy ourselves we did.

The greatest difference between ourselves and our predecessors in the art of stalking lay in the rifle. In the practice of the art itself there has been but little change, for the necessity of procuring food goes back to the dim red dawn of man. The truth of this has been forced on us during the last few years when venison, formerly the chosen dish of kings, which prior to 1939 had almost been refused even when given away, rocketed to fantastic prices in the black market and was often unprocurable. But weapons had, in truth, changed. The spear was replaced by the bow; the bow by the firearm; this developed into the flintlock, and this again into the percussion cap. Then came the old black powder rifle with which I began my stalking career. Now we have the modern high-velocity small bore. Deadly in the hands of the expert, it is apt to encourage the novice or one who is not a real stalker into taking long shots, and the neglect of the art wherein lies the real pleasure of stalking.

Ill-used would the young man of the present day consider himself were he sent to the hills with the weapon which I used to carry. Ill-used, too, he might consider himself if compelled to catch "the mail" at six o'clock in the morning in order to reach his rendezvous with the stalker at the appointed hour. There were no motor-cars then, and had there been I should have forfeited the memory of that leisurely early morning drive, the mist rising from the still waters of the loch as the sun appeared above the eastern hills.

Then we had a collie, an enthusiastic animal with a perpetual grin, whose duty it was to pursue any stag I might have the misfortune to wound and bring him to bay before he could gain the recesses of the wood. Fortunately his services were unnecessary. It is rare now to see a dog taken on the hill, though I do not know that their absence is due to any improvement in the shooting. That it should have improved can scarcely be questioned, for it is very much easier to make accurate shooting with a modern small bore, and at longer ranges, than it was with the old black powder rifles. That such weapons have increased the likelihood of wounding animals at excessive ranges is also true.

Fifty years ago there were very few lady stalkers. Before the war one could scarcely open the paper during the stalking season without seeing that Miss So-and-so had "grassed" a fine stag (I never quite realise the distinction involved!), or a snapshot, carefully posed, of some female in the fashionable headpiece of the period, labelled "Miss —— shooting at a deer."

We all know what British women did in the war years, the dangers they faced, uncomplaining and unafraid. We viewed with admiration their magnificent courage, efficiency and hard work. For all of them I have a profound admiration and respect, but I have a particular feeling for those who in my youth were classified as "ladies," young or old, brought up in luxury, waited on, spoiled if you like. They undertook tasks which they never expected to be called on to perform and did them with an efficiency and speed which those who previously had been paid to execute them seldom equalled. They cooked, cleaned their houses, looked after their menfolk, tended their gardens, did heavy manual labour and contrived at the same time to maintain an outward appearance which might have been expected to deteriorate. The work they did in the deer forests during the war years will not be forgotten by those who witnessed it. They not only stalked and shot but they acted as gillies, they dragged in deer (no one who has undertaken this task is likely to underestimate its difficulty), they groomed the ponies, they spent hours drenched to the skin on open hillsides. Tired and weary they yet contrived to look after their male belongings and provide them with hot baths and meals when they returned tired after a hard day. Respectfully and admiringly I take off my hat to them.

In those days before 1939 every season produced the usual crop of letters on the "Deterioration of Scottish Deer." Then, as now, remedies were suggested and "Laudator temporis acti" explained how such deterioration could be remedied. Then, as now, those who had studied the subject knew quite well how improvements could be effected, and also that under existing conditions such improvements could never, generally, be carried into effect.

It seems to me, looking back, that heads are more intelligently analysed than they were when I was a boy. I never remember hearing much about measurements of heads. A head was "good" or "very good," and that was about all. There was, to my recollection, no real standard of comparison. That such a change should have come about is all to the good, and if stalkers would learn how to measure a head properly, instead of wildly guessing, as many of them still do, it would enable one who had not seen a particular trophy to estimate the category to which it belongs much more nearly and accurately than would otherwise be possible. A head described as "very fine" may be so for the ground from which it comes, and very mediocre from a forest a few miles away. One read in some sporting paper: "The record stag for the past seventy years has been shot: 21 sts., clean, and a royal." This sort of statement may delight the casual reader, but to the experienced stalker it means nothing. It *may* be quite true, but many stags of 21 sts. have been killed in the past seventy years and a great many royals. If the writer of the paragraph had given the measurements of the head he might have been justified in his opening statement; as it stands it is quite valueless.

Fifty years ago we should not have been roused by the news that an American sportsman had suggested bringing his light aeroplane for the purpose of "spotting" the deer. There were few Americans in Scotland then (they are rare now as lessees of deer forests) and no aeroplanes. Nor should we have experienced a gratifying sensation on reading the comment in connection with the above statement that "the idea is frowned upon by British sportsmen"!

The whole outlook of stalking is now completely altered. Rents, suffering a blow in 1914 from which they never recovered, had dropped by half or more in the years intervening prior to 1939. The whole future is completely uncertain, save that it is entirely unlikely that deer forests will ever recover any of their former standing.

Whether such changes as have taken place press more

hardly on the young or on their elders is difficult to determine. We knew something of the great days; they only by
hearsay.

Up to 1912, which I put as the peak year, we in the little
world on whose outskirts I revolved, knew what was happening in the North. We knew to whom which forests and
whose moors were let, many on long leases. We knew who,
on the 12th, would get the record bags (usually it was the
Hargreaves family at Gaick). We knew from which forests
would come the best heads. It all seems so futile now, that
narrow little circle which made our lives, when we read
that Mr. Molotov has again said "no"; that there has been
some further development in the atom bomb, or puzzle
over some new word of which previously we were completely unaware. We were happy then, and those whom we
met seemed happy. There was none of the class hatred
which seems now to permeate the atmosphere, though less
apparent in the north than in the south. Civil greetings
were not regarded as marks of subservience, and if some
were better off than others we were not taught to regard
them as public enemies, unworthy of consideration and
marks for hatred and malice. Good manners were regarded
as an asset, for they, after all, in the highly artificial atmosphere in which we exist, are but a portion of the cement
which keeps the whole structure from disintegrating and
at least serve to make human contacts pleasant and bearable.

That the outlook of those whom we now meet is different
to our own a chance encounter brought home to me. I had
stopped at the Glen Affaric Hotel, that little inn which I had
known for so long and where I purchased for ten shillings
four volumes on Prince Charles Edward, which was the
original cause of the motor trip referred to by my old friend
Lionel Edwards in his reminiscences and from which came
A Stuart Sketch Book. There was a magnificent assemblage
in front of the inn; a general air of haste and excitement in
contrast to the peaceful Highland surroundings which were
so familiar. I counted eight or nine cars and thought that,

unwittingly, I had encountered some royal progress. I was wrong. The haste was caused by the advent of some ministers to whose names I had not yet become accustomed, inspecting the possibilities of the Highlands. They departed, and I got into conversation with some of the dregs who remained. They were full of enthusiasm for the future. We discussed Highland industries, factories, modern improvements and hydro-electric schemes. They had visited Glen Cannich and inspected the site of the great dam. The water, if restrained, would eventually submerge Benula lodge in which I had spent many happy hours.

"Don't these people mind having their houses put under water, though?" suggested one of the enthusiasts.

"Wouldn't you mind having your house put under water?" I asked.

"Oh yes! But that's quite different," lightly rejoined the lady. It is. Quite different.

When I was a boy the journey to Inverness and back was an event. It was nearly 50 miles. Relays of horses had to be arranged. For several days discussions took place as to who was to be permitted to go, and elaborate lists were drawn up in order that nothing might be forgotten. The road scarcely permitted the passing of "machines." Altogether the whole expedition was a thrilling affair. Tourists were never seen. They were all safely ensconced on Messrs. David MacBrayne's swift mail steamers.

The road now is changed beyond recognition. Buses even can pass each other with comparative ease. In place of the lovely birches which clothed the hillsides and gave the traveller so much joy to contemplate, ranks of firs grow in orderly rows. White-harled cottages stand where they did, though their gardens have diminished in size to add to the width of great arterial highways. On them, as of yore, you may meet the tinkers, who have not been transformed as have the scenes through which they journey. Occasionally one finds that a cart has been replaced by a broken-down Ford car; but still through tousled hair weather-beaten faces, rude with health, peer as you pass; rabbit skins still dangle from the axles.

Places hitherto inaccessible are easily reached, and a type of visitor formerly unknown is to be seen in the main centres. Foreigners, smitten with the charm of the country, even take up permanent residence there, and having practised assiduously before a looking-glass, proudly display their nether extremities in kilts of their own design. I have often wondered, were they to select some of the more remote Pacific Islands as a place of residence, would they appear in the local equivalent of a fig-leaf; or in, say, the Austrian Tyrol be found yodelling upon the hillside in leather shorts and jaeger hats? Their females in the tweediest of tweeds open bazaars, and for a time, to the delight of the local inhabitants, enact the rôle of lady bountiful. The wealthier of them may bring money into the country, but they always remain aliens, and do not as a rule like deer stalking. When, involuntarily, one compares them with their penniless predecessors, one cannot but feel a pang, for the latter were at any rate sportsmen.

The hiker is another difficulty. I am all in favour of hiking. With their aims the average stalker has every sympathy, though the feeling is not always reciprocated. A certain type of hiker—I think the rarest—is roused to fury at the thought of anyone having enough money to appropriate to his own use a large tract of land for two or three months in the year. This is the type which makes hiking unpopular in the Highlands. I know very few owners or tenants of forests who would refuse a stranger permission to go on their land at any time save only in August or September. These, unfortunately, are the two months when hiking is most popular. Even so, were the hiker to approach the occupier of the lodge and ask him if he might climb a certain hill he would almost invariably be treated with courtesy. If a stalking party were going on this particular beat he would probably be allowed to accompany it. It is the man or woman who marches into the middle of the forest unwittingly, as is usually the case, moving large numbers of deer of whose presence they are probably unaware, to whom the stalker objects, and rightly. To expect anyone who pays heavily for his pleasure and who employs a large staff to acquiesce tamely in having his enjoyment and sport ruined by those who would be the first to object were the positions reversed is to be less than reasonable. Ordinary courtesy on both sides is all that is required to regulate the position, and where this is shown matters are usually adjusted quite amicably. I know of one stalker who was motoring along a lonely glen preparatory to reaching a suitable spot before beginning an ascent of the hill. Having left his car and proceeded half a mile on his appointed path he looked back, and was surprised to see a quartette of strangers, who had also abandoned their car, following him. He is not blessed with a particularly even temper, and demanded somewhat tersely the meaning of their presence.

"Oh," said the leader, "we thought you looked as if you knew your way about here, so we followed you!" They did not follow him for long.

On another occasion a stalker was just getting into his stag when a party of hikers appeared on the sky-line above it. In order to appraise him of the whereabouts of his quarry they kindly waved their handkerchiefs to indicate the direction in which it had gone. His feelings are better imagined than described.

One owner told me that in a single day he had seen twenty-two parties of hikers on his ground. This, again, is not conducive to good sport.

Certain forests are, of course, much more likely to be disturbed than others. Anyone who contemplates taking a forest can easily find out whether the ground he is thinking of taking is an "infested" area, and act accordingly.

Now, however, there are but few who are in a position to rent deer forests after five years of war and such reflections are out of date.

There has been a change, as I have said, in the stalking

rifle and everything has been made much easier. To this the
late Lochiel attributed—I think rightly—the decline which
has taken place in the popularity of stalking as a sport, at
any rate to some extent. The type of stalker has changed. In
Hunting and Stalking the Deer I have written more fully
some of the differences.

The other day, when I was in Inverness, a lady came into
the hotel lounge where I was sitting. We had met before,
and I knew the forest which she owned. We fell into conversation, and presently she introduced me to her stalker.
Someone came up and spoke to her, and I started to write a
letter. While I was doing so the stalker came up to me and
explained that he had not known who I was, but that he
wished to thank me for the pleasure he had derived from
my book. This to any author is pleasing, but what he went
on to say gave me greater satisfaction.

"There is one comment you made which delighted me,"
he continued. "You spoke about that cigarette-smoking
habit. If my father saw me smoking a pipe even when I was
talking to the gentleman with whom I was stalking, I got
a cuff on the head, and if I see any of these gillies doing it
he gets one from me."

The socialist may, no doubt, enquire, "Why the devil
shouldn't he smoke if he wants to?" Quite so, but no one
with any politeness would dream of smoking a pipe in a
lady's drawing-room without permission. It is a question
of ordinary courtesy, and none of the old type of stalkers
would have been guilty of such a breach of good manners.
It is only ignorance. The majority of Highlanders have a
natural instinct for good manners which many so-called
gentlemen might well envy. The conversation and charm of
the generation of stalkers with whom I had so many happy
days on the hill as a boy, and whom I am proud to have
called my friends, has left me with many memories which
the passage of time will never efface.

But if there is much that has changed, the hills themselves
are still there, and in spite of roads, Forestry Commissions,

hikers and new owners, to a great extent unchanged. I am
sometimes asked what I consider the finest deer ground in
Scotland. It is rather similar to being questioned as to the
most attractive woman you know, and who could reply to
such a query? There are many forests in which I have never
stalked. I doubt, however, if there is finer hill country to be
seen in the Highlands than that which is bounded on the
north by Kintail and on the south by Loch Morar. This
area comprises part of Affaric, Kintail, Cluanie, Glen
Quoich, Barrisdale, Knoydart, Glen Kingie, and Meoble.
Certainly the finest views I know are Sgur-na-Ciche from
the narrows of Lòch Nevis; the Five Sisters of Kintail from
the mouth of Loch Duich; and the panorama of hills which
are seen from above Loch Hourn. For rugged grandeur
Corrie-na-Gaul I have always held to be the finest in Scotland. Knoydart, on the whole, contains the finest scenery,
for stretches of water are always present, and for a view to
be really satisfying there must be water. Since first I saw the
latter forest, over thirty-five years ago, I have always considered it the most beautiful of any in which I have been
privileged to stalk.

I shall never forget one October day on which I sailed
from Knoydart to Kinloch-hourn on my way to Glen
Kingie, where I have spent so many happy days. As we
moved out from the bay of Inverie I could see the house of
Scotus and the islet on which the Prince lay hidden that
July day before he walked by night to Morar. Sandy bays
crept down to the water's edge, the red of the bracken
which fringed them contrasting with the greens and umbers,
ochres and yellows of the grasses. Beyond the blue of the
water astern the misty purple cone of Sgur-na-Ciche rose
through a gap in the rocks. In front lay Armadale and the
Sound, with Eigg to port and the outline of Rhum. A
white cloud of gulls rose from their feast of herring fry,
betokening the presence of a whale. In the distance a plume
of smoke and the red funnel of the *Fusilier* showed against
the horizon. Dotting the fields which led down to the Point

of Sleat were little white-harled houses dancing and fantastic in the haze. The blue and jagged outline of the Cuchullins lay dead ahead, rising above the intervening ridge. Sharp against the hillside the lighthouse of I. Oronsay was reflected in the cerulean and eau-de-nil waters of the Sound. To the north, above the entrance to Loch Hourn, rose hills pink in colour. As we drew closer in-shore before rounding the point, past rocky islets, each tenanted by its little colony of gulls, the reflections drove me to despair, so impossible did it seem to catch their fleeting hues. Warm greys alternated with pink, sienna, green, vivid ultramarine, and wonderful oily flashes of light from the ripples in our wake. Loch Hourn seemed anything but gloomy that never-to-be-forgotten day, despite the meaning of its name. Arisaig gleamed white in the sun, with beyond Barrisdale, Glen Cosaidh, and Corrie Ghorkill. Let anyone who desires the sight of colour unsurpassed and in his heart peace beyond believing accomplish this journey on such a day. He will never regret it.

If, like me, at the end of his voyaging he is lulled to sleep by the roaring of stags and the sound of the burn as it rushes beneath Meal-na-Spardain; if, lying in bed, he can see by the light of the moon the very cave which for a day gave shelter to Prince Charlie, he will fall asleep on the very wings of romance.

For it is, after all, the surroundings which make stalking the sport it is. Compared to the shooting of big game it may to some seem tame. There are many arguments to be adduced by which it can be made to suffer. It *is* artificial, but when all is said and done it approaches more nearly the genuine thing, satisfies more completely the primeval hunting instinct than any other form of sport to be had in these islands. The experienced stalker is quite happy even when he is not engaged in killing. There are only two kinds of deer he really wants to shoot: an old bad head or a real good one. The latter are not found every day. It is the search which makes a day's stalking enjoyable. You will see country which perhaps you have never seen before. There is probably a story attached to each hill. The modern stalker may not know it, but at least there is no harm in asking him. Your question may open the door to conversation which you had no idea could be so interesting. The stalker's natural shyness may have been mistaken by you for taciturnity. If he sees that you want to learn he will open out in a manner which will surprise you. A little knowledge of Gaelic is very useful in ascertaining the meaning of different local names.

Some of the old legends connected with the place-names of forests are of great interest. One that I heard had an amusing sequel.

A noted stalker many years ago had got within shot of a hind and was taking aim when, to his astonishment, he found that it was no deer at the end of his sight, but a lovely young woman. Lowering his weapon, he thought that he must have made a mistake, for there stood the hind as before. Raising his piece, he took aim a second time, when he immediately perceived that he had not been misled, for there again stood an attractive young female. This occurrence was repeated, when, becoming rather bored with this transformation scene, he put an end to it by shooting. The hind fell dead, but on going up to it a wraith-like form ascended from its still warm body and an irate voice informed the murderer that from henceforth a hind should always haunt the glen in which he had perpetrated such an enormity.

Not far from the spot, as years went on, rose a small and compact shooting lodge which could at a pinch hold three rifles. Here the host and his guest were awaiting the arrival of a second one evening in October.

"Here he is!" exclaimed the host, as at length the sound of wheels was heard. Presently the new arrival, fed and warmed, was enjoying a smoke before the fire. The talk, as was natural, turned on the forest, to which he was a stranger. The day's doings were discussed, heads and weights were duly canvassed, and the story of the hind which I have set down was in the course of conversation related.

"You're going to the far beat to-morrow, so you'll have to start early," was the host's final remark to the new arrival as they went to bed.

It was late the following evening when the latter returned. His host had not been out, and the other rifle, having killed his stag, was home early. They had finished their dinner, and following a hot bath the late arrival proceeded to the dining-room, whilst the others smoked in the sitting-room on the other side of the passage.

Drowsy and replete, they sat in comfort till a despairing cry from the dining-room galvanised them into activity.

"Help! Come quick!" came a strangled shriek. Dashing across the passage, they flung open the door.

White as a sheet, anguish and terror stamped on every line of his pinched features, his hair ruffled, and his hands frantically gripping the edge of the table, crouched their friend, whilst unconcernedly nosing the viands spread before her at the end nearest to the door stood a large and handsome hind!

It was not until she had been summarily removed by the horrified wife of the stalker, whose pet she was, that the tension relaxed and that explanations made the whole matter clear. "Long and loud," to quote from a book I used to love as a boy, "rose the laughter in the smoking-room that night"; but I fancy the chief actor still thinks that there was something a little uncanny about his visitor.

The Duke of Portland, in his entertaining volume, *Fifty Years and More of Sport in Scotland*, mentions having seen a menagerie proceeding along the Helmsdale road. An elephant was part of the procession, and at this apparition some stags near by fled into the woods and never emerged for the rest of the day. "Whether it was the sight of him or the smell," the Duke concludes, "I could not decide."

This incident reminds me of another story. Two stalkers who had made a night of it and were not quite so fit as they

might have been were out together in a forest in Aberdeen-
shire. Through it ran a main road. Presently they sat down
to spy. After some minutes one of them kept his glass
focused on a particular spot. At length, removing it from his
eye and sighing deeply, he proceeded to take it to pieces and
carefully clean the lenses. This operation completed, he
rather hesitatingly again focused it on the same place.

Glancing at his companion, who was spying the opposite
hill, he laid it carefully by his side, and with a troubled
expression lay back in the heather. His friend's glass came
swinging round, and eventually rested near the same point.
He, too, gave a gasp, lowered his glass, and turned to his
fellow stalker. They stared at each other for some moments
in guilty silence.

"Can you see it, too?" at length quavered the first.

"See what?" queried the other.

"*It!*"

"Well——" They both focused again.

"It can't be," said one.

"It is!" said the other. Then, in unison, "An elephant!"

It was, too—one that had escaped from a travelling circus!
The two stalkers went home full of good resolutions.

I once told Johnnie Millais a stalking story which,
months later, he said was the best he had ever heard.

"By the way," he finished, "what was it?"

I tried several, but they were none of them right, and
from that day to this I have never been able to recollect it;
which is a pity. The following, however, I believe to be true.

A certain very distinguished personage arrived at the spot
from which he was to start his day's stalking some two
hours after the appointed time.

"Well, Duncan," said he, greeting his old friend, who
placidly leant on his stalking stick awaiting his arrival, "it
was a narrow shave this morning! I've got a bit of a cold,
and the Duchess didn't want me to come out. In fact, she
very nearly made me stay at home."

Duncan gravely pondered this explanation, and then gave

vent to his feelings in a manner which left no doubt of their intensity.

"The betch!" he remarked coldly, and, turning, led the way up the hill. His mind, centred wholly on the day's sport, resented any extraneous factor which might interfere. The personage, realising this and choking with laughter, meekly followed.

Another stalker had his patience sorely tried. Placed in charge of a distinguished foreign artist who had never seen a stag in his life and was panting to kill one, he was much incensed by the latter's behaviour. He, overcome by the beauty of Highland scenery and the picturesque appearance of his attendant, insisted on wasting much valuable time in making a series of sketches. His artistic urge being satisfied, they proceeded on their way, when, to make matters worse, he missed an easy chance. Nothing daunted, they continued to advance, and were presently rewarded by the death of a fine stag. Overcome with joy, the successful shot flung his arms around the stalker's neck and kissed him on both cheeks. Not content with this expression of delight, he next, to their intense surprise, embraced the gillie and the pony boy.

I narrated these happenings to a matter-of-fact friend of mine. When I had finished he frigidly enquired, "Didn't he kiss the stag, too?"

I heard a story about myself the other day, though I am not sure that it is altogether to my credit. However, it dates back a long time ago, when I was young, so perhaps I may be forgiven for the slur it casts on my character.

My wife and I were sitting in a car by the side of Loch Ness in a vain endeavour to locate "the monster," which was causing a good deal of stir at the time. A policeman hove into view riding a motor-bicycle. Him I recognised as an old friend with whom in times gone by I had spent many days on the hill. Blowing my horn I brought him to a standstill, and we settled down to a long crack. One remark led to another, till he said:

"Did you ever hear the story about Archie, when he was with a gentleman up on the march waiting for a stag to rise?"

It appeared that Archie, of whom some of my readers may remember I have written before, had stalked a good stag which fed over the march and lay down. The stalking party watched him for some hours, hoping that he would rise and feed back. At length, tried of waiting, Archie suggested that this preliminary was quite unnecessary, and that a good deal of time might be saved were his gentleman to assassinate him where he lay. The corpse could then easily be dragged to the right side of the march; that anyhow, what with all these rocks and heather about, it was very difficult to tell exactly where the march was, and that it was a very easy shot whatever.

This specious reasoning being rejected with horror, as of course it should have been by any right-minded sportsman, the party settled down to another long wait. Not, however, before Archie, with an anguished look at my informant, had been heard to whisper in a muttered aside, "Oh, that I had Fraank Wallass here!"

I refrain from comment.

With regard to the inviolability of the march opinions vary. An arrangement is sometimes made between adjoining forests by which, where no harm can be done, a wounded stag may be followed. Stags, unfortunately, are sometimes wounded, and when they can easily be got at without disturbing the ground it is much better that they should be followed up at once and killed. This is not always possible, its practicability depending entirely on how far they have gone and the local conditions prevailing at the time. When the wind is right and the wounded beast is not near other deer it is foolish to leave him. On the other hand, an inexperienced stalker may ruin his neighbour's beat and spoil a stalk if he rashly follows a wounded animal without fully weighing the consequences.

There are, of course, no "rights" in such a contingency.

K

To talk as if there were is as foolish as a discussion which took place some years ago as to the "rights" of ownership of a head shot by a guest. Some misguided individual, suffering from an imaginary grievance, argued that the head belonged to the person who had shot it. It seems fairly obvious that a stag, alive or dead, belongs to the person who has paid for it—namely, the owner or lessee of the ground on which it is shot. If he is generous enough to allow a friend to shoot it, the latter has no more "rights" in the animal than has a stalker to follow a wounded stag on to adjoining territory.

When neighbouring forests are owned by men who know and trust each other, each can feel confident that he is safe from undue disturbance when they have mutually agreed that a wounded stag may be followed for a reasonable distance over the march.

Mention of "the march" never fails to conjure up some experience in the mind of a stalker.

I was once staying in a forest on the West Coast which contains some of the wildest and steepest ground on which it has ever been my good fortune to be invited to stalk.

One corrie in particular holds my affections. A long and narrow glen branches into a huge semicircular basin whose steep and rocky sides, strewn with huge boulders and riven by cascading burns, sweep round to a sheer rock-wall broken only in one place by a narrow track which crosses the march on the sky-line. Over the crest the steep hillside descends from a height of nearly 3,000 feet to a river which eventually wends its way eastward across Scotland to the North Sea. On the other side of the watershed, but a few yards distance, water seeking the sea has but a mile or so to flow ere it empties itself into the Atlantic.

Up this narrow glen my host and I were proceeding on a fine September day. The wind was right, which implied that we could explore the recesses of the corrie without moving deer over the march. One drawback existed. Before reaching the top of the ridge for which we aimed we were bound to give our wind to the east side of the glen. This was inevitable, as in any other wind the corrie was unstalkable. There might be good stags there; they might, when moved, remain at the far end of the glen; they might, on the other hand, be feeding round the corner of the basin, in which case all would be well. It is, perhaps, superfluous to mention that they *were* feeding on the east side of the glen and, of course, got our wind. It was two miles to the pass on the sky-line from the spot where their moving forms first drew our notice. Nothing could be done, and simultaneously we sat down to examine their heads. Deer, when thus moved, may settle after a comparatively short distance or, even though not greatly alarmed, keep moving. On this occasion, strung across the hillside, they moved steadily forward towards the pass. Their first headlong rush over, they stopped occasionally to stand and look back, but the sudden trot of some old hind would set them moving again, which was the more aggravating as we could see some fine stags among them. When there are several good stags together any head above the average stands out unmistakably. The sun was in our faces, which made spying difficult, but having swung my glass up and down the line of moving deer, I kept bringing it back to one particular stag near the head of the line. Appearing and disappearing as he crossed from one dip in the ground to another, swallowed by deep burns and re-emerging on the far bank, it was not easy to make out his head. That he was good was quite evident, but whether he belonged to that select band whose few extra inches carry them into a class beyond was not so certain. On the crest of a ridge he stood, turned his head and looked back. I could make out six points for certain on one horn. Of the other I was not so sure.

"That's the stag!" said my host. "He's the royal we saw last week. I wish he'd stop."

Before I could make out the other horn he had turned and moved on.

The leaders had already reached the pass. Each head we

noted as it appeared on the sky-line. Into the haze which shrouded the base of the cliff the big stag moved. In the blue shadows it was hard to define even his form as he moved steadily upwards. Then the tips of his horns came into view silhouetted against the sky. My host was right. Three on each top. Then his whole form stood revealed. Double brows! He stood for a second looking back, then passed out of sight.

"He's over the march," said my companion. "He may cross back in the evening. He's worth spending the whole day over. We'll go right round the top."

Presently the last of the herd, clearly cut as they stood on the crest of the ridge, had passed out of sight and we rose, shutting our glasses.

There was no need for hurry, so slowly and steadily we faced the long climb to the top of the ridge. It was two hours later that we reached it and three before we had crossed the shoulder of the peak whose cone-shaped summit dominated the corrie. Here we gazed across to the western islands and to a sea of blue whose loveliness comes back to me in my dreams.

We had finished the climb, but were still far from the pass by which the deer had crossed and which intervening ridges hid from our view. It seemed likely that, having put danger behind them, they would settle near the march close to the spot at which they had vanished. However, this we could not ascertain until we had reached the end of the far ridge. Following its crest we walked steadily on. The ground sloped steeply on both sides. A stone thrown from either hand would have fallen hundreds of feet. No deer were in sight either on our own ground or in Naboth's vineyard. Full of hopes and fears, we drew near to that last top which would decide our doubts. At last we reached it, crawled the last few yards, and peered round the corner of the rocks. The burly figure of my host stiffened.

"I can see them," he announced in a hoarse whisper. There they were, lying facing towards us on ground which sloped gently from the summit of the pass before plunging steeply to the burn which flashed in the late afternoon sunshine so far below.

Our glasses were out in a second, and simultaneously and ungrammatically we exclaimed, "That's him!"

He was lying slightly above the other deer and beyond them, quite close to the march. A few yards to the north, could we have got within range, he would have been an easy and legitimate shot. But those few yards made all the difference.

"I wish he'd move," said my host, looking at his watch. "We can't do anything if he stays there."

This was quite true and it was getting late. We resumed our inspection of his head.

"Good points, but he's a little thin," said my companion. "I wish to goodness he'd move."

That he would eventually move there was no doubt, but whether he would move in time was quite another matter.

"Suppose," I began, "a hiker came up from below the pass, and didn't know he was there, and came suddenly round that corner, he'd go back on to our ground."

"Don't be an ass!" snapped my host peevishly. "There isn't a hiker."

"No," I said, "but there might be."

My host took his eye from the glass and looked at me, the dawn of comprehension in his eye.

"You mean——" he began.

"I don't mean anything," I retorted, looking at the stag. The stag continued to stare rather drowsily down the hill.

"I wish to goodness he'd move," said my companion again.

"He doesn't look much like moving," said I.

"You couldn't get there without him seeing you," he went on.

"Get where?" I asked.

"There—where you said the hiker might be."

"No," said I carefully; "but if a hiker was with us now

and he crawled to that rock below us and didn't know the stag was there and walked on, I think the stag would jump up and bolt back over the march."

"Why should he crawl to that rock if he's going to get up and walk about afterwards?" asked my host, entering into the spirit of the discussion.

"Oh, I don't know!" I answered. "Hikers do funny things at times."

"Well, it wouldn't do us much good if he did," said my host. "The stag would still be out of shot."

"No, he wouldn't. When you saw the hiker coming you'd have gone back and round below the ridge and be waiting just below the pass. When the stag came back over the sky-line he'd only be about one hundred and fifty yards off. And if you can't hit a stag at one hundred and fifty yards," I continued offensively, "it's time you gave up stalking."

My host giggled.

"Look here," he said, "I'm going back."

"All right," said I. "Lead on."

"You're not coming," he went on. "I'm going back below the pass, and you're going to stay here and be a hiker."

So back he went and I hiked.

I crawled down to the rock below me. I admired the view. Then I peered round the rock. The stag still lay about 500 yards off, looking very drowsy.

I gave a parched whistle. He remained entirely undisturbed. I gave another whistle. A hind below him raised her head, stared in my direction, and resumed feeding. I showed my head and whistled again. The deer took not the slightest notice, though a mere whiff of wind had sent them clattering up the glen in the morning as if the devil were after them. For ten minutes or more I continued to whistle without causing any change in the attitude of the deer. I even waved my cap, but they remained obstinately unconcerned. I hit the rock with my stick, I threw stones down the hillside, all with no effect. I was in a quandary, for if suddenly alarmed it was quite likely that they might bolt down the hill in the wrong direction, when all my labours would count for naught, to say nothing of incurring the wrath of my host.

I was debating what course to pursue when a slight noise —a slight noise after all my efforts!—caused me to glance backward out of the corner of my glasses. A large red mushroom had apparently come into being by the side of my protecting rock. Very strange!

Suddenly a furious whisper hissed in my ear: "What the devil are you doing? Why on earth are you messing about like this? We want to *move* the stag!"

Not a mushroom after all, but the empurpled and blazing visage of my host!

"Well, there's the stag!" I hissed back, rather ruffled. "You move him! I've whistled and shouted and waved my cap, clattered my stick and hurled rocks, and I might just as well have been sitting in the lodge for all the notice he takes. I think he's bewitched."

The onus was off my shoulders, anyhow. If the stag took it into his head to bolt down the hill the responsibility would not be mine!

Casting caution to the winds, we stood up. Not a sign of interest from the deer! We walked boldly into the open. That did make him take a little notice. Raising his head, he stared at us. Two of the hinds stopped feeding and turned, facing us with cocked ears. Then the stag rose to his feet. The deer bunched together. Next moment they were off, and in the right direction. Ten minutes earlier and my companion would have had a shot and avoided many future exertions. As it was we reached home after a long, tiring walk with no stag.

The next day I stalked an outlying beat while my host went in pursuit of the royal.

The Red Corrie, adjoining that in which we had seen him, ran north and south, the southern ridge forming the western end of the long glen which eventually merged into the main strath, distant 12 miles or more. A long search failed to reveal the well-known form, and it was late in the evening that he was discovered far down the glen, and too late for a stalk. It was not until long after the dinner hour that the weary but undaunted stalker returned to tell us of his odyssey.

Down the glen he went on the following morning and round the main ridge until he reached the spot where it was possible to spy the position in which the stag had been left. He was not there, nor did a prolonged spy reveal him. Up the glen went his pursuer, almost to its western end, and there at last, almost within shot of the pass he had crossed two days before, he was again found. A long stalk failed, and the royal moved back into the Red Corrie. Here at last, after three hard days' stalking, and when it was almost too dark to shoot, he met the doom he had so long evaded.

That he was well worth the exertions entailed the keen stalker will realise, for his horns measured over 33 inches, with a span of just under 30 inches. A rough calculation made that night with the aid of a map enabled us to estimate that at least 60 miles over some very rough country had been covered in pursuit of this stag.

Judging by some of the articles one sees in the press, there are critics who consider deer stalking an effete form of sport. I wonder what they would have said that last evening?

XIII. A STALKING MEMORY

"Let us go up to the mountain."—ISAIAH ii. 3

O N the mind of a young stalker the entire sequence of events leading up to the death of his first stag is so vividly impressed, so clearly does every detail recur to his memory, that he may think that it will always be so. As the entries in his game book increase he realises, and with a pang, that such is not the case. Some consolation, however, lies in the reflection that the really noteworthy stalks in his career stand out with a freshness all the greater as his experience is enlarged. Factors which at one period would have seemed all-important, incidents which would once have served as landmarks, are eliminated. It may not be his best heads which carry with them such a train of pleasant recollections, though most likely they will, for the stalker of experience knows their value. Heads which at the

outset of his career would have satisfied him he will decline
to shoot. At any rate the fruits of such stalks, if not intrinsi-
cally the best heads, will be the heads he values most.

Such reflections arose from the contemplation of the head
of a ten-pointer I killed some years ago. The brows are
miserable, the trays short (there are no bays), and though
the tops and symmetry of the horns redeem it to some
extent, it would make but a poor show beside even the
second-class heads of a good season. No stag that I ever
stalked, however, gave me so exciting a chase or eluded me
so persistently. For two whole days did we pursue him, and
made seven distinct stalks in our endeavours to circumvent
his watchfulness. When at length he fell I knew that no
other stag would loom before the sights of my rifle for at
least another ten months.

The Exception and I were stalking together, a fact which
greatly delighted Archie. "Andra" had taken to himself a
wife and abandoned his career as gillie. Otherwise things
were much the same as on the day six years before when a
ten-pointer had died in the morning, and in the darkness a
stag, shot through the head, had fallen at the bidding of the
omnipotent James.

Unmindful of her former success, the Exception had, in a
moment of undue excitement, missed a stag. We sadly
watched his retreating form, and stalking deer for the
moment seemed but a poor game! He was an old beast with
a weak head, and as we gained a knoll we saw him, with his
hinds, join and mingle with a herd of deer of both sexes.
There were four or five fair stags among them, but not until
we had successfully got round and below them did we sight
the beast which was to cause us so much anxiety. The deer
were moving slowly along the base of a hill just out of shot.
There was a chance that by running parallel with them,
sheltered by the ridge, we might obtain a chance, but this
hope proved of no avail. They continued steadily forward
and the ten-pointer which had aroused my hopes remained
out of range. His tops were good, though we could not

obtain a clear view of his lower points, but he carried himself like a gentleman and was undoubtedly the best stag in
the herd. We had two more distinct stalks after him, both of
which were frustrated.

Towards evening he, with about thirty hinds, fed close
up to the march, whilst we, hotly but stealthily, followed on
his tracks. The sun was setting directly over the low hills
which formed the march and shone straight in our faces.
By twos and threes we watched the hinds, silhouetted in the
glow, merge among the rocks and heather. High up on their
left were two or three young stags which effectually blocked
our line of approach. They were uneasy and cast suspicious
glances in our direction. The Exception, Archie and I
crawled and slithered onwards, praying fervently that we
might yet get within shot before the darkness fell. At last
we reached a hollow from which we dared not move. We
were within three hundred yards of our beast, who continually roared, but the younger stags were very much on
the alert. As we lay one suddenly made up his mind, and
with cocked ears and twitching nose deliberately minced
down upon us. Lower and lower we crawled, still on and on
he came.

"He's no a ba-ad stag!" I heard in a hoarse whisper behind
me. "Indeed he is no a ba-ad stag!" This time more em-
phatically. But I was determined to deal in no half-measures.
It was to be the ten-pointer or nothing, and as that soft,
whining, persuasive Highland voice was raised for the third
time I snapped out, "Shut up!" I did not turn my head, for
the stag was within ten yards, but without looking I pictured
Archie's expression, the pathetic upward roll of the eye
eloquent of depressed resignation. Still the stag came on,
and now his horns, black and magnified against the blaze of
glory beyond, almost persuaded me that I was in error. So
close he came that I could actually have touched him with
the rifle; but I knew that I was right in my determination.
He was a young, improving stag and his death would have
been no compensation for what might otherwise prove a

blank day. Then with a stamp and a snort he wheeled round and galloped madly like a beast possessed over the march. There was no need for concealment now, so snatching the rifle I dashed after him.

"He's off!" I heard Archie groan, but whether he meant me or the stag I did not stop to inquire.

From the ridge I could just make out the dim forms of the hinds, and slowly moving after them that of the ten-pointer. It was almost hopeless, and as the shot rang out I knew we had a blank day behind us so far as dead stags were concerned.

A six-mile walk carried a somewhat depressed party to the lodge in time for a late dinner, when we resolved to attempt the same beat next day.

The morning was cold and squally, but a spy at the far end of the ground about two o'clock revealed a herd of about seventy hinds lying and feeding in the shelter not far from a large loch. We could not at first distinguish the stag, but at length to our joy made out the ten-pointer of the previous day. He was in a very difficult position for a stalk, and though the broken peaty ground gave good cover at times, it was, on the whole, very flat, while the scattered hinds made it a hard task to get anywhere near their lord. The Exception remained behind a convenient rock whilst Archie and I, flat as soles, wriggled and squirmed through a morass. There Archie was dropped and I wriggled on alone. For nearly ten minutes I lay there with the scattered hinds twenty yards distant. Then the stag showed clear against the sky-line about a hundred and seventy yards off— and I missed him! At least so it seemed, though as they galloped off his uneasy movements betrayed a slight wound.

We had some hope that they would remain in the shelter a mile or so away, and our expectations were justified on finding the hinds quietly feeding about a burn. The stag, however, had disappeared. Then he came into view from behind a knoll, but he was not the ten-pointer, and our glasses revealed a beast with a head of eight points which we had seen the previous day. The ten-pointer could not be far off, and a careful search revealed him sulking in some long heather and gazing at his successful rival.

It was difficult to decide what plan to adopt, as it was impossible to get at our stag without disturbing the other deer. We decided at last to try for the eight-pointer, trusting that the other stag, who was evidently hit somewhere, would not move far. We accordingly began our stalk. The greater part of the herd were out of sight during our advance, and I knew the shot would be at close range. As we drew near I took the rifle, and the precaution was justified, for we came suddenly on the eight-pointer, who gave me a snap at his neck as he bolted across my front. Fortunately it took effect and we had the satisfaction of seeing the ten-pointer rejoin his hinds and move quietly down the ridge with every sign of satisfaction at the sudden disappearance of his rival.

Giving them time to settle we cleaned the dead stag, and rather anxiously, for it was getting late, followed our beast. Our difficulties were increased on locating them by finding that another stag had captured about forty hinds and was roaring defiance on a flat below the ten-pointer, who occasionally answered. He was on a rocky heather-covered knoll which sloped very steeply to the flat, bathed in the late afternoon sunshine. Slowly, down to the place where we had last seen our beast, we began to crawl, but on reaching a point above it, found ourselves unable, owing to the slope of the hill, to see any deer save a few hinds.

While we were watching, a number of deer began stringing up the hillside to our right. We could see no stag with them, and the question arose to which of the rivals they belonged. We had to proceed with the greatest care, for the deer were already alarmed and a false move on our part might have cleared them off the ground for good, as we were then only a few yards from the march. We crawled on and then, seeing no sign of our stag, crawled back.

Such an occasion is one of the most trying which the

stalker can encounter. He has to proceed more or less blindly, and yet quickly, for delay may be fatal. The great thing is to keep cool, eliminate impossibilities, and reason out his chances. Hidden from the flat we stood up, and walked back along the ridge. A narrow dip separated us from another ridge. As this came into view we both dropped, for there, peacefully lying within a hundred and twenty yards, were the ten-pointer and a score or so of hinds. I thought it unlikely that he would run down wind into our ground if alarmed; his most obvious route was up the dip and over the march past us. A shot, if it missed, would certainly make him rise, so taking everything into consideration, I determined to take him lying, though it is a kind of shot I loathe.

Very carefully I settled myself and took aim. My pressure on the trigger was greeted with a sharp click. A missfire! Two of the hinds jumped up facing me; the stag turned his head. Somewhat flurried I took aim a second time. At the shot the stag jumped to his feet, turned, and galloped past me towards the march, two hundred yards distance. I had missed again! With a coolness born of despair I stood up and as he drew level, clear of his hinds, some sixty yards away, I fired just in front of his shoulder. There was no mistake this time, and though the hinds galloped on unharmed, he crashed to the ground and before we reached him was dead. He weighed only fourteen stone, but no stag that I ever stalked gave me more enjoyment, and the sight of his head always recalls two of the most enjoyable days I ever spent on the dear hills I love so well.

XIV. THE DEEP BURN

"Let me hide myself in thee."
ROCK OF AGES—A. M. Toplady

IN the course of my stalking career, which now, alas!
covers a great deal longer period than I care to remember,
I have been fortunate to visit many forests in Scotland.
Varied as they are in character, from Langwell in the north
to Blackmount in the south, from Invermark in the east to
Knoydart in the west, they all have one feature in common,
even if, with it, I may not be personally acquainted—they
all have a "deep burn." It may be on high ground, it may
be on the flat, it may be wide, or more likely narrow, but
somewhere within their confines its course will lie and from
its banks many a good stag has been laid low, or missed.

There is one in particular which for ever holds my
affections. From a small round cup or hollow on the crest
of a ridge it falls abruptly through a miniature chasm some
thirty feet deep, with steep and rocky sides where tiny

ferns, drenched with the spray of the fall, find a precarious
foothold. From this point it meanders through high, peaty
banks until it emerges on to the flats half a mile away.
How many times, with Archie, have I not in the past scaled
its rocky sides, and though it is now many years since I
wandered through its recesses I feel that there is not a nook
nor corner of it that I should not greet as one does an old
friend. I remember one occasion well when it served me in
good stead. I was then young and active and having discovered a herd of deer, to the number of eighty or more,
not, strictly speaking, I regret to say, within the boundaries
of the gate, I manœuvred it by a series of cautious appari-
tions at selected points and a skilful use of the wind, into
the cup to which I have already alluded. Though not more
than four hundred yards across it was almost impossible to
obtain a shot within its confines. I only once remember
doing so and that involved a long and very flat crawl, as,
until one reached the centre of the bowl there was no cover
of any kind. However, on this occasion the deer moved
straight across it and over the ridge to the south of the burn.
Waiting until they had all disappeared I scrambled down the
waterfall and made my way down the course of the burn
until I reached a point from which I could see the flats
below. The line the deer had taken was diagonal and on
reaching my vantage point I found them scattered along the
hillside, just out of shot. The stag I wanted was, of course,
on the far side of the herd, and though I managed to steal
a few more yards, on this occasion the burn failed me and
my previous exertions, added to a rather guilty conscience,
saved him.

On the slopes of the Kingie valley is another deep burn.
Its characteristics are entirely different. Save a scar high up
on the top of the Kingie face there is practically no sign
of its presence unless you stand on the path below and look
up the hillside. There it stretches, a long, narrow line running
up the hillside, with sides so steep that only at two points
throughout its length is it passable for deer. The first stag

I ever killed at Kingie was within a few yards of the top pass.
At Gaick, so different in every essential from west coast
forests, on whose rounded tops deer paths, deep and
narrow, run through the mosses, there is another deep burn.
It winds almost straight at times, through the peat hags, and
from its shelter a great area of ground is covered. So smooth
and even is its course that one might almost imagine oneself walking along a pathway. Provided that deer were in
the right position all that would be necessary would be to
walk up to a given point, look over the edge, level one's
rifle and fire. No stalking would be necessary. Probably,
however, the deer would *not* be in the right position, but
they would have to cross the burn at some point, or go
down a sheer face if they wished to move their quarters.

Had it not been for another deep burn I should never
have killed the finest Highland stag it has ever been my good
fortune to stalk. It was at Wyvis whose great shoulders are
so conspicuous a feature of the eastern side of Ross-shire.
I had stalked him all day and it was not until the evening
that he turned back, following his hinds across the burn,
and gave me, from its shelter, the chance I had worked so
hard to obtain. Elsewhere I have described in detail all that
happened on that eventful day.

I remember another deep burn in a large forest, again in
Ross-shire, which I visited after an absence from the hill of
two years. During that interval I had hunted in Poland,
Austria and Germany and had had my previous opinion
confirmed that stalking in Scotland, poor though the
trophies may be when comparisons are made, is vastly
superior to many forms of Continental sport. Of these latter
the best in which I have any experience is undoubtedly
chamois stalking.

The forest in which I was a guest on the occasion of
which I am writing had not been let for a long period. One
might have reasonably expected that some good heads
would be on the ground. There was one, a royal, but he
was a young stag and my host, who was a true sportsman,

L

refused to shoot him. It seemed to me that he was paying a high rent to shoot stags which never ought to have been at large on any forest.

Most of the ground was shrouded in dense mist on the morning after my arrival and I was sent out on the sheep ground marching with a very famous forest which annually produced some of the best heads of the season. I entertained a faint, a very faint hope that one of these monsters might be sufficiently misguided to put in an appearance, consequent on which I looked forward to pulling the leg of the rightful owner when I next saw him. Alas! that now I shall never have the opportunity of doing so, for he has passed beyond the hills he loved so well. However, late in the afternoon we came on a ridge and into the shelter of a deep burn which poured its waters over a precipitous face of rock and so to the loch which lay stretched far below.

Peering over the edge I saw a small stag with horns, literally, not more than a foot long. He would have weighed about 9 stones. The stalker peered about for some moments, then suddenly crouching down, turned to the gillie and hissed, "The rifle! The rifle!" I was behind him, but being taller could see over his shoulder. I thought that one of the monsters had materialised and was hidden from my view. Taking the rifle I slid in beside him where he beckoned and peered over the edge of the cliff. "Tak' him. Tak' him!" he whispered.

I "peeped and peered," as Mr. Wentworth Day would say, but nothing could I see but this wretched little knobber.

"Where is he?" I queried.

"There he is! Tak' him now," was the answer.

I could scarcely believe that he meant me to shoot the poor little beast and said so.

"He's a' richt," said he.

"I'm not going to shoot that wretched little thing. He's an absolute baby. Look at his head."

"Tak' him," he repeated. "*Look at his body!*"

I must say, I was rather disgusted. He would never have

made a good stag. Had it been the general practice in this forest systematically to shoot such rubbish, as ought to be done everywhere, I should have had no objections to offer, but one more or less would have made no difference to the improvement of the stock and I declined to shoot, much to the annoyance of my friend the stalker.

I inspected, with my host, the fifty odd heads which comprised his bag for the season. Only once have I seen them equalled and that was on an even larger forest which a friend of mine took on a long lease. It had been very much neglected and he started off by killing every bad head he saw. At the end of three years there certainly was a difference and had it not been for the war he would by now (1941) be getting many good heads every year. In the total of which I am speaking there was not one single head in the whole fifty with any sort of a top. The majority were switches, six-pointers and freaks.

"One really ought to be paid for shooting this sort of thing," said my host ruefully.

"There's the answer," said I, pointing at the rows of heads going back to the early years of the century which adorned the outside of the gillie's quarters, the larder and the usual offices.

There was no denying it, for they were in the main a very nice lot of heads, though many of them never ought to have been shot as they had, obviously, not reached their prime. Nearly every one had nice tops and, in many cases, double brows.

My host, when he had taken the forest, had been asked by the owner not to shoot certain stags which had been spared the year before. He had, rightly, I think, refused to agree. His argument was that he had paid a large sum of money for what amounted to practically six weeks' sport, and that if he saw a stag he wanted to shoot he was going to shoot it. Here is the point. He had not killed a single one of the promising young stags which were on the ground, which many tenants would have shot during the first week of their tenancy. This includes the royal I have already mentioned. That he was perfectly within his rights to do so I have no doubts. That he did not was because he was a genuine sportsman. The owner only did what I should have done myself had I been in his place, but he did not know his tenant as I did. What is sticking out a mile is that after the war there is no one either willing or in a position, even if they wanted to, to pay large sums for the privilege of killing absolute rubbish. After all, the main thing which everyone who stalks really wants is a good head, and the chances of getting such a head, at any rate on forests which are let from year to year, and not on long leases, are becoming increasingly rare.

I remember, too, another occasion on which Archie and I found a deep burn useful. We were walking to our beat "proceeding west" as he would have put it, when, from the shelter of this burn, defining the march, we heard a roar. Neither he nor his hinds could we see, but we knew from the sound that he must be very close. The hill rose gently on our left from a marsh dotted with heathery knolls and small lochans. It was from this broken ground that the roar came and I realised that my shot would be a quick one. The ground was sodden after days of heavy rain and mist. We squelched loudly in the soaking, peaty soil, the water often over our ankles. The roars continued as we crept forward when, on a sudden, from behind a knoll trotted a fine stag. My glasses were dim and blurred by rain and the heat from my body (those who have been similarly circumstanced will realise my feelings!) but I knew from the sketchy glimpse I obtained of his head that he was a good beast. As we sank into a pool of water he trotted away down the flat, then slowed to a rapid walk. "That's him!" cried Archie, unconsciously plagiarising the Jackdaw of Rheims. As he spoke a resounding roar came from the burn.

"It's not," I retorted.

"Here, tak' you the rifle and rin," he cried.

I snatched the rifle as he thrust it at me, and doubled in

behind the knoll. Peering round the edge I saw the stag still making away from me, stopping occasionally to sniff the ground. Why he had not winded us was a mystery, for it was blowing dead on my back.

Waiting until the ground hid him, I splashed clumsily forward until, wet and panting, another knoll was gained. Throwing myself in among the heather, I scrambled to the top, hoping he would be within shot. He had disappeared so there was nothing for it but to continue. The next knoll revealed him trotting away, head up, at twice the distance he had been at the start and with every indication that he knew there was something wrong, without being definitely frightened. Beyond the next knoll the flat swelled into a miniature plain, 300 to 400 yards in extent. If he reached this and went on, I knew there was but little chance of a shot. As he disappeared I doubled forward again with hopes steadily diminishing. A hasty glance backward showed Archie a small speck—with, I knew, anxious and puckered eyes straining above his red beard—in the distance.

I reached the last knoll, and saw the stag standing, ears cocked, on the sloping ground on the edge of a burn at the far side of the flat. He had evidently got my wind and was preparing for a final disappearance. As I looked, I heard a loud roar from the burn. The stag heard it too, for he turned his head sharply. The unknown roared again, and my stag took a few steps forward. The next roar seemed to me the sweetest music I had ever heard. The stag, wrath conquering his fears, plunged down the hillside and across the flat. It was an anxious moment as he came straight in line, for the breeze came from my back, but he still held on. As he crossed my front, I cut in behind him and knew that I was safe so far as the wind was concerned.

The burn was very close and as I stole forward in the direction in which he had vanished I cocked the rifle, for any moment might bring me on top of him. I heard another roar, very close this time, and crouched low as I drew near the crest of a slight rise in the ground. Slowly raising my

head I saw the tips of his horns. The little pocket Zeiss—
invaluable to short-sighted stalkers—showed three points
on each top. Thrusting the glass into my pocket, I crawled
forward, keeping my head low. Then, raising it, I saw the
stag. He was standing, with swollen neck, bloodshot eyes
and distended nostrils, snuffing the grass within twenty
yards of me. Everyone has missed such shots because they
are so easy, but the remembrance of past moments of bitterness came to my mind, and, aiming very low, I had the
satisfaction of seeing him fall and when I got up, of finding
that he was a very pretty wild royal. Though there were no
particular difficulties in the stalk, if stalk it could be called,
it was a very exciting twenty minutes and very interesting as
showing how an animal will ignore a danger he is aware of
when other senses are roused. Of the stag which had roared
in the burn I saw nothing, and he must have slipped away
over the march after I had fired.

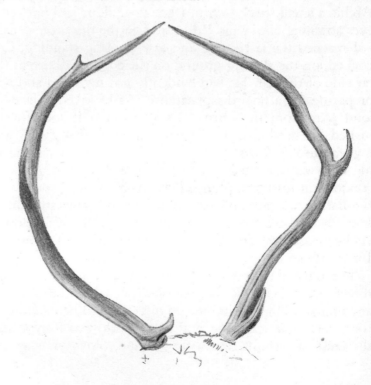

XV. THE STAG AND THE "WATTCHER"

"Sent to spy out the land."

NUMBERS xiii. 16

To shoot a stag is one thing; to kill *the* stag is another and quite different matter. Anyone who is lucky enough to be asked to stalk in Scotland on ground which may reasonably be termed a forest is pretty certain, provided he is a tolerable shot, to kill a stag.

It is *the* stag which the experienced stalker always hopes to encounter and which lingers in his mind when it and the hills he loves are but a dream. *The* stag may have a good head or a bad one. He is usually old and cunning and at times develops into *the big stag*, attaining rank in the mind of his pursuer equal to that of the Muckle Hart of Benmore. A guest's chance of being placed on terms with him when this apotheosis has taken place are remote.

The stag has come my way on more than one occasion. The first—barring that shabby eight-pointer which fell, now, alas! so long ago above the birchwood which used to delight my eyes beyond Loch Meiklie, and which, too, has vanished with so much else that was lovely—was a royal whose death on the edge of a turnip field I have already recorded.

The last came to his end only a year or so before the last war, beside a burn which laughs and sings its way from the high tops which look across to Skye. He carried nine points and was an old gentleman who loved his food. Had he restrained his appetite and carried a better head he might be alive now, but a stag with a bad head will, relatively, eat as much expensive food as will a dull guest at a fashionable restaurant, and will be just as little welcomed by his host.

For years my friend had turned up regularly at the winter feed, and my, and his, host was not at all pleased with him. He shouldered better animals out of the way, ate his fill with an occasional savage jab at any intruder, and then, full up to the back teeth, staggered across the march to a nice sunny slope facing due south, where at the time when he was first pointed out to me at the end of September, he had collected quite a respectable harem. These and his condition he flaunted openly before the eyes of his unwilling entertainer, only crossing the burn which marked the limits of his winter debauches at the fall of darkness.

"Get the old brute if you can!" was my host's parting injunction as I set out with the stalker on the morning after my arrival. As we climbed the slopes opposite to those on which he lay, we decided to try and get a stag on the top of the ridge, descend again to the level of the burn and await developments there.

Having successfully accomplished the first part of the programme, at about 3.30 p.m. we were in a position to make further plans. The stag and his hinds were in full view, strung out in the nook of a grassy hollow which led down to the flats on which they were accustomed to take their evening meal, and which extended on both sides of the burn defining the march.

Convenient knolls and the remains of a ruined cottage

were strewn along its banks and to the latter we cautiously made our way, cheered by an occasional lazy roar. "We'd have a better chance if we got under the bank on the other side," I suggested.

Guttural noises at the back of M.'s nose indicated that though this point of view was undoubtedly sound, it was rather hampered by the fact that we should be trespassing. However, as our presence there could not possibly do any harm when I had promised not to shoot until I was in a position to do so legitimately, he agreed. Very slowly and cautiously in full view of the deer we wormed our way among rushes and whatever other cover we could find, until we got under shelter of the bank, waded across the burn and crouched in a heathery hollow which gave an unrestricted view of the deer.

As the afternoon drew on the hinds began to move down the hillside. The stag slowly followed them, occasionally making a short rush at a hind, halting to have a mouthful of grass, and roaring at intervals.

These are always among the most pleasurable moments of stalking. There is no need for immediate action. You have done all that there is to do and the rest is on the knees of the gods. You discuss possibilities, weigh chances and try to make out exactly what the head you are after is like. We were engaged in this pleasant occupation when, as I took down my glass, a movement somewhere behind us caught the corner of my eye.

Turning my head I saw a figure clad in dark clothes sauntering along the path which led from the lodge in full view of ourselves and the deer. Making no attempt at concealment, the figure ensconced itself in a conspicuous position and drew out a glass.

"Who on earth's that?" I enquired.

"He'll just be the wattcher," replied my companion.

"What's he think he's doing?"

A sheepish grin illumined the stalker's face.

"He'll just be seeing what happens!" he remarked.

As nothing much seemed likely to happen, except that in all probability the deer would "take to the hill," the problem seemed to require but little elucidation. Awkwardly and self-consciously we slid back into the burn, crossed it, and slunk again through the rushes to the shelter of the ruined cottage. Throughout this manœuvre I was aware of the "wattcher's" eyes, to say nothing of those of the deer glued on the small of my back!

Having reached safety, a look through the glass disclosed the fact that my fears had been unnecessary. The hinds were still in the same position; the "wattcher" was still serenely surveying the scene, apparently quite unconscious of the commotion he had caused. We discussed his conduct. M. agreed that it was unpardonable. My own comments were distinctly unfavourable. M. conceded that, though strictly legal, his behaviour was unsportsmanlike, unnecessary and entirely superfluous. I was left with the impression that his mind was filled with doubt as to why an all-seeing Providence permitted such a creature to live! Whilst thus relieving our minds the gentleman in question ostentatiously rose, replaced his glass, and withdrew his unwelcome presence. The deer, apparently accustomed to these invasions of their solitude, watched him disappear down the track and quietly went on feeding, though distant not more than 400 yards.

It was getting late, and my previous optimism had waned. In an hour's time it would be dark, and though it was obvious that the hinds had every intention of crossing the burn, there was a time limit of which they were ignorant, and whether these factors would coincide in our favour was a matter of considerable doubt.

Several hinds and young beasts were feeding on the brink of the burn, and if they once started to cross I felt that our chances were pretty good. Then the stag disappeared!

We had marked his position though he was often out of our sight, and where he had got to I could not imagine. M. was equally at a loss, and for ten minutes or more we craned our necks round broken masonry and through derelict windows in an endeavour to locate him. Every stalker who has pursued *the* stag will appreciate our feelings and the qualms that beset us.

Was he, through some uncanny instinct, going to defeat our plans when they were on the verge of success? I have known stags which have, for no apparent reason, gone clean away, abandoning their hinds when it seemed certain that in a few minutes at most an opportunity would be given for a successful shot. Was this to be our fate?

Then once more hope revived.

"I haave him," came in a hoarse whisper from M. "He's awa' up the hill after yon hind and calf."

In the gathering dusk I at length made him out, a quarter of a mile or more above the burn, steadily climbing towards a hind and calf who apathetically watched his approach. The apathy was more apparent than real, for as he drew near the hind gave a sudden cat-like turn and started at a canter up the hill.

The stag gave chase, galloped off sideways, turned her beneath a steep bank and, to my delight, charged savagely down the hill behind her, uttering short grunts of annoyance. In a ridiculously short space of time, or so it seemed to me after all my doubts and fears, they reached the flats. Here, it was quite apparent that their lord and master was not going to have any more nonsense. Rounding up his female belongings with a skill which I secretly envied, he plunged—like Mr. Pennybone—into the burn and emerged dripping on the other side.

But we were no longer hidden in the ruined cottage. Crawling, panting, with sidelong dips and runs, we had gained the cover of the knolls fringing the burn, another couple of hundred yards distant from the deer, but with an easy approach from above to the flats, where they were rapidly moving along on our side of the march. Out of sight below us, triumphant roars led us in that last-minute struggle with time.

The first quick look over the bank proved that we were too far behind, for the stag, still last, was just disappearing round a corner. A quick duck back and a final rush brought us to a knoll, the flat covered with deer below us and, most glorious sight of all, *the* stag, his head thrown back, standing transfixed, looking at the skyline which hid us. That is the moment which remains clear in my mind.

It was 7.15 and a dark night before we were ready to leave, and as I lit my pipe I said to M.: "We were lucky to get him. I thought that watcher had done us!"

"I thought so, too," said he.

"Dirty dog! By the way, who is he?" I asked casually.

"He's my wife's brother," said M. It was too dark to see his face.

XVI. DEER STALKING IN NEW ZEALAND

"Sport claims its numerous votaries who roam."
THE HAWARDEN HORACE—Charles L. Graves

IT is over forty years since I visited New Zealand, lured there by tales of the enormous stags which, descended from imported Scottish stock, had thriven on the rich slopes and thick woods abounding in the South Island. Johnnie Millais used to say that the hardest walking he had ever experienced in pursuit of game was after the reindeer of Norway. He gives a graphic description of the country in the *Gun at Home and Abroad*. I do not think I have ever known harder climbing and stalking than in Otago. I was young and fit, and enjoyed every minute of it, but it is a young man's game. Red deer, it is sometimes forgotten, are naturally woodland animals, and in New Zealand live in dense bush, from which they emerge in the early mornings and late evenings to feed in the glades about the river flats, and on the grasses which grow on the rocky tops 5,000 or 6,000 feet above. A day on the steepest and rockiest corries in Scotland is child's play compared to one in this type of country.

Lord Dalhousie's two stags and three hinds, from which the Otago herd has sprung, were liberated in the Morven Hills in the year 1870. The Dingle, close by, when I visited New Zealand, was played out and the ground full of rubbish. The Hunter Valley still held some good stags, but the best heads were coming from the Makarora, then comparatively unknown country. As we were rather pressed for time we decided to go to the Hunter Valley.

The best head I killed was a fourteen-pointer, and though at that time he might have been classed as a moderate second-class head, he sinks into insignificance beside the magnificent trophies which have since been killed by other stalkers. Even now the recollection of all those incidents which go to the making of a day's stalking are vivid in my mind.

Every morning, circling round the tops, we had endeavoured to circumvent some amateur Caruso less wily than his fellows. Every evening we had returned with tales of some immature wanderer whose distant roars had brought joy to our hearts, and a closer inspection of his head a muttered anathema to our lips. A long hot day in the bush had given us nothing but stiff necks, sorely-tried tempers, and huge appetites. Once, a two-hours' stalk had revealed a startled seven-pointer, whose emulous roars had deluded us into the belief that his head was equal to his voice; and now, on the seventh day, we were despairing.

Stags there were in plenty, as one could hear, good ones too; but never were the beauties of an Eastern harem so securely shrouded in coy obscurity, and though the imagination might run riot over their secluded charms, distance still continued to lend enchantment.

So we determined on a change of camp, and though, our

resolution taken, the red god smiled upon us and delivered two victims into our hands, it is not of them that I shall tell.

It was on the morning of April 17 that I was awakened by the calling of the Paradise ducks as they flew in pairs to meet the dawn, and some two hours later started off down the valley, whose boundary peaks, 5,000 feet above us, were still swathed in mist.

We had a long, tiring day; and until three o'clock lacked any reward save the distant view of an ugly seven-pointer and his harem, preceded, as we climbed the hill, by that of a nice ten-pointer whose safety lay in his youth. At that hour, high up at the head of a big rock-slide, we saw the little royal, though what he was we did not then know, who indirectly, and in spite of many disappointments, brought us to my big stag and the end of my stalking trip. We did not realise all that lay before us then, and when at four o'clock I laid the tape along his horns and found that he was scarcely better than a Scottish head, I was disappointed that the reward of all our toil should be so meagre.

Half an hour later we started down the southern side of the corrie, not the northern, as we should have done had we not seen the royal, and so came in sight of some scattered specks about a distant grassy slope.

The rock-scarred hills sloped steeply away beneath us until they were swallowed up in the sea of bush which swayed and eddied in their depths. Great bunches of snow-grass flaunted their waving streamers in the evening breeze until, 1,000 feet below, they melted into one indistinguishable blue. Across the valley more hills threw their craggy tops athwart the sky, rising stern and forbidding, with none of the melting appeal which emanates from every knoll and corrie of a Highland glen, yet for all that majestic and imposing. Over a distant ridge Lake Hawea caught the eye with a myriad scintillating points of light. From the rocky barriers which confined its waters a thousand twinkling reflections were thrown, and in turn caught back and tossed about by the very wavelets from which they had first sprung. Beyond, again, lay a range of snow-capped hills dominated by the cone of Mount Aspiring, dwelling aloof from the turmoil of a busy world amid the regions of eternal snow. It was very still, and save for the monotonous though musical call of the keas who circled uneasily around, we might have thought ourselves the only living things upon the ridge. On the ridge's summit indeed we were, but from the depths of the bush, though gradually drawing nearer to its edge, came a strange hoarse roar which was answered and re-echoed ere it had time to die away.

Close by the keas settled, and with twisted heads regarded us dispassionately from behind a tuft of snow-grass. Reassured, they waddled clumsily out into the open and croaked hoarsely. Once again from down amid the rustling beech leaves a stag poured out his love-sick challenge in a long-drawn wail which came floating up about the heights encircling the corrie. Buckley looked at me significantly. "He's getting close," said he. "There's another hind," he continued. Even half a mile off we could see her every movement, so clear and rarefied was the air.

Its very transparency detracted in a way from the beauty of the scene which it pervaded. Nothing was left to the imagination, and the outline of a hill 10 miles distant stood as hard and sharp as one within a few hundred yards. Incidentally it became possible, as a matter of course, to take a shot which one would have regarded as something of a feat in a more humid atmosphere. For a few minutes the hind stood there motionless, the leading member of her lord's customary advance guard, apparently drinking in the calm beauty of the scene. Then she soberly moved, and was shortly followed by three companions. Presently, their fears at rest, all fell quietly to feeding. Before my glass was out another roar fell upon our expectant ears. Then out of a little basin walked a stag with a head which in that light looked enormous. "One, two, three on his left; and two on his right!" said Buckley. I agreed, so far as the failing light would let me see, but it was hopeless to think of going after him so late, and rather regretfully, but full of hope, we finished the long walk back to camp.

The next morning by eight o'clock we were sitting at the foot of the hill waiting for him to emerge from the bush; or, at least, to hear his welcome roar.

In this expectation we were doomed to disappointment, though a regular menagerie of animals beguiled the time. With subdued quacks a pair of Paradise ducks flirted close to a swamp turkey, who poked about amid the flax bushes, his handsome indigo plumage and red bill contrasting strongly with the green foliage among which he paraded. A seagull busily stuffed himself within a few yards; three or four hawks quartered the flats about the river-bed. A couple of black rabbits (lucky omen!) hopped, conspicuous among their drab relations, until the advent of a lank black and white cat, who came sneaking along in search of what she might devour. At length, tired of waiting, we started up the hill, and despite the delay caused by the appearance of a hind with her calf, reached a spot commanding the corrie.

The wind was all over the place. At the foot of the hill it was blowing up; at the top, down. The mists crawled sluggishly up the valley; clouds sailed steadily across it in precisely the opposite direction. Under the circumstances it was somewhat difficult to decide what to do. The stag might be in either of the corries whose lower slopes were covered with bush, and it seemed best to get above them and to trust to luck that our beast would feed out in the evening.

It was three o'clock when we reached the top of the first ridge, then, as society novelists say, "events moved rapidly to a conclusion."

Hardly had we seated ourselves behind a large tussock of snow-grass, horrible stuff to walk on, than a stag roared in the gully below us.

He was only a small beast, and as I watched another and still smaller stag walked out of the bush close to him and proceeded to thrash a tree in the approved manner of his elders. He would get the stem (it was a small celery pine, and

M

through rubbing these trees many of the New Zealand stags' horns are stained a bright red) between his horns and would then rub it vigorously up and down, repeating the performance on his neck. I have seen stags do this many times; it appears to afford them satisfaction in the rutting season.

The stag who had first roared could hear, but could not see, him. He rose to his feet, cocked his head on one side and listened, but apparently could not make up his mind as to the next event on the programme. Then he gave a tentative and somewhat subdued roar.

At this the smaller stag stopped his warlike demonstrations on the tree, cocked *his* head on one side, and also listened.

They were too far off to watch closely without a glass, so as my eye was getting rather tired I had my lunch. By the time I had finished and had another look they had vanished, which was disappointing, as I had anticipated some amusement from their encounter.

Buckley, too, had disappeared. Presently I heard a whistle, and looking round saw him making frantic signals for me to join him. Seizing my rifle, I made my way as quickly as possible over the tussocky grass. "Come on!" hissed Buckley. "He's there." It was needless to enquire who "he" was; so contenting myself with the laconic enquiry, "How far?" I received the equally laconic reply, "A hundred." Behind me I heard the stalker say, "Quick, a hind's seen me!" and I peered over the low knoll in front of us. A hind within 50 yards of the knoll was making preparations to decamp; higher up the hill were some seven or eight beasts standing in a huddled group, all staring in our direction; whilst all by himself, and wonder of wonders! on the near-side of the hinds, was my stag. His head was up, and the afternoon sun glinted on his wide-spread antlers as he strove to draw from some tainted channel in the air that message which he never lived to receive.

The great red gods, Diana, or my guardian angel, I know

not which, held my hand steady. He gave a great leap, gal-loped 50 yards down the hill in a spasmodic rush, and I knew that his head was mine. Then he stopped, trembled all over, and as his knees gave way went rolling down a tiny creek until a ledge far below us checked his downward career.

"He's got four on this top," cried Buckley, as we scrambled down the hill. "Four on the left, too," I answered. "He's a thirteen!" we both exclaimed on reaching him. But he wasn't; he was a fourteen-pointer, and a beautifully sym-metrical head at that. A broken bay snapped off short had misled me. Practically skin and bone, in addition to his broken bay he had smashed one tray point, one top badly and the other slightly.

Then it was that I blessed the little royal, for had I not stalked him I should never have seen the fourteen-pointer at all.

I had great luck with this stag all through, for only chance—or was it something else?—led Buckley to explore that little side basin. Had I not killed him then I should never have done so at all, as it started to pour with rain the next day, thick mists overhung the whole valley, and four days later the conditions were precisely the same. But little we cared that evening for rain or mist, or for the long walk back to camp.

Of the post-war condition of the deer in New Zealand I had learned nothing at first hand until Lord Belper visited the country in 1925. He secured what is probably the best bag which has ever been got there in one season by a single sportsman. Summing up his impressions, he wrote in his diary:

I had no idea of the difficulties of the country. Unless the stalker is prepared for real hard work and very stiff climbing on very difficult and sometimes dangerous ground, he will do no good. Good heads are few and far between, and one has to work hard to get them. Of course, not nearly all the good stags are seen, as many never come out of the thick bush. We were in about the best country on the fringe of the herd, which keeps gradually spreading out.

The fact that the herds have in the past been allowed to increase unchecked, to which I drew attention in 1907, is now producing the inevitable results. The districts in which the older herds were originally liberated are now, I think I am right in saying, without exception entirely useless from the stalker's point of view. Rubbish of both sexes is predominant, and as Lord Belper points out, the keen stalker who wants a really good head has to penetrate into the very rough country to which the best deer have worked out. It is sufficient comment on this point to say that after his trip with Lord Belper, Con Hodgkinson, probably the best guide in New Zealand, was going out to "cull" the deer, and expected to kill at least 800 head.

Lord Belper could not speak too highly of the consideration, sportsmanlike behaviour, and kindness which he received from Major Wilson (who arranged his trip), Mr. Forbes, his guides, and, indeed, all the New Zealanders with whom he was brought into contact. Since then, another major war has given many others in this country an opportunity of endorsing this opinion.

Starting on March 14 from Pembroke by launch for the Makarora, the party left their main camp three days later to go up the Landsborough Valley. To illustrate the difficulties which the stalker in Otago has to encounter, it may be mentioned that it took ten hours to advance 10 miles through thick bush, four hours being occupied in traversing Harper's Bluff, a lateral distance of about half a mile. In this type of country the only paths are deer tracks, usually well marked, on each side of the rivers, but difficult to follow when they branch off. Subsequently, Major Wilson reached the top of the valley, which had not been done since Arthur Harper discovered it about thirty years ago.

On the 18th Lord Belper killed his first royal, the first stag ever shot so high up the valley. Five days later, after much hard work, nothing sufficiently good to shoot having

been seen, from his second flying camp the stalker's perseverance was rewarded. The rest of the story may be told
in his own words:

About 2.30 we were on a fairly large flat, when we suddenly
heard a roar in the bush not far away from us. It sounded a very
good roar, so we decided to wait and see if the stag would come
out and show himself. We waited for four hours, when suddenly
five hinds came out, followed by the stag. I saw at once that he
seemed to have a very big head, but had no time to put a glass
on him, as already the hinds were very suspicious. I crawled
hurriedly up to within 175 yards of him and took a snap shot
just as he was turning to go back into the bush. I got him, and
when we got up, found to our great joy a wonderful head,
probably the best ever shot out of this herd in New Zealand.

Lord Belper estimated the weight of this stag at about
600 lbs. (nearly 43 stones), which is by no means improbable.
The skull weighed 25 lbs. before it was boiled, and the horns
carried sixteen points. Comparing these figures with those
of big Continental stags, it may be mentioned that in *Happy
Retrospect* Count Wilczek mentions the heaviest European
stag he ever killed was at Mühlleiten with the Crown Prince
Rudolf, September 1, 1885. He estimated the weight at
43 sts. 6 lbs., and thought it would have weighed more immediately after death. It was not weighed until the following
day, when it scaled 300 kilos without the head and antlers.

Subsequently the river rose too high to be forded, and
several good stags which had been seen on the far side had
to be left. Food ran short, and the party moved down, after
encountering various difficulties, to the base camp, and then
on to the Makarora, a march of over 70 miles. For the first
30 miles Con Hodgkinson carried the big head on his back
through thick bush. Those alone who have tried it can
realise what a feat of this kind implies. His only remark was
that "it was a pleasure to have carried such a splendid head."
Lady Belper joined her husband before proceeding up the
Blue River in the Makarora.

In her diary she notes the absence of birds, all the large wingless birds which formerly abounded having been killed in a few years by the stoats which were imported to keep down the rabbits.

Heavy rain delayed the travellers, and not until April 10 was camp pitched at Blue River Flats. From the camp a good stag was spied, and after fording the river, which was icy cold, and a long, difficult stalk, Lady Belper killed him, to find a very pretty even fifteen-pointer. A heavy storm came on, soaking the camp and rendering a supply of food from the base camp impossible. However, on the 11th Lady Belper killed a wild-looking thirteen-pointer with long horns and good points, and Lord Belper a good royal. On the 12th Lord Belper killed another very good royal in the bush itself. After an exhausting day, with very little food, the party reached camp, to find that at last fresh provisions had arrived from the base camp.

The 13th, a fine day, but very cold (the alterations of temperature are very trying, as it may be extremely hot in the bush and freezing on the tops), again brought luck. To quote from Lady Belper's notes:

For the last few days we have been spying what we judge to be a very good head on the mountain-side beyond the river opposite the camp, but he has been perched on the edge of a precipice, and would crash many hundreds of feet if shot. This morning we cannot see him, and A. decides to go and look for him, if it is possible to get up to where he was. From the camp it looks too precipitous to climb, being sheer rock-face and huge waterfalls. However, full of hope at 9.30, A., Jim, and Con cross the river and disappear into the bush. . . . At 4.30 they return with a magnificent fourteen-pointer, and give us the following account of the stalk. They had thought at times they would never reach the top, so steep it was, with no footing on the rock-face of the mountain, and a sheer drop of many hundred feet below them. The waterfalls had to be crossed, too, where one mistake would have meant instant death. As they neared the top they had to cut steps in the ice, and when at last they reached their goal, wading through snow, no stag was in sight. They rested for an hour, and terribly disappointed, started for home. Suddenly they saw some beasts below them, and among them, lying down, the fourteen-pointer. He was sheer below them, 100 yards or so, and A. had to fire into the middle of his back, using Con's shoulder as a rest. It took the two guides about an hour to get down to him, cut the head off, and return.

This beast was shot 5,000 feet up.

After this the weather got really bad. There was a heavy fall of snow, and four feet round the camp. It was vitally important to get across the river before a thaw, so, hastily packing what they could carry, the party abandoned their tents, and after crossing the river only just in time, with the water up to their arm-pits, reached their base camp.

Luck, no doubt, plays a certain part in the success of a trip of this kind, but no one who has ever stalked in New Zealand—and as I have already mentioned, I have never met harder stalking ground in any part of the globe I have been lucky enough to visit—will deny that a stalker who really works for his heads deserves every bit of luck which may be coming to him.

The chief point about the sixteen-pointer is its somewhat top-heavy appearance, due to an apparent weakening in the lower points and the extraordinarily massive character of the tops. It is much more symmetrical and well balanced than is usual with heads of this type, and is one which a stalker gets a chance at only once in a lifetime. The fourteen-pointer (it might be called fifteen, as there is a small point on the right top) is an ideal example of what a fourteen-pointer ought to be, and is one of the most beautiful I have ever seen, from New Zealand or anywhere else. All the points are long, its symmetry and proportions are pretty nearly perfect, the horn is thick and rough, and the tops magnificent.

The lack of span in Lady Belper's thirteen-pointer is atoned for by its wild appearance and length of horn; and though of Lord Belper's three royals it is not difficult to pick out the best, he would have been lucky to shoot either of the other two had the former been absent. The following are the measurements of these heads:

No.	Points.	Length.	Beam.	Span.	Spread.
1	8 + 8	48	$6\frac{3}{4}$	$33\frac{3}{4}$	41
2	7 + 7	$45\frac{1}{2}$	6	$31\frac{1}{2}$	41
3	7 + 6	$44\frac{3}{4}$	5	27	$34\frac{1}{4}$
4	6 + 6	$44\frac{1}{4}$	$6\frac{1}{2}$	$31\frac{3}{4}$	$40\frac{1}{4}$
5	6 + 6	$40\frac{3}{4}$	$5\frac{1}{2}$	$28\frac{1}{4}$	35
6	6 + 6	$38\frac{1}{2}$	$5\frac{1}{2}$	$33\frac{1}{2}$	$42\frac{3}{4}$
7	8 + 7	38	$5\frac{3}{4}$	$28\frac{1}{2}$	$36\frac{1}{4}$

I commented very unfavourably on the manner in which the New Zealand authorities were controlling the deer herds when I was there. Apparently conditions now are even worse.

The block system, an excellent one, by which the country was divided up into blocks of stalking ground, the allocation of each block being by ballot, has been abolished in the principal deer forest in the South Island. Licences, also, have been done away with, and there is no control over the movements of stalkers.

The Government were apparently influenced in their decision by the agitation of people who knew nothing of the real conditions, and by "crank" societies. These drew lurid pictures of the destruction done by deer to trees and the danger to native bird life. A sum of £6,000 was voted in 1932 for the destruction of deer, and I understand that something like 33,000 animals were slaughtered. All through the summer of 1932 official gangs were at work in the best forests in New Zealand, and when Acclimatisation Societies applied for protection in their deer forests in the South Island, they received an official reply stating that they had been advised that it was wrong to declare the deer a pest and at the same time protect them during the stalking season. Protection was apparently granted to Southland, where the quality of the heads is nothing like so good as in those forests to which protection was refused.

These stalkers, paid by the Government, hunt in pairs, and are usually experienced men. They are twelve in number, and do not have an easy time. When deer are regularly hunted they will not leave the bush, which grows up to a height of 3,000 feet, until after dark, and do not return to it till daybreak. Consequently they can never be approached, as their positions are unknown unless a stag is heard to roar.

Wapiti and moose, which inhabit a national park with very heavy bush and holding much native bird life, are not included in the "pest" class, which seems a little illogical, as one would have supposed that they were just as likely to cause damage as red deer. A writer in the *Field*, commenting on the introduction of these two species, states, incidentally, that those who stalk them reckon themselves among the aristocrats of the sporting world, and that there is a very perceptible difference between the man who has a moose or wapiti hanging in his smoking-room and the man who has but a humble royal. The difference may be apparent to him, but I fancy a good many possessors of humble royals would question his remark!

The whole question of destruction by deer is, of course, greatly exaggerated. Deer in large numbers undoubtedly cause damage and annoyance to farmers and to young plantations. That they would cause serious damage to well-grown timber I cannot believe. Deer have lived for centuries in the forests on the Continent which still survive, save where they have been destroyed by man's agency. "There are vast areas of land in the South Island of New Zealand that are of no use for anything but game animals, which, managed sensibly, would provide an attraction for local and overseas sportsmen." I quote from an excellent article by Mr. Forbes, the well-known New Zealand stalker, which appeared in the *New Zealand Fishing and Sporting Gazette*. From this article I have derived much useful information. The deer, as I have mentioned, were originally liberated in the neighbourhood of the Dingle Burn, which flows into Lake Hawea, and here the best heads for some years were killed. Spreading further, they extended from the Hunter Valley and the Makarora to Westland, and to the basin of

the Haast River formed by the Landsborough and Clarke
Rivers. Captain Haggas, who obtained some good heads in
a pre-war trip, tells me that they are now in the Matetake
Range, the Moeraki and the Paringa. The stags winter on the
west coast, in which direction they have been spreading for
years, and from this virgin country come back very fat to
the hinds. In *Stalks Abroad* I gave some particulars of
weights. Thirty-stone stags are common; one weighed
recently in pieces and without blood was 30 sts. 7 lbs. In
1914 a stag weighed near Lake Hawea was 44 sts. 4 lbs.
One is safe in saying that a big stag killed in virgin country
would be over 40 sts. It will be noticed that the best stags
have always been killed further west, as the deer spread, and
I have no doubt that there are still many fine stags in inaccessible country, in spite of the prevalent slaughter.

But it is only in such country that the best heads will be
got. It is difficult, unless one is on the spot, to gauge the
situation correctly. When I was in New Zealand the management of many of the deer herds was in the hands of men
many of whom had never seen a deer in their lives. A similar
state of affairs prevailed before the war. I have no information as to what has happened with regard to the deer since
1939. Had the deer been properly controlled—a difficult
matter in such country, I admit—the sensational clamour of
ignorant busybodies with an axe to grind would have had
but little effect. That there is damage by deer, that some have
grievances, I have but little doubt. The evil has gone beyond
control, which gives the agitator his chance, and deer have
been slaughtered wholesale to satisfy the clamour this class
has raised. Had the deer not been allowed to get beyond
control the situation could have been simplified to a great
extent. If all malforms, bad heads, and bad breeding hinds
had been ruthlessly shot; the Morven Hills, Timaru Creek,
Lower Dingle, Mount Jones, and Longslip districts practically cleared of deer, and the numbers reduced by properly
appointed stalkers who knew their job, the present situation
would not have arisen. All the old deer country which I

knew is, of course, entirely worthless. It is no longer possible to exterminate worthless deer. If the Government butchers killed all they could, spared good heads (which they do not) and promising young stags, and were kept out of the deer country during the stalking season in March and April, it would still be possible for local and visiting sportsmen to enjoy a measure of sport. This at present seems to be the only possible solution.

It is a thousand pities, for, properly managed, the New Zealand authorities had a heritage which would have provided not only fine sport for New Zealanders, but an attractive inducement for visitors with money to spend, and trophies which might have been the admiration of sportsmen all over the world.

XVII. DUNCAN'S RIFLE

"Tell me now, could you hit any given acre of land at fifty paces?"
THE ART OF DEER STALKING—William Scrope.

THE story was told me by Archie, who was for many years a great ally of mine; his only drawbacks being that where deer are concerned he was absolutely unscrupulous, and that he was a vile shot. The following incident illustrates both of these failings.

He had taken an inexperienced gentleman out stalking and brought him up to within a hundred yards of a good stag which was feeding away from them into the wood. They occupied a good position, but in spite of all Archie's directions and explanations, to the novice the stag was invisible. "There, by yon white stane!" hissed the exasperated stalker. The stag still remained unseen. At last he could stand it no longer. Hurriedly seizing the rifle he took a hasty aim and fired. The stag was hit very far back and they found him dead in the wood the next day, but it was only

Archie's reputation as a stalker that saved him from dismissal. Apropos of this he told me the following yarn as we were returning from the hill one evening last autumn, the moorland breeze blowing softly in our faces, and the sun, low down in the west, casting long shadows at our feet.

Twenty years before, when Archie was a lad of fifteen, his father, Duncan, had been stalker in a certain big forest in the north. They lived the healthy open-air lives such men do and, on the whole, were supremely happy. There was only one thing which Duncan secretly longed for, and that was—a rifle. There were two other stalkers in the forest who each possessed a weapon of sorts—not accurate small-bores of the present day, but good enough to knock over a hind in winter at a hundred yards—and it was gall and wormwood to Duncan to feel that in this respect he was their inferior. He racked his brains for a means of getting the wherewithal to buy that second-hand ·450 he knew of in Inverness, but in vain. His small croft coupled with his wages and well-earned tips left him comfortably off but with nothing to spare on luxuries when there was a family of eight children to feed and educate.

Now, there chanced to come as a guest to the forest a certain captain in Her Majesty's army. He became a very distinguished general, but having in view the end of the story and the fact that it is a true one I forbear to give his name. He had never been in Scotland before, and his great ambition was to kill a stag. He was a good target shot, and provided there was a stag within range, thought he would answer for the rest. So he told his host, when that gentleman, the morning after his arrival, wished him luck as he started for the hill with Duncan. An hour's walk from the lodge brought them to the spying-place from which they could obtain a view of some of the best ground in the forest. The captain awkwardly pulled out his new glass, and in a strained position, which he intended to be a close imitation of Duncan's, proceeded to spy the opposite corrie. After a minute or so he got tired of it, and, shutting up his telescope, began to interrogate his companion as to their chances of getting a stag. Duncan slowly replied that "he wass seeing deer," and later that one of them was a "gude beastie." Archie was there as gillie to lead the tracker, and he told me that, on Duncan's remark being translated to mean "a shootable stag," he never in his life had seen anyone so excited. He and his father had both seen bad attacks of stag fever before but they were none the less somewhat astonished when the excited warrior promised Duncan a five-pound note if he killed a stag.

There was no difficulty in getting him to do what was wanted. He crawled through bogs, slithered down banks covered with long heather which only just concealed sharp pointed rocks, tore his hands and knees on burnt patches, in fact there was nothing he would not do provided he could get that stag.

The stalk was not really a hard one, and within half an hour from the time when the deer had been first spied, Duncan and the gasping novice were ensconced behind a friendly rock within a hundred yards of the unconscious herd. Archie, with his collie, had been left in the shelter of a burn, whence he got a good view of the subsequent operations. "Tak' your time," said Duncan, "they're aal feeding." Presently the object (no other word describes him at that moment) to whom his remarks were addressed began to take a rather more personal interest in the proceedings as his gasps became less frequent, and Duncan, drawing off the cover of the rifle, put the weapon into his hands.

"D'ye see yon staag, the thirrd frae the richt," he began in a long, careful whisper, "him with the red coat? Tak' him when he gies ye a brroadside chance!"

The stag, a nice nine-pointer, little knowing what a change of position might mean to him, fed slowly on. At last, in order to get a better bite at a clump of fresh young heather, he turned his shoulder to the anxious pair.

"Noo!" said Duncan, looking on the fiver as already his. Bang! went number one, and bang! again went the second barrel as the herd galloped madly away. A dip in the ground hid them almost immediately, and by the time the discomfited marksman, following Duncan's example, had doubled hastily to the edge of the bluff they were a good four hundred yards off. The stalker noted his companion's jaw mutely working and sympathised, but laying his hand on the rifle he only said, "Likely they'll be stopping east a bittie!" and then pulled out his glass.

They did indeed "stop east a bittie," but not in such a position that the crestfallen soldier was able to retrieve his reputation as a shot, and it was a disconsolate quartette which returned to the lodge that night. However, a hot bath, dinner and cigar sent the captain to bed in a more equable frame of mind, fully convinced that it was his long train journey plus lack of exercise which was responsible for the morning's blunders.

Two days later he was given another chance of "being blooded." The morning dawned clear and bright, with a strong wind blowing from the north, and, as Duncan remarked going up to their beat, "a graand morning for a stalk!" On they went past lonely hill tarns watched over by the eagle they could see above them, past the herd of hinds and knobbers which gazed at them from the sky-line, on up the narrow winding path until they were at the far march, forty miles from the nearest station, and, as the guide-book says, "in a place lonely and inaccessible to a degree." To the captain's inexperienced eye it looked most unlikely ground for deer, but a day's practice with a glass had made him rather more accustomed to its use, and now, following Duncan's directions, he managed to make out several dim red forms on a far-distant slope of green. He, of course, could not tell whether they were donkeys or deer, but Duncan's keen eyes made out some good stags, so, closely followed by Archie, they started.

Once again they crawled, climbed and slithered, and once again Duncan's skilful manœuvres brought them to within eighty yards of the deer.

"Tak' plenty o' time and aim steady," he said quietly, whilst the object of his exhortations cast a despairing glance at the rifle he was pushing cautiously round the corner of a stone. The muzzle, resting as it did on Duncan's cap, remained fairly steady, so did the stag. There was a nice light, and, as I said before, the intended victim was only eighty yards off, broadside on. Yet the fact remained that at the shot the stag cantered away apparently unharmed, nor, as the herd bunched together and a second shot rang out, did they leave one of their number prostrate on the ground. With a hearty oath the captain flung his rifle on the ground, and, shaking his fist at the retreating deer, literally danced with rage.

Now, Duncan, in spite of his quiet advice, had not been unprepared for a miss, and, while they were coming up the steep hill path in the morning, had evolved a scheme by which, should such a contretemps as he had already witnessed occur a second time, all parties would be mutually benefited. A few hasty words in Gaelic were sufficient to give Archie his directions, then, whilst the captain was still uttering heartfelt wishes concerning his own and the stag's ultimate destination, he picked up the rifle and disappeared at a trot in the direction taken by the deer. The captain, somewhat ashamed of himself, was about to follow, when Archie, laying a hand on his sleeve, told him to lie down as his father thought one of the stags was hit. They watched him out of sight and then, their impatience and excitement getting beyond control, started to follow. For a time they continued their cautious advance, and then, as they saw no signs of either man or deer, lay down again. For ten minutes or so nothing came to disturb them; then, just as they were making preparations for another start, the sound of a shot came crisply to them, and, a second later, another. At this they could stand the inaction no longer and hastily crawled to the summit of a neighbouring knoll. Arrived there they had a good view of some big corries, and Archie soon saw Duncan coming up to them from the flat below. As he drew near he cast one quick look at his son, and then answered the captain's eager inquiries.

"Aye, sir, ye hutt the first staag vera hard. He's deid on the flat there, and I'm thinking likely we'll be getting the seccund too." Saying this he turned and, leading the way, strode on ahead. He occasionally looked round with caution when the jubilant warrior's excitement threatened to break forth into open song, beyond this making but few comments. Before long a red mass lying in the grass on the flat caught the captain's eye and, plunging forward, he found himself wallowing full length in a peat bog. Nothing daunted, he continued his mad career, and only brought up when almost on top of the dead stag. His delight knew no bounds, for there before him lay a fine ten-pointer, the blood yet oozing from a red hole behind his shoulder; but, as Duncan gravely explained, the movements of deer when hit through the heart are governed by no stated laws, stags frequently running four or five hundred yards when hit in this manner, "and, sir," he wound up, "yon was a graand shot."

"You shall have the five pounds I promised you for this stag, Duncan, and, by Jove! if I've got the other too, you shall have ten!" exclaimed the grateful soldier.

"Weel, sir," said Duncan, touching his cap (perhaps to hide the sudden twinkle in his eye), "I saw both the staags was hutt when I got the glass on them; I fired twa shots at the seccund, and I'm thinking he'll be deid by yon knollie." Slowly and cautiously they reached the knoll, when Duncan, motioning his companions back, crawled carefully forward. For a long time he scrutinised the surrounding country with his glass, and then beckoned the others to approach. In a low voice he explained he thought he knew the position of the wounded stag, and, handing the captain his rifle, told him to have it ready in case the beast should jump up suddenly. As they advanced, the stalker on hands and knees led the way past a little hollow. For some strange reason a still dun form lying in it escaped his attention. Not so his followers. A furious tugging at his elbow apprised him of

N

this fact, and he turned to see the hitherto quiescent captain wildly stabbing the air with his forefinger.

"Have you the rifle ready?" he said quietly and crawled a little nearer. Still no movement. "Ye'll no need it now," said Duncan gravely, "the staag is deid!"

He was indeed, as a red stain on his neck showed. I need not describe the final rites, the "blooding" of the captain, the walk home and the triumphant arrival at the lodge. Anyone who has stalked will appreciate the captain's feelings, and any stalker will appreciate Duncan's when, on the morning the former left, he handed him two crisp banknotes for five pounds each.

But though he felt fully convinced that he had killed two good stags, what had really happened was this. Duncan, on seeing that none of the deer had been hit, left the others and rapidly made his way to a pass in the hills for which he thought the deer would make. Sure enough, about half a mile from where the shots had been fired, he found them walking slowly forward and occasionally stopping for a backward look. They had not seen him, so a slow, cautious retreat followed by a hasty run forward brought him within shot. Singling out the best stag he fired and had the satisfaction of seeing it give a convulsive leap which he knew betokened a hit. As the rest of the herd topped a ridge he took quick aim and fired again. The deer were out of sight the next second, but Duncan had seen his victim give a sudden lurch at the shot and knew his own powers. He, accordingly, made his way back to the others with the result which I have already described.

All that happened many years ago now; Archie's father is no longer a stalker, but, though nearly eighty, he still occasionally has a day at the hinds. His rifle is a ·450, and the accuracy with which I lately saw him kill a beast at a hundred and twenty yards convinced me that his brain and eye are still as cunning as on the day, twenty years ago, when he earned that trusty weapon and the lasting gratitude of a very distinguished man at one and the same time.

XVIII. PRIDE GOETH——!

"My high-blown pride at length broke under me."
KING HENRY VIII, Act III, Sc. 2—W. Shakespeare

I RECENTLY became engaged with a distinguished stalker in a discussion on our favourite sport, and in particular, on the question of the shot itself.

"What," I asked him, "do you consider a good average percentage of hits to cartridges?"

"You mean taking every shot into account?" I agreed. He pondered for a little.

"Would you consider three shots per beast good?" I went on.

"Very good indeed," he replied. "Four to five, I should say."

His answer interested me very much and a week or so later I had an opportunity of proving its truth. I know that many stalkers lacking his experience would fail to agree with him, but experience teaches one a great deal. My proof in practice came about as follows. It was February and I went out to kill some hinds. The weather was cold and frosty with very little wind, such as there was from the north-west. Stalking under such conditions is never easy, particularly with any snow on the ground, for sound carries far and deer very frequently hear the stalker before he can get within comfortable range. I found a number of hinds and calves, stalked them, but owing to the reasons I have mentioned, failed to get a shot. They moved off, not much alarmed and, after going for a quarter of a mile or so, quieted down and started to feed. A low ridge separated them from me, on the other side of a peaty flat 150 yards across. Having successfully negotiated this I found myself comfortably ensconced within 50 yards of them. To the number of thirty or more they were scattered beyond the ridge, the most distant being a little over 100 yards. She was a good hind and fell at once. The others bunched, not knowing where the shot had come from. I killed four more in as many shots, all good hinds.

I confess that I was rather pleased with myself. My shooting had been accurate and I had picked the right hinds, which is not, altogether, an easy thing to do. I returned home glowing with self-satisfaction.

A week later I went out again. Weather conditions were much the same though the light was bad. Patches of snow lay in the hollows and such conditions, as all stalkers know, are very trying. It is the easiest thing in the world to pass over deer when spying such ground and the judging of distances is difficult. I found some hinds. They were not in a good position for a stalk and I could not get nearer than 150 yards. The deer were below me and there was no cover to speak of. They were quite ignorant of my presence, so I sat up, rested my elbows on my knees, took careful aim and missed. A second shot had a similar result. The deer vanished over the march so, retracing my steps to the crest of the ridge, I turned back. My route led past a narrow strip of fir plantation. Walking slowly along its edge I caught a movement to my left and saw a solitary hind trotting rapidly across the flat towards me. At the edge of the trees she stopped, facing me. I sat down and fired. Another miss.

She stood and I missed her again. Then she started to bolt. A third shot killed her stone dead. Five shots—one beast.

I had noticed some hinds on the edge of a wood rising above a little loch and made my way to a knoll from which I could get a good spy. They were not to be seen, but cautiously advancing I saw a hind feeding among some bushes about 100 yards off. There was no need to stalk. I crept a few yards, sat down and fired. The bullet hit a patch of snow just over her back.

She made off and I climbed the ridge behind me, hoping to catch sight of her and get a second shot. I had got halfway up when two hinds galloped past the spot where she had stood, slowed down, eventually stopping among some trees. I ran back, rather flurried, caught sight of them again and got a shot. They moved on, stopped, and I fired again. I knew one was hit and could just see her through the trees. I fired again. They turned down into the wood. I followed and to make a long story short fired several more shots at the wounded hind, the view partially obscured by the trees. She disappeared and I followed her into the wood. The second hind suddenly dashed past below me. I fired, missed and fired again. Then she moved into the open and I had several more shots—all misses. The first hind I found, lying dead in the wood. Result, fourteen shots for two beasts.

I had seen more deer, a mile or so away, not far from the road. We dragged the two hinds home about a mile distant, had a bite of food, got the car and went round to see if we could get to terms with the deer beside the road. After some careful spying I found a hind feeding among some trees at the edge of a wood. The stalk was not difficult though the wind was bad and a considerable detour was necessary before I could feel safe. Stalking among trees on the edge of a wood is always tricky, as great care is necessary in order that one's presence is not detected before making quite certain where the deer are. The appearance of trees is very deceptive from different angles and it is easy to mistake one

point for another. However, I got up to a convenient knoll
and saw the hind facing me among some trees about 120
yards distant. Misses are usually high or low and a facing
shot is not really so difficult as it sounds, as so large a vital
area is exposed.

Accordingly I took what I thought was careful aim and
fired. She never moved. A second shot produced a similar
result. The third hit her and she moved slowly away among
the trees. I fired again, she walked on. Not until the fifth
shot did she fall. Nineteen shots for three beasts.

Without trying to excuse very bad shooting I may say
that I consider the modern soft-nosed ·275 bullets, which
appear to be all that it is possible to procure at present, are
very unsatisfactory compared with the pointed copper-
tipped bullets which were the standard type of ammunition
for this bore prior to the First World War. They were the
best bullets I ever used and with them I never lost a single
beast after it had been hit. They seemed to paralyse all the
nerve-centres, whereas with these soft-nosed things you
never know, at least I don't, whether the beast has been hit
or not.

The next day's hind stalking went as follows. From the
spying place I saw a few hinds and calves scattered about a
flat by the march burn. They were not easy to get at and a
long detour was necessary to get the wind right. Then I
discovered that there were thirty or more hinds at the far
end of the flat, some of them good yeld hinds. The proper
hinds to shoot are the old ragged ones and the late calves,
but I agree that it takes a certain amount of determination
to do this, especially when shooting for meat and not,
primarily, for the good of the forest.

We proceeded above the flat and out of sight of the deer
until we reached the shelter of a burn with narrow rocky
sides which led on to the flat. Unfortunately, as so often
happens in such cases, its shelter terminated abruptly just
where it would have been most useful and in the wide
expanse of yellow grass, interspersed with tufts of heather

and patches of snow, there was not a patch of cover which would have enabled us to get within range. Three or four hinds lay beside a drain which ran diagonally across the flat a couple of hundred yards from the main body. Whilst we debated on the best means of approach a heavy snow shower came on which kept us cowering in the shelter of the burn for half an hour. When it had passed we saw that the hinds still lay there, powdered with snow, and all we could do was to retrace our steps until we had reached a point from which we could ascertain if the remainder had moved. They had passed the flat and were feeding on the edge of a ridge, a few hundred yards distant from a straggly birchwood whose outposts ran down to the edge of the burn. Back we went again and came to the edge of a ridge which extended, not to the flat directly, but to some broken hollows with steep sides which precluded a clear view. I thought they had moved on to the wood and was making for its edge when I saw the head of a hind emerging from the broken ground behind me. Gaining the cover of a knoll I saw half a dozen more within shot and others feeding rapidly forward. Getting into position I took steady aim and saw a hind fall. A second gave me a good chance and she too fell. The remainder bolted up the hill, down wind, for deer when frightened will always make for home. It was bare, open, heathery ground and before I could gain any cover they had seen me and stopped. I could not sit or they would have been out of my view, so I knelt, an attitude for shooting which I have always loathed. They galloped past me, about 70 yards off, broadside on.

I fired six shots. One hind broke off from her companions and made off in the opposite direction. I fired three more shots and she lay down. I could not see where my shots were going but I imagine high, as this is the most usual form of miss. I gave the wounded hind a little time and then stalked the place where I thought she was lying, as it was not actually in sight.

Apparently she was not so badly hurt as I thought, for

I was barely in view when she rose and moved off. I crawled to a knoll, fired twice, and missed both times. Eventually she trotted off, apparently not much hurt, and that ended the day. Result, thirteen shots for two hinds, and thirty-two for five beasts, an average of about six shots per beast. "Not," as the Boy would say, "so good!"

I give a rather detailed description of these days' stalking in order to show the vicissitudes which befall the stalker for no apparent reason. When one is stalking continuously every day for several weeks such catastrophes do not so often occur as one gains confidence and is able to correct mistakes. Over-confidence is a fault to beware of, and the most frequent cause of bad shooting in the case of experienced shots. The light, I admit in my own defence, was bad, and though I have always had bad sight I am much more adversely affected by poor visibility than formerly. Such bad shooting, however, was inexcusable, even though on account of advancing age and defective eyesight the standard of youth cannot be maintained. The account of such an experience may, however, be of some interest to others who have sustained similar disasters.

XIX. AN EXPEDITION TO CHINA

"And these from the land of Sinim."

ISAIAH xlix. 12

I SUPPOSE that every hunter of big game has in mind
certain trophies which he covets most. He may or may
not have got them.

The head of my dreams is that of one of the great Asiatic
sheep, and I always break the tenth commandment whenever I look at the beautiful 60-inch argali killed by Lord
Elphinstone, or the slightly larger head which my friend
Jack Miller obtained before his untimely death in the First
World War. These I prefer even to the heads of those wonderful sheep named after the great Venetian traveller. He it
was who found them while traversing those dreary wastes
so many years ago in a manner but little different from that
which the wayfarer pursues today.

These sheep and the wild goats of Asia provide the
finest stalking in the world, and the death of a good specimen the climax of an achievement which no other form of
sport can equal. Next to one of the big sheep I would hang

the head of an Astor markhor with its beautiful, open, corkscrew-like horns; and third, an ibex from the Tien Shan. Alas! they are but dreams, and their shadowy horns fill a void only in my imagination.

I have shot wild sheep in the Rockies, burhel on the heights of Kansu, and ibex in the Red Sea Hills, and in the Sierra di Gredos in Spain. These, to the heads I covet, stand in the same relation as do the horns of a little Highland stag to those of his giant relatives who lurk in the forests of Galicia and about the banks of the Danube.

Next to this trio of my choice I would place the giant sable of Angola, a really good kudu bull, a bongo, and Lord Derby's eland from the Bahr-el-Ghazal. A first-class Alaskan moose, a 60-inch wapiti with twelve points, and a big Galician stag's head, with no "ifs" about it, would complete my list, with one addition—a perfect Scottish roe head. The latter is the only trophy that comes within the bounds of possibility, and then only if I have such luck as to practically exclude it! I have been trying for him for fifty years and have never yet seen him in the flesh, nor do I suppose that, now, I ever shall.

Such a display is unknown on the walls of any single individual, nor is it likely that it ever will be envied as the result of perseverance on the part of one man. The dreams with which we set out have to be modified, and in these days to have secured any animal comparatively unknown is, at all events, to have achieved something, and to have stored up happy recollections for those days "when anno domini has you in his clutches, and the rifle and spy-glass are kept but to be looked at."

This I have accomplished.

It was in 1911 that Captain George Fenwick-Owen asked me to accompany him to China in an endeavour to secure specimens of that strange animal, the takin. Major Malcolm McNeill had a year or two previously killed a female deer to the west of Tachienlu which was new to science, and the species had been named in his honour. Various other species had been rumoured as existing, and we hoped that we might have the good fortune to come across some fresh variety in the centre of China. This seemed to be the most likely neighbourhood in which to attempt to find the main object of our search.

Very little was known of the game to be found in the interior of China, few sportsmen had shot there, and its possibilities as the home of unknown species were considerable. This still remains true. I should never be surprised to learn that a new race of, say, sambhur or sika had been discovered. The literature of sport in the Middle Kingdom was, and is, meagre. The only work, so far as I am aware, to be published since Mr. E. H. Wilson's *A Naturalist in Western China* is *Trailing the Giant Panda*. This is an account of the Kelly-Roosevelt Field Museum expedition undertaken in 1929. The country described is to the south of our own wanderings. Ascending the Irrawaddy in Burma, the party crossed into Yunan, struck north into Szechuan, and returned by Yunnan-fu. It may be added that the expedition was successful and secured a specimen of the giant panda, which, though like a bear in appearance, is in reality a member of the racoon family. It was discovered by Père David in Mupin in 1869. M. Berezovski encountered the species on the Kansu-Szechuan border in 1892–93. None had been shot by a white man until my old friend the late Colonel (he was then Captain) Brocklehurst killed the magnificent specimen in Szechuan in 1935 which was exhibited at the Berlin Hunting Exhibition in 1937, and in London in 1938. To obtain this he travelled over 28,000 miles and climbed to over 13,000 feet. "Brock" was one of the few people who could successfully have undertaken so arduous a trip. The Roosevelt Expedition was not successful in securing a takin, though traces of the animal were found. This uncouth creature ranges through difficult mountainous country extending from the Mishmi Hills on the northern frontiers of Assam into Szechuan, Yunnan, Tibet, and Kansu. They are said to exist in Northern Shansi.

The latest information with regard to the position of the takin in the animal kingdom appears to come from Mr. H. P. Pycraft. In *The Illustrated London News* (February 17, 1934) he writes:

On the subject of the affinities of the takin there are many opinions. The teeth, which are extremely important guides in this matter, it is to be noted, resemble those of sheep and goats, and differ conspicuously from those of oxen. It is unfortunate that no complete skull is known in England, but the remains in the British Museum show that it is remarkable for the great depth in front of the eyes; while the relatively short and highly arched nasal bones cover an enormous nasal cavity. This is a well-known feature of animals which live in the rarefied atmosphere of great elevations. We find a similar nasal cavity in the chiru, or saiga antelope of Thibet, and of the Thibetan domesticated goat.

One authority suggested that the takin is "essentially a serow." This is a goat-like antelope, represented by several species, ranging from the Himalayas, through China and Japan to Sumatra, linking up with the oxen through the musk-ox on the one hand, and the sheep and goats on the other. But there is really no justification for this association with the oxen. Another supported the view as to the relationship with the musk-ox, basing his conclusions on the striking shortness and great width of the cannon bones, the shape of the skull and horns, the small and strangely shaped ears, the hairy muzzle (like that of sheep or goats), the shortness of the tail (a mere stump), and the large lateral hoofs.

It is worth noting that one finds such phenomenally short cannon bones only in the takin, the musk-ox, and the Rocky Mountain goat (Oreamnus). That these three animals are indeed related seems to be indicated by the fact that they are linked by two extinct species—*Euceratotherium* and *Preptoceras*—found in certain caves in California. That the ancestors of these two came from Asia is practically certain in the opinion of the late Richard Lydekker, one of the foremost authorities of his time on fossil animals; and they represent an assemblage of ruminants of which the takin and the serow are the sole survivors.

This, then, was the animal we set out to pursue.

Mason Mitchell, who was American Consul at Chungking in 1907, claims to have been the first white man to shoot one. In *A Naturalist in Western China* Mr. Wilson gives the honour to Mr. Zappey, though Mr. C. H. Mears ran him very close. The former killed his animal near Tachienlu on May 27, 1908; the latter's, a cow, succumbed three days later. Mr. Wilson ignores Mitchell's claim. Mr. Roy Andrews and Mr. K. K. Horn have, since our expedition, shot the Kansu variety, and in the same locality. Col. John Stanford hunted them successfully on the Yunnan frontier in 1938–9. He is even more famous as the author of that shooting classic, *The Twelfth*. These, so far as I know, are the only ones killed by white men.

In *The Big Game of Central and Western China*, and in *The Gun at Home and Abroad* I wrote fully of the appearance and habits of the takin. To these works I would refer the reader who is in search of detailed information. A brief description of this rare animal may be forgiven. Probably no creature in the world has so seldom been the object of pursuit on the part of the white man. A conspicuous golden yellow in colour, the profile is decidedly semitic, whilst the back-view inevitably calls to mind that of a Teddy bear. His horns resemble to some extent those of the African wildebeeste, but there are marked differences. I was once amused to see at an exhibition of trophies held in London a pair of takin horns which had been detached from their cores and mounted on a boss back to front! From a spectacular point of view the head is a poor trophy: its interest lies in its rarity and the position of its original owner in the animal kingdom.

By the natives they are regarded as savage. Roosevelt emphasises this point in *Trailing the Giant Panda*. Personally, my acquaintance with them was too limited for me to speak with any authority on the subject. Though I do not consider the takin capable of domestication, it is a fact worth noting that many animals which in their wild state are the most wild and intractable become, when adapted to man's uses, the most docile and tame. One who had only seen sheep and goats in their native condition would scarcely believe that it is their descendants which provide us with both food and clothing.

Travelling in China is a long and wearisome business. It is not a question of stepping from a train or steamer and finding yourself within easy reach of your shooting ground. It took us many days' hard going after landing at Shanghai to reach our goal. The traveller, even in civilised countries, is often at the mercy of circumstances over which he has no control. China is not yet civilised according to Western ideas. In addition, when the wayfarer is ignorant of the language of those who control his destinies, the difficulties are increased to an extent which at times reduces his over-wrought nerves to a pitch bordering on frenzy. Travel in China, even thirty years ago, was like travel in no other part of the globe. The country is so old, so tired that one seems to have wandered into a world immeasurably more ancient than that which has been left. Its age is perhaps what strikes the observer most. One reads in the Bible of walled cities. There are walled cities in other countries. In none have I seen any which brought to my mind with such emphasis the connotation of these words. Small wonder that they are so frequently used to denote a place of refuge. On top of the walls of cities such as Peking or Sian-fu could be driven four motor-cars abreast.

The cities after the last named we left behind on our journey across the plains, slowly progressing day after day through the deep dusty layers of loess, or ploughing a sea of mud in which, not infrequently, the carts became almost submerged. A nation of crofters are the Chinese. Painfully they till and cultivate each scrap of soil. If from the road they can steal a few inches, they do so. Gradually the road contracts until it can barely accommodate the traffic it is designed to support. On the loess plains, which stretch interminably in the centre of China, the original roads during wet weather sink into oblivion. Another is formed as some

muleteer, more callous than his fellows, drives his team
along the edge of some unfortunate's crop. A second follows, and a new road is formed. This again goes the way of
its predecessor, and a third comes into being. You may,
perhaps, see the traces of as many as five roads within a few
yards of each other.

It is a long, dusty, tiring journey to the hills. It seems as
if such things as clear running water, cool, aloof tops flushed
with the dawn, the pleasant shade of leafy trees cannot
exist in the same land as holds the parched, dusty heat
through which you have struggled. At your journey's end
they do exist, and here it was, above the thickets of bamboo,
the clumps of rhododendrons, and the wild flowers, that
we found at last the quarry we had come so far to seek.
Not at once, for, having toiled up 5,000 feet of rough hillside, we spent day after day soaked to the skin and swathed
in mist, cowering beneath an overhanging rock, termed by
courtesy a cave.

At last one morning blue sky appeared, and having
climbed another 2,000 feet or so above our temporary
resting-place, we spied, on the far side of the great rocky
basin which stretched below us, the yellow forms of the
rare animals we had come so far to seek. From the narrow
ridge on which we stood the view was magnificent. To the
west spread range after range of mountains, the highest
peaks topped by fleecy clouds; to the north extended a wide
valley stretched far below us, the whole panorama, save for
the rocks and slides which gashed the sides of the hills, of a
vivid green. In this setting the takin, tawny as lions, moved
in a somewhat uncouth and clumsy fashion.

The wind [to quote from the description I wrote at the time]
was from the east. A detour round the top of the basin was our
only means of approach. The actual distance was not great, but it
took us an hour to reach the spot from which the descent had to
be made.

Here a higher and even rockier top than those which we had
already traversed confronted us. From its side sprang an enormous

jagged spur, which stretched into the depths of a deep gully to
our left. Stopping for a spy, we almost at once found another herd
of takins. They were lying in the sun directly above a stone shoot,
or narrow gully, which seamed one side of the spur and descended
in an unbroken drop for 1,000 or 1,500 feet. There were eight in
all—three bulls, three cows, and two calves. Two of the bulls
were sparring, while the calves played about among the rocks.
They were in a much better position for a stalk than those which
we had seen from the far side of the basin, so we decided to try
for a shot. An hour and a half later we reached the summit of the
mountain, attaining a height of 11,000 to 12,000 feet. The ascent
was very similar to the type of ground we had already crossed.
In the saddles, open grassy patches bordered by stunted larches
on which were laid long roof poles and coffin boards, for the
country swarmed with wood-cutters. No tree was of any size, for
in a land where fuel is precious every large tree, with a happy
disregard for the future, is cut down and cast into the fire. Others,
saved from this fate, are sliced into coffin boards, transported
down to the valleys on the backs of the wood-cutters, and so by
mule-train to Sian-fu.

Replanting is unknown. Bluebells, gentians, vetches, forget-me-
nots, orchids, poppies, edelweiss, and an amazing variety of small
rock plants grew, scattered among the rhododendrons and
azaleas; meadow pippits darted among the rocks; a Siberian mink
flung himself headlong across the path; a blood pheasant called
from the valley below and was answered by the flippant cry of
a fir-crow. Ever and anon the unmistakable scent of a fox was
borne to our nostrils.

Both our hunters were very excited, laughing and gesticulating,
leaping among the rocks in their rope sandals in a manner which
was highly aggravating to anyone in heavy shooting boots.

At length we reached a spot from which it was possible to spy
the takins. They had moved a little distance from the place where
we had originally seen them and were lying among the rocks with
which the hillside was strewn. One bull looked considerably
larger than the other two, though these were full grown. His
horns were slightly longer and his bulk greater. A little apart from
the others he lay, overlooking the stone shoot, in an ideal position
for a stalk.

Continuing our advance, we gained a position on very rocky

and precipitous ground 400 or 500 yards above the animals. Here we put on some spare hemp sandals which, though very small and uncomfortable, were a necessity, as it would have been impossible to get within shot in our heavy foot-gear without making a noise. Even so I was within an ace of dislodging a large boulder, but fortunately managed to steady it in time.

We drew lots for the first shot at the big bull, my companion winning. We agreed that on hearing his shot I was free to do what I liked. A steep crag of rock, sloping into lesser pinnacles, rose immediately above the bank of dwarf rhododendrons, sprinkled with wild flowers, on which they lay. I watched my companion and his hunter get into position, and then crawled down among the rocks. In this type of country one can often obtain a close shot, but none the less I was a little startled, on looking over my peak, to see a bull and two cows, blissfully unconscious of my presence, lying within 20 yards. The big bull I could not see, nor the third, which was tucked away beneath an overhanging rock lower down the hillside.

Cautiously I thrust my rifle over the rock, took a sight on the bull's neck, and waited. It seemed an age before the shot for which I was listening rang out. At last it did, and before my bull could spring to his feet he was dead. I heard a crash from below; the two cows dashed past me, and as they did so I fired again. As my hunter seized me by the arm another full-grown animal suddenly appeared, to fall among the rocks out of my sight.

On comparing notes a few moments later we found that we had the big bull, though, unfortunately, in falling over the rocks, the tip of one horn had been broken; a cow which had pitched straight over the edge of the stone shoot and was smashed to pulp; the two other bulls and the second cow.

Thus ended an exciting five minutes, during which we had secured a very rare animal. No particle of the meat was wasted, and though, reading this description, it might be thought we had indulged in somewhat wholesale slaughter, it should be remembered that we had travelled long and far to obtain specimens, which it was not likely we should encounter again.

o

We were lucky in finding these takins in a place where it was possible to stalk them under such favourable conditions. In bamboo and rhododendron thickets it is quite another story. The game hears the hunter approach and loses no time in making off, as we subsequently proved, killing another cow and losing a bull after fourteen hours' strenuous exertions.

Having got our takin during the only spell of fine weather we experienced, we decided to move camp, and though before hunting the Kansu stag we spent some time after burhel, it was with the former animal that I will deal next, as, after the takin, he was the most important variety of game we obtained.

This fine animal was named from a female shot by the companion of our trip, Dr. J. A. Smith. The reader may have already gathered that in China, to render certain the success of a shooting expedition, an interpreter is an absolute necessity. Although a native would have been cheaper, they are not always to be relied on, and I count ourselves lucky to have had Dr. Smith's services. He had shot this hind in the mountains to the south of Tao-chow, in Kansu, at an altitude of 11,000 feet, in March, 1911. It is a species closely allied to the deer found in Szechuan and Yunnan, and though carrying typical wapiti horns, approximates more nearly to the hangul of Kashmir.

One of the reasons why any member of the deer tribe is hunted with relentless ferocity by the natives of China is for the fictitious value attached to their horns. These are greatly prized and ground down into medicine. They even keep animals in captivity for this purpose, and a miserable time these unfortunate captives have. Such deer are consequently extremely hard to get and very difficult to approach.

To procure information from natives as to the locality in which a certain animal may be found with any degree of precision is far from easy. They will generalise to your heart's content, but when it comes to pinning them down to a definite statement they will either give the answer they think will be most pleasing to their interrogator, or one which by devious ways leads to their own greater advantage. Our half-Chinese, half-Tibetan hunters stoutly declared their conviction that we should kill stags with enormous heads. In an endeavour to get accurate information we pumped them dry, and poor Dr. Smith was continually interpreting and translating until he must have been sick of the very word "maloo" (wapiti).

This sort of conversation would take place:

"Oh, Doctor, ask him if there are many wapiti."

Lengthy reply, interjected with murmured assents from the doctor.

"He says there are many wapiti, but not so many as there were."

This probably means that there are very few!

"When do they roar?"

More conversation.

"He says they roar from the hill-tops every night. Their excellencies will not be able to sleep for the noise." Pleased grins and much nodding and smiling from the hunters as we digest this piece of information.

"I mean, what time of year do they roar?"

"The middle of the eighth moon."

"When's that?"

"He means the end of October."

"How many days' journey from here shall we find them?"

Consultation between the hunters.

"He says there are wapiti two days' journey from here, but it would be better to go five days."

"Why?"

"Because he knows a party of wood-cutters have been all over the ground."

Signs of restiveness on the part of those undergoing the third degree, and much to the interpreter's relief, for we are all very tired, we close the court for the time being.

The eventual annihilation of all members of the Asiatic deer tribe in districts in which it is impossible to give them the protection of efficient game laws is certain. What I wrote at the time of the Kansu deer applies with greater or less force to all of the cervidæ within reasonable distance of China.

Although realising the passion of the Chinaman for hartshorn taken medicinally, we were not altogether prepared for the actual state of affairs.

The Kansu wapiti has about the most uncomfortable existence of any animal it has been my lot to encounter. From the moment he can run he has scarcely one moment's peace. The native hunters kill indiscriminately. A hind or calf represents meat to them at any time of the year, and a close season would be too ludicrous to be considered seriously. Having attained the dignity of horns, the young stag's life is even more burdensome, for he carries with him wherever he goes that which represents a certain sum of money to the indigent hunter. Even a small head such a man would never dream of sparing in the hope that it might grow bigger, for he would have no surety that he would be the one to shoot it. So it comes about that the wretched stag has but two months' immunity from slaughter—May and June. His head is even more greatly prized when the horns are in velvet than when they have hardened, and the man who shoots a good head in this condition may reckon on getting from fifty to sixty taels (£7 or £8) for it. Such a sum, far more than he can hope to make in any other way during the year, represents a small fortune to him, so that we can hardly blame him for his zeal. It is peculiarly maddening, however, during a stalk, to hear the cannonading of native guns (and these make quite good shooting up to about 200 yards); to realise that neither age nor sex is spared, that the worth of a fine stag is estimated, not by the actual excellence of his horns, but by their value as reduced to avoirdupois; and last, but not least, that your sport for the day is over. Ethical estimates of sport do not trouble the native. He is out for blood, and when he can he gets it.

I had several long, tiring days when we reached our hunting ground before I saw a beast. He was a small stag and I left him. On the last day of October it started to snow, and at daybreak the next morning my hunter and I were

on the top of the ridge above our camp. We heard roars
and saw some hinds and a stag with a head of nine points.

The method of hunting adopted by the natives is to start
before it is light, locate a roar, return home, hold a council
of war, and start out again in the afternoon in order to
catch the stag when he emerges from the wood in the evening to feed. They usually appear fairly close to the opening
in which they have had their morning meal. I did not realise
this almost invariable procedure on the part of the natives,
and we wasted a great deal of time owing to the reluctance
of my hunter to attempt a stalk. When I did eventually start
it was too late, and the stag had gone back into the wood.
I followed him again in the afternoon, but he had moved
into dense timber on the other side of the ridge.

The following day we stalked a nice ten-pointer, who
caught sight of us as we crossed an open place on the hillside, and rather reluctantly, it seemed to me, moved his
hinds, three in number, over a ridge and out of sight. It
was a bitterly cold night, and early the next morning, after
two hours' steady climbing, we found in the snow, which
still lay deep in the shadows, the tracks of the deer we had
seen.

For several hours we sat on top of the ridge waiting in
vain for the sound which would betray their presence. The
forest was thick, but sadly thinned compared to what it had
originally been. Timber in China is cut with no thought of
the future. Only about the villages stand groups of noble
trees, and the disappearance of the forests, like the disappearance of the deer, is only a matter of time.

Carefully I spied each patch of open ground, but no dun
form, standing motionless in the shadows, rewarded my
expectant gaze. On a distant crest across the valley a wild-
looking figure suddenly crept into the field of my glass and
peered cautiously round. Over his shoulder was slung a
long gun with its forked rest. His flowing rags floated in
the wind and in his hand was a thin-stemmed, tiny-bowled
pipe. Presently I made out another squatting immovable

among the rocks. Two of the local murderers out for blood!
At any rate, they were too far off to disturb my plans that
evening.

It was an hour later that the sound of a muffled grunt
fell on my ears. Only one animal could have made it, and
I roused my hunter, who had been peacefully slumbering.
Then it came again. After that, for nearly an hour, silence.
Then as we stood on the edge of the wood it was broken
by a magnificent roar from the opposite slope.

The ground was very difficult on which to make an
approach. Sparsely scattered trees rose from patches of
frozen snow, which crackled loudly at our footfalls. The
rhododendron leaves rustled in a manner which I felt sure
must advertise our presence, but when we reached a spot
on the edge of the timber and were enabled to get a view,
there, 600 yards distant, was the stag we had seen the night
before, accompanied by his trio of hinds.

It was hard to know what to do. The light was going and
the deer seemed to be moving on a course which would
bring them to within 100 yards of where we stood. Would
they get there before it was dark? Very cautiously we started
to advance. The deer at times were out of sight. Once I saw
the stag standing on the sky-line 250 yards off. He walked
quickly out of sight, and we scuttled as quickly as we dared
to the spot where he had disappeared. The noise we made
seemed to me deafening as I slithered through the snow to
the knoll from which I hoped to see him. Peering over, I
caught sight of the hinds, their heads up, within 60 yards.
Of the stag I could see nothing, but I knew he must be
close. Then below me down the hill his branching horns
swung into view. The shot was not an easy one, for the long
grass nearly hid him and the light was atrocious, so that I
was disgusted only, and not surprised, when I missed. He
trotted slowly off down the hill, and despairingly I fired
again. This time there was no mistake.

In addition to the deer whose pursuit I have described is
another variety whose horns I saw exposed for sale in some

of the shops. They are called by the native *yung-loo*, or sheep-deer, and were described as being smaller than the deer of Kansu and larger than a roe. Spotted in the summer, the hair is red and becomes darker in the winter months. They carry four points on each horn. This description seems to apply to some variety of sika. They are said to be found in the hills not far from Minchow.

The roe, rather larger than the European variety, are otherwise very similar in appearance. They are smaller than the *Pygargus* found in the Tien Shan Mountains. Mr. Edgar N. Barclay, in an interesting paper on these animals which appeared in the *Annals and Magazine of Natural History* (ser. 10, vol. xii, p. 66, July, 1933), concludes that:

1. The roe-deer of Shansi, China, very closely resemble the roe-deer of Sweden (the type-locality of *C. capreolus*) in all characters.
2. The roe-deer of Central Asia, though resembling the roe-deer of Shansi and Sweden, are larger, but this difference in size is no greater than is the difference between local races in Europe.

The further conclusion he draws is that "there is but one species of roe-deer, and the names *pygargus, bedfordi,* and *coxi* should therefore be regarded as synonyms of *capreolus*" — or in other words, as local races, but not distinct species.

I spent many days in their pursuit, for the roe has always been an especial favourite of mine. I saw one very good buck, but alas! my toil was in vain, and he eluded me. The ground on which they are to be found is very difficult to stalk and the roe, small in size, is very difficult to locate. I killed only one buck, sacrificing several chances in the forlorn hope that fate would be kind and that I should get a good chance at the one whose horns I coveted.

One of the reasons which makes hunting in China a matter of difficulty is the distance separating the homes of the game you wish to secure. These are widely scattered, with journeys of many days intervening. It was on August 6 that we had secured our specimens of the takin, and many miles away lay the ground on which we hoped to get sheep.

The burhel, or blue sheep, is in appearance more like a goat. Indeed, with the latter animal he has many affinities, and probably indicates the transition point between the two species.

I have never seen the head of a Chinese burhel which in size approached the best heads from India. The record head of the latter is well over 30 inches, the best Chinese specimen only about 26 inches. Fortunately, however, length of horn is no criterion of the sporting capabilities of any animal, and the blue sheep of Kansu is a sporting little beast. To obtain the head of any variety of mountain game a great deal of hard work is necessary, and he is no exception to the rule. Burhel are found at an elevation of between 10,000 and 17,000 feet, which necessitates many a long climb. The reward for such exertion, even if no sheep are found, lies in the satisfaction of an accomplished task; the wonderful air; the sense of fitness; the freedom from mundane cares and responsibilities; and the enjoyment of any wild life you may happen to encounter. This is why stalking in Scotland is still popular among those who appreciate such sensations, which, of course, are all intensified when the stalker is in country that is practically untouched.

Feelings such as these underwent a rapid change on one occasion when I was stalking a herd of sheep. We had climbed, and it *was* a climb, to a point not far from the summit of the range, and intended to come down on the sheep, which were undisturbed and had no notion of our presence. Suddenly they rose and stared intently down the corrie. Up through its centre, blissfully unconscious of the murderous feelings which animated my breast, came a party of wood-cutters shouting and yelling at the top of their voices, as is their usual habit when indulging in conversation. Then they saw us. They gathered, I fancy, that their presence was not altogether welcome, and vanished over the ridge. So, unfortunately, did the sheep. All through that long day did we pursue them. Several times, having at last located them after the mishap of the morning, did we get to within a quarter of a mile. Always something occurred to thwart us at the last moment. I had, in fact, given up all hope of a shot, when late in the evening, on coming over a ridge overlooking the corrie where they had first been spied, we found them peacefully feeding among the rocks, and returned to camp late that night with the head of the ram.

One of the rarest animals to be found in this part of China is the white-maned serow. The natives usually hunt them with a scratch pack of dogs. Serow inhabit thick woods of fir and are seldom seen in the daytime. We tried a drive of this description and, wonderful to relate, for such tactics usually end in failure, secured a good specimen, which fell to the rifle of my companion. A second drive had no result. I tried stalking them, and saw one which stood on a slope a mile off in a position which rendered a stalk impossible; and another at which I did get a poor chance and missed. Dr. Smith, who did not want to shoot one, invariably, of course, ran into them whenever he went out. One evening an old male walked straight out of the wood across a bare hillside in full view of him, and on the following morning utterly defeated the diminished remnants of the scratch pack. That is always the way. Whenever I go to stalk roe in Scotland, these, which up to the time of my arrival have been practically feeding from the hands of the domestic staff, who take not the slightest interest in them, vanish completely, to reappear with unfailing regularity on my departure. So I never got a serow!

It was after this, having waited for the stags to begin roaring, that we hunted the Kansu deer, with the result I have described. We each got one stag. The Revolution, which had broken out a few weeks earlier, was gaining ground, and it became obvious that were we to attempt to return by the route we had planned through Szechuan and the gorges of the Yang-tse we should be in for a very difficult time. Accordingly, after a good deal of delay, we decided that the only practicable road home lay across the Gobi Desert.

On December 2, 1911, we left Lanchow-fu on our long journey. It was March 25, 1912, when we reached Omsk.

During this period we shot only five animals, all belonging to two species of gazelle—Przewalskis and the Mongolian varieties. They are typical gazelle in appearance, but instead of the short glossy coats of their African relatives, carry long, soft hair, without which they would soon perish in the icy cold. There is little of interest to describe in the manner of their approach, so I will say no more.

In all, during a trip which had occupied very nearly a year, I had shot, exclusive of one or two animals for meat, well under a dozen specimens. This, to one who has shot only, say, in Africa, may appear a ridiculously small total for so great an expenditure of time. China, I have endeavoured to make clear, is no big game butcher's paradise. Let me again quote from Mr. Roosevelt's book:

It is no country for the inexperienced hunter, nor for the one who wishes to secure a large bag without undue expenditure of time and effort. An experienced hunter who is not obliged to hurry can, however, secure a varied bag, and be certain that practically every animal he collects will prove of great interest, with a very definite possibility of finding it a new species or sub-species.

He would indeed be an adventurous hunter who attempted now to undertake a journey into the interior of China in search of unknown species of game. Such would, in fact, be almost impossible. Though born fifty years too late I have been lucky, in my youth, to have seen some of the wonders of this fascinating country.

XX. BENEATH THE SOUTHERN CROSS

"The old and gentle Australian bush."
RED HEIFER—J. D. Davison

FROM the point of view of the hunter of big game, Australia, though it possesses many other advantages, does not rank very highly. Indeed, the only "big game" to be found there is imported, namely, the Asiatic water buffalo, pig, and a few fallow deer. Kangaroo and wallaby are, of course, indigenous and provide good sport when hunted on horseback with hounds. Quail and duck shooting are to be had in places, and there is excellent fishing; but so far as big game is concerned it is limited to the animals I have mentioned.

I had left New Zealand and its red deer some weeks previously, and after an all too short stay in Tasmania, had arrived in Sydney via Melbourne. I had no thoughts of shooting when I landed, and then I fell in with Pat!

It is curious how the lilt of a song, the scent of a flower, or the sight of an unexpected face can carry your thoughts in the fraction of a second to scenes far distant from those in which you move. In a flash, at the sight of his lean, bronzed face, Australia had vanished and I was back in Scotland beneath a Lowland sky.

Above me, on the hillside, a furze bush bristled aggressively against the skyline; down below a clump of rushes stirred in the evening breeze and through their green spears I caught the glint of a gun barrel. Before me was the grey stone dyke, just such another as that before which Greer of Lag set the steady-eyed Covenanters and shot them for their faith. Beyond, again, the yellow bloom of a stubble, tinged with grey, the green shoulder of a hill, a glimpse of bracken and more dykes. From out of the golden west and the fringe of the moor came a desultory line of black dots, topping the farthest dyke. For a second they seemed to hang, stationary and motionless, then bobbed to the bloom of the stubble and came gliding silently onwards to the wall from whose shelter I watched. The greater part of the pack vanished silently over the ridge. Of their number they left three, inert feathered tufts, lying behind the dyke. One old blackcock came steadily on, straight for the clump of rushes below me. As he drew near he seemed instinctively aware of some hidden danger, and started on a long swinging curve which would have brought him to me. He was not allowed to complete it. Above the rush clump I saw a dull gleam, behind it a grey cap. The old cock seemed on a sudden to falter, crumpled, hung for a second, and fell on the stubble with a dull thud. The Right-hand Gun emerged from the rushes, picked him up, and the drive was over. Little did I think, as I saw him climb the dyke, that the next time he and I met would be 12,000 miles away beneath the Southern Cross. Yet so the Fates had willed, and as we rode out of the station gates later it was a very different scene which met my eyes.

In place of the soft grey lowland gloaming the fierce

Australian sun beat on us out of a cloudless sky. The bracken and furze had changed to blue gums and the low dykes to miles of wire fences. They stretched before us in long, straight lines until their ends were swallowed up in narrow spits of bush which wandered down the dried-up creeks, or behind the undulating swells which rose out of the reddened, dusty plain. Wherever the eye chanced to rest it fell on the ubiquitous gum trees, stunted and low on the hills, in the open tall and erect, grey, lifeless ruins, so dead and gaunt that it seemed impossible they could ever have held a spark of life.

The dried yellow grass had given way to thistles, good cover, as I found, for quail; they, on occasion, to stretches of greensward, looking strangely fresh and out of place in so parched a land.

A little flock of spur-winged plover flopped clumsily away as we topped a rise, and the wailing cry of a crow, uncannily like that of a child in distress, followed us into the still, hot recesses of the wood. Then that ceased and everything was quiet save for the clink of the horses' feet against some chance stone.

Every now and again a bare open space showed us a distant glimpse of more flats and deadened gum trees, which stretched their ghastly arms in writhing entreaty to the mocking sky. Scattered among them were other trees strange to me: willow-like hickory; wattle, which we know better as mimosa; the oak; stoneless cherry, though there is a small stone outside the fruit; and many another whose names I do not know. The sun was high in the heaven when we found what we sought: four dark forms which moved slowly out of sight into the shade of the bush. Dismounted, we tied up the horses and reconnoitred. Presently we made them out, three does and a small buck. A narrow, hump-backed hill rose from the plain, blistered and rocky. Dry creeks ran up to its summit and made red scars on its baked surface. A tangle of brushwood hid its sores in places and the whitening limbs of dead gum trees strewed the ground. In such a spot the does fed, and it seemed unlikely that anything more desirable would appear.

I said as much to Pat and he assented. The does quietly fed up a dry creek bed. We sat on a huge rock, ate our lunch, and after this short rest, continued our circumnavigation of the hill.

It was my companion who saw them first, two deer under a tree, and it hardly needed the glass to tell us they were bucks, one with a good head.

They were about 300 yards off and seemed slightly suspicious, for they fidgeted round the tree as if unable to make up their minds to any definite course of action. For ten minutes we watched them, then the bigger of the two came to a decision, and moving out from the shelter of his tree started at a trot towards us. The smaller beast followed him. Between us there lay a hollow, slight but deep enough to hide all but their horns. These I could see bobbing above the grass, but their owners came steadily on as I slithered down behind some dead gums which, prone as they were, gave so great an air of desolation to the scene.

The two deer came steadily on until a bare 40 yards separated us, and that, as many a stalker knows, is a very deceptive distance. It looks so easy, as in truth it is, just to put up the rifle, fire, and over goes your victim. But in its apparent simplicity lies its danger, and many a time at so close a range the bullet whistles over the target's back, and he, poor wretch, lives to die another day.

One of the bucks put up his head, but which I could not tell, for the waving grass hid it and I dared not stir. One, I knew, was a considerably better trophy than the other and I wanted to make sure of him first.

Slowly I raised myself behind the fallen log. The tips of the horns I watched swing swiftly towards me. In a tremble I aimed where I thought his shoulder would be, then fired. I got my deserts. There was a rush and scurry in the grass and the deer dashed past me, fortunately into the open. Across a bare patch they raced, the big one last. As he reached the lip of a dried creek bed he made his own mistake and gave me my chance. In a flurry of dust they shot over the edge, but only the smaller one emerged on the opposite bank. He dashed on, and two hasty shots merely threw up spirts of dust beneath him. Just on the edge of the bush he stopped, turned broadside on, and gave me a beautiful chance. He dropped like a stone and never moved.

Behind me I heard yells, and turned to find Pat waving and pointing. Out of the creek bed the big buck was slowly making his way, looking very sick and stopping every few yards with hanging head. Presently he lay down, and as quietly as the dry ground permitted we began our stalk.

When within 50 yards he jumped up and made for the bush, but we headed him off and into the open. A moment later his sufferings ended.

My companion went back to the horses and then to the station for a cart to take the dead beasts home, whilst I stayed to perform the final rites, and made one or two rough sketches. It was late when he returned, and by the time we had everything finished the day was at its close. So in the evening light we rode out of the wood and into the glories of the setting sun. His opalescent hues put to shame in their vivid colouring the sunsets of a northern clime. Splashes and rifts of intense electric blue split the background of glowing gold with transverse bars. Here it changed to carmine, there to purplish-grey. Slowly the grey crept up the sky. The blue and gold faded before it into intangible half-tones, and ere we reached the station gates the world around was lost in the hush of the velvety night.

The morning following was dull and cloudy, but Pat, knowing my predilections, had arranged that we should try for a kangaroo, and I had delightedly acquiesced.

Out of place in Australia seemed the grey mist which swept in long wisps about the low hills, yet even as we rode it vanished, slowly curling about the rocks and thickets to reveal, stretching away in the distance, a yellow plain whose shallow basin had once held a great lake. No lake was there now—the brazen sun had seen to that—but it was an easy matter to cheat oneself into the belief that the jutting peninsulas of rock which here and there ran out into the flat expanse were lapped about by cool lagoons lying beneath the shimmering waves of heat. An easy matter: yet as I drew near the blue lagoons melted imperceptibly into dried and withered grasses, and I was left wondering at the unimagined transformation.

About the illimitable sweep of plain there was something stupefying, and a sense of relief came to me when I saw it end in low hilly tops which held a depth of blue, such as you find among the Surrey hills upon an early summer's day.

From the plain we rode into a region of stunted bushes and low hills. Here the ubiquitous gums had climbed in vain endeavour. Perished were their gaunt outposts, the broken remnants of an invading army, grey and ghastly, warning the survivors in the valley not to attempt so impossible a task. From a distance came the harsh cry of an English crow, and looking up I saw some thirty or forty white cockatoos settling on a dead tree. They showed up at a great distance and looked remarkably picturesque. These were not the only birds I saw, for later on we came across black jays; crows; magpies, with their white heads, smart liveries and musical call; but no "galahs," the pink and grey variety of cockatoo which make the best talkers and are sometimes seen in mobs of as many as a thousand. Presently we came to a little rocky knoll, and out among the bushes hopped a strange elf-like creature, which peered curiously at us with distorted neck and then vanished. He seemed quite in keeping with the strangeness of our surroundings, and though we were off our horses in a moment he had been too quick for us and effectually vanished. So we rode on amid the gum trees and presently caught sight of another wallaby. He had heard us from afar, long ere we discovered his existence, and went bounding away in long tireless jumps and was dodging in and out among the bushes and lifeless trunks when first we sighted him.

A crowd of gorgeously coloured little parrots chattered from tree to tree as though rejoicing at his escape, flashing into the bush, their gay red and blue plumage gleaming brilliantly in the strong sunlight. As they disappeared a large dark bird swept silently away close to the ground, and then, as luck would have it, sharply up on to a withered branch, showing the orange colouring of his under-wings. It was a black cockatoo, and Pat told me that he had only seen two in his life. Their export is forbidden, and I never heard of one in captivity, even in Australia. Their appearance is supposed to portend heavy rain.

It was by this time nearly noon, and as we had made an early start we had lunch before riding out into the dusty plain, alive with rabbits whose tails flickered and bobbed at every fresh alarm. We passed them by while Pat called down every imaginable form of destruction on their heads. It is difficult, unless one has actually seen with one's own eyes what a curse they are to Australia, to understand the hatred which flares up at the sight of them.

From the plain we came to a park-like opening among the trees, and in a flash two great mouse-coloured forms went leaping into the shadows. They were kangaroos, and disappointed as I was at their hurried exit, it was something, at all events, to have seen them.

As with the wallabies, the clinking of the horses' hooves had warned them of their danger, and one day's kangaroo hunting convinced me that a combination most likely to succeed in this form of sport would comprise rubber-soled shoes, a thorough knowledge of the country, and an infinity of patience. Ultimately I was successful, but I do not pretend for a moment that unaided by good fortune and Pat I should have accomplished anything. The most exciting method of pursuit is to hunt them with dogs, but this I had no opportunity of witnessing. The old kangaroo dogs

P

were greyhounds with a strain of bulldog or mastiff. Now they are more or less a breed of their own, not unlike a heavily-built greyhound. A cross between a greyhound and a Scottish deerhound makes a good beast.

Where this form of hunting is practised the hound will get up near his quarry and, as the kangaroo jumps, will go for his throat and endeavour to pull him over. Kangaroos are dangerous beasts when cornered. They are often brought to bay in a water-hole, and in such a situation have an advantage of which they make the most, for, seizing with their forearms any hound which approaches within reach, they will hold him under water until drowned. They have been known to attempt the same trick with a man. It is hardly necessary to add that they can inflict a very deadly wound with their abnormally powerful hind-legs.

They are extraordinarily quick at dodging a blow, as those who saw the Boxing Kangaroo in London many years ago will realise.

When hard pressed, the female snatches her young from her pouch and throws it aside into some bush or long grass. Whether this is done in an attempt to save her own life by ridding herself of an encumbrance, or in an endeavour to give her young a chance of safety, I leave the reader to determine. When going strong a kangaroo will jump about 18 feet. There are two varieties: the Red Kangaroo found in Southern and Eastern Australia, and the great Grey Kangaroo, widely distributed over the whole continent. The former inhabits rocky districts, while the latter is essentially a plain dweller. A full-grown male of either species will weigh as much as 200 lbs.

They feed early and late like deer, and in bush country are found, as a rule, in much the same sort of places as one would expect the latter animal to frequent, assimilating very closely to their surroundings.

It was useless attempting to pursue the two beasts we had seen, so we crossed a flat covered with bracken and the stumps of dead gum trees. Hardly had we left it than I

caught a glimpse of something moving. Pat reined up and
cried in a whisper, "It's another kangaroo!"

Sure enough it was. On our right lay a dried creek bed
7 or 8 feet deep. To avoid us the beast would have to cross
this, so giving Pat the reins of my horse I ran to the lip
of the creek and sat down. The kangaroo came past about
140 yards distant, dodging the trees in long, lazy jumps. I
hear my companion calling to me, as I thought, to fire,
and had a snap, but missed. It turned out afterwards that
he was saying the beast would stop. Directly after I had
fired it did, but behind a bush, and never gave me a chance.

I can see it all so plainly, even now. The burning sky,
the parched valley between the blistering hills, the gaunt
gum trees stretching on every side and beating the desolation of the place into one's brain, here and there little
patches of green as though to bid one hope, the kangaroo
dodging off through the trees, and Pat watching with
puckered eyes as he held the horses.

For an hour or so we saw nothing, then late in the afternoon, as the shadows lengthened, came on three wallabies
sitting out in the open grass. It was the first really good
view I had had of them. They looked very red and large,
with something suggestively rat-like in their appearance. I
was just getting the sights on one as he sat by a bush when
he made off and was hidden in a second. When going at top
speed in the open, one requires cool judgment and a quick
shot to bring one down; in the bush it is about as difficult
shooting as one could imagine.

I was getting rather disheartened at our want of success,
but went on, and presently came on another, leisurely hopping about among some useless peppermint shrubs. He
stopped for a second, gave me a good chance at about
130 yards, and this time I got him.

He was a full-grown male, but I had no time to take any
measurements. We skinned him, an operation which did not
take very long, and, tying the skin on to a saddle, went on.

Half an hour later, as we were getting down to the flat

where I had seen the kangaroo in the morning, something
jumped out of the bracken and made off up the hill. I recognised the colour and black tip to the tail before Pat cried out,
"Quick, it's a kangaroo!"

Half hidden by a tree it stopped, but I could see the head
and shoulders and fired. The horses plunged and reared at
the shot, for I was very close, but Pat hung on and I saw
the kangaroo going hard up the hill. I was in despair, as I
feared I should lose him, and ran up, hoping for a snap
through the trees. Then Pat yelled, "He's down!" and I
saw a grey mass under a tree. The effort had been his last,
for both shoulders were broken.

So that was the end of my day after kangaroos in New
South Wales, and very lucky I considered myself, for in two
days' shooting I had got a couple of fallow bucks, a kangaroo, and a wallaby.

We had some little difficulty in crossing the creek bed,
but eventually reached the station. A few hours later I
drove down through the gum trees for the last time. White
and ghastly they rose as the moon silvered their despairing
branches and cast long black shadows on the ground. Out
of the darkness beyond the white riband of road the station
lights showed brightly, until they were swept into obscurity
by a shoulder of the hill. Kind voices yet rung in my ears,
and I realised again that the worst moments of travelling
are those which must inevitably come when a hand grips
yours for the last time and that sad little word "Good-bye"
haunts one's memory with its mute appeal.

XXI. HIS FIRST STAG

"Love of sport makes the man."

Sir James Outram

"I wish he could see you now," said the Boy.

"Who's 'he'?" I asked.

"You know when you came down to Eton last time you were quite well dressed," he went on.

I remembered the occasion well and felt gratified that I had earned the Boy's approval. I had taken a good deal of trouble over my appearance. One has to on such occasions. I had worn a Foreign Office hat. I was pleased with my suit. My shirt and tie were all right. I had gone to the reckless extravagance of ninepence on a carnation. In fact I was rather pleased with myself.

"Yes. I remember," said I smugly.

"You were rather pleased with yourself." The acumen of youth deserves no encouragement.

"Nothing——" I began.

He interrupted me. "One of my little school-mates asked me the next day who the frightful old Poonah was I was with."

I was not quite sure if I liked being called "a frightful old Poonah."

"He didn't mean anything," went on the Boy, noticing my expression which I hoped, without being quite sure about it, conveyed a sense of dignity above such trifles, "derok—— What's the word?"

"Derogatory," I supplied hopefully.

"Yes, that's it. Derogatory. He just meant that you were a bit of a swell."

I experienced a feeling of elation.

"That's why I said I wished he could see you now."

Old stalking clothes, if they really are old stalking clothes, are not calculated to foster one's sense of self-esteem. My coat was baggy. The cuffs were frayed. My nether-garments had inserts on each knee. The back portion had started life as part of an entirely separate and distinct piece of tweed. My shoes had been darned, and all this happened several years ago. I appreciated the contrast implied in his wish.

"Well, they're all right for the hill," I said, as we started.

I find that a day on the hill with the Boy not only clarifies what knowledge I possess about the habits of deer, but also of stalking, for I have to give a reason for everything. It also increases my knowledge of slang, largely Americanised.

The questions began at once.

"Do you like stalking alone or with a stalker?"

I hesitated. After roe of course there is only one answer. You must go alone if it is possible to arrange it. A roe requires much more circumventing than a red deer. Any-one with you doubles the chances of being spotted. There is always great satisfaction in pitting one's skill against a wild animal on ground of its own choosing. It is necessary to be on the alert the whole time. Nor can one relax a sense of watchfulness for a second from the moment one's quarry

is first sighted until the rifle is aimed. There is no leisure to
drink in the beauty of the surroundings, the light on the
hill, the gleam of water winding amid yellow grasses, to
appreciate the beauty of dreams come true. It is this necessity for tense and strict attention to the business in hand
which, at times, compels me to prefer the throwing of
responsibility on to someone else. This I told my companion.

To stalk for someone else is again different. From it there
is to be derived enormous satisfaction. The responsibility is,
in one way, greater than when stalking alone. Another is
dependent on your skill save in the matter of the shot. That
is out of your hands; but to have chosen the right line of
approach, to have circumvented the pitfalls by which you
were surrounded and to have brought your companion
within shot is to experience a feeling of satisfaction which
few other pursuits can equal.

Our hunting ground was minute but it contained everything save high hills. Its chief drawback lay in the fact that
if a mistake was made and deer moved the whole of our
territory was cleared at one fell swoop.

In the broken ground below the loch which presently
merged into a flat through which ran a little burn defining
the march, I presently discovered a small stag.

"I can see a stag."

Instantly my companion was all excitement.

"Where? What's he like? Show me," he exclaimed, pulling
out his glass.

I indicated the position of the animal and waited for his
comments.

"Good Lord! What an awful little twerp."

I agreed. It was a very small six-pointer.

"I don't want to shoot a thing like that for my first stag,"
said the Boy reproachfully.

"Well, you needn't," I remarked. "We'll try and find
another."

Climbing to a knoll we sat and spied almost the whole of

the ground. We could also spy a large part of Naboth's vineyard. Here there were stags in plenty. Stags by themselves and stags with hinds. Stags that roared and stags that were silent; but on our own ground I could see nothing. I regretfully said as much.

"What about going for that old brute just over there?"

I pointed out that we should be over the march.

"No one would ever know," said the Boy coaxingly. "You know no one's stalking there and," he added virtuously, "we should be augmenting the meat supply." This was, no doubt, true, but the ethics of the case remained unaltered, though I seemed to remember using similar arguments many years before.

Then in the broken hollows where the trees grew thinly I saw something yellow. I put my glass on it. A hind showed. A careful scrutiny revealed another, her head just rising above the ridge. This wanted looking into. I told him what I had seen.

"Come on. Let's go to that knoll. There may be some more. There may be a stag."

From the knoll we could see a bit more of the gully. There were more hinds but I could see no stag. They lay, drowsing, to the number of fifteen or twenty.

"I can't see a stag."

"What do we do now?"

I was getting a bit tired of this. I didn't know what we could do, except wait. I said so.

This evidently displeased him. "Why?" said he. "Let's get closer. We may not be able to see them all."

I gave my reasons, which satisfied him for the moment.

Presently a hind rose and started to feed. Then another. At the same instant a stag walked into view from behind a dead tree and roared.

"He's all right, isn't he?" asked the Boy anxiously.

He was an eight-pointer with double brows, just the sort of stag which ought to be shot. His head was not big, but a decided improvement on that of the "twerp," and a very

much better head than that of my own first stag which had
died over forty years ago.

"Come on," cried the Boy. "Let's get to that rock."

He was terribly keen and had picked up the essentials
extraordinarily quickly. The stalk was easy, but I explained
that we should be uncomfortably close and that he might
have to take a quick shot. He was at that happy stage
when you think that the closer you are the easier the shot.
When within a hundred yards of the rock we lay down and
crawled. At first I could see nothing. Then very close, within
thirty yards, I saw a hind's head, which had materialised,
apparently, out of nothing. We stared in mutual disgust and
slowly, very slowly, I lowered my head.

"Come on," I hissed.

He crawled up beside me and very gently we raised our
heads. The hind's head had been augmented by about
twenty bodies and forty eyes, all staring intently in our
direction. They started to run. The stag cantered behind
them broadside on about thirty yards off. The Boy fired.
The deer vanished and that was that.

"I'm awfully sorry!" said a small voice. I looked round.
His face was puckered into an expression of intense misery.

"That's nothing," I explained. "Those sort of shots are
the most difficult. They look so easy. It's always the same
when you get very close. The hinds see you; you get a bit
flurried and nearly always shoot high. We'll get them again.
They won't go far." I was not so confident as I sounded.
They might go far, in which case it looked as if we were
done. However, there was some hope, as they were not
much frightened and might stop on the far side of the
wood.

Through the latter in a leisurely manner we proceeded.
Marks of their passage were evident in the soft mosses, torn
and cut by their sharp hooves. Here and there, the bracken,
russet and gold, was broken. The trees, tall slim birches,
began to thin. We were getting to the edge of the wood.
Very cautiously, taking care not to tread on the twigs

which strewed the ground, we made our way. Then, just outside the trees, I saw a broken branch showing against the sky. But was it a broken branch? My pocket Zeiss told me that it was not. It was one of the horns of the eight-pointer. The hinds had disappeared. The Boy crept up beside me. I pointed. The Boy nodded. There was a tree-trunk dead in line with the head, and by signs I showed him what to do. He took the rifle and crept on. I saw him take aim. Then there was a sharp crack and the head fell over. The Boy had shot his first stag.

That was on October 5. On the 12th we went out again, the Boy blooded and free of the hill.

This time we struck up to the top of the wood, for the wind had changed. There was much more roaring but on our tiny strip of ground there appeared to be nothing save one young stag. He had nine points, long and sharp but with no length of horn, and lay brooding by himself on the disadvantages of youth. I explained that he was a young stag, that he would improve and in a year or two might have a good head.

How did I know he was a young stag? I gave my reasons. He pondered over this for a bit.

"Shall we go for him?" I asked.

He had only killed one stag in his life, there was nothing else on the ground and, as far as he knew, no chance of a shot. I was very pleased when he declined any closer acquaintance.

There came a loud roar from below us. It was answered by another.

"What about putting the cross on one of them?" said the Boy.

The first roar had come from a beast with about thirty hinds. They were feeding on a slope below some rocks in quite a stalkable position, and the stag had a very nice head of eleven points with thick rough horns, the sort of head which would have been welcomed in any forest.

"They're all over the march," I answered firmly.

"Not much over the march!" said the Boy coaxingly.

It was very tempting. "If they came down to that ridge," I said weakly, "they wouldn't be very much over the march; but if they did I don't think we could get in. It's all very exposed."

We lay and watched them for over an hour. The stag lay down. The hinds lay down. Then the stag got up, roared and lay down again. We watched for another hour. A hind rose and started to feed. Then another until they were all up save one. The stag rose and walked up to her. She got up too and they fed slowly along to the ridge.

Between us there was a wide, open flat through which ran a burn. To its edge it was possible to go under cover of some sparsely scattered trees. By keeping their trunks in line with the deer we reached the burn. A broken-down wire fence defined the march. With an uncomfortably guilty feeling I crossed it, striving to allay my conscience by the thought that no one would stalk on this ground for nearly another year. On the far side was a stone dyke. It was no longer really a dyke but a low, irregular line of piled-up stones, with great gaps between. Slowly, very slowly and very flat, stopping whenever there came a gleam of sunlight, we worked our way along its length. Such a crawl is, to me, a painful necessity. I cannot see through the tops of my glasses and have to focus through the centre. This gives me a kink in the neck which threatens to become permanent. We reached the end of the stones without being spotted and I heaved a sigh of relief. On such occasions the memory of Archie, of whom I so often have written, comes to my mind. He was an adept at such stalks. I wondered if he watched us on the hillside on which we had so often been together and which he loved so well. He would have loved the Boy too. The rest was easy. Within ten minutes we were lying behind a rock within a hundred yards of the deer. The Boy was quite cool. Indeed I marvelled at his composure. He might have been stalking for years. He took the rifle, nodded to me and crawled up to the crest of the ridge.

Then he put the rifle to his shoulder. At the crack the hinds broke along the hillside, but no stag followed them.

The Boy turned his head. "I've given him the works," said he.

"For God's sake talk English," I snapped. I wanted to see the stag. We looked over the rocks but there was no stag to be seen. Beyond the place where the deer had fed there ran a ridge and to it we went. The Boy was behind carrying the rifle. Very incautiously I came into view over the ridge and at the same moment saw the stag. He was looking very sick but at sight of us flung up his head and made off. I rushed back, snatched the rifle and regained the ridge. The stag was cantering now, and well over the march. There could be no hesitation. I sat down, fired and missed. And again. Despairingly, as his yellow form blended in with a patch of bracken, I fired a third time. He disappeared. Hot and excited the Boy joined me. Feeling more guilty than ever we reached the patch of bracken. After some search we found him. He was quite dead, though the Boy's shot had hit him low and a little far back. It was several hundred yards to the march and the ground was very rough. It took us nearly an hour to reach the burn and I felt as if someone had been beating me with a heavy stick.

He weighed well over 15 stones and I can testify to the roughness of his horns, for my hands felt as if they had been rubbed hard with emery paper. But I had my reward as we stumbled home in the dark.

The Boy slipped his arm through mine. "We do have fun together, don't we?" he said. We do.

XXII. MR. HODGE FINDS HEAVEN

"Heaven will be what we love most on earth."
THE SETONS—O. Douglas

"FUNNY little chap!" I remarked to my wife as Mr. Hodge drove slowly away from the hotel. "His name's 'Hodge.' I looked at the label on his rods."
"Where's he going?" asked the latter.
"To Balnacoil. He's a bad colour."
"I liked his eyes."
This remark I ignored.
"Apparently he's taken the fishing there for the last three years," I went on. "Rum little devil." Then we forgot all about him—till later.

Mr. Hodge drove sedately on. He was not thinking of his own colour but of that by which he was surrounded. The bright purple of the bell heather at the side of the road which twisted up the glen; the tender loveliness of the birches; the green and red of the firs.

He had "discovered" Scotland ten years before. It had been a revelation to him. Once a year for a fortnight, since then, he had revelled in it. During the remaining months he fulfilled his duties as Messrs. Baxter & Webb's head clerk, dryly and with efficiency. Short, insignificant and unremarked, he passed his days as do thousands of others. But Mr. Hodge possessed an imaginative mind which was at once his heaven and his hell. He had never married. Most of the married people he knew seemed to lack happiness; but he had his dreams. He had often thought of marriage, but that was long past. He was getting old. Even his employment had begun to irk him. Then he had seen Balnacoil, the house of his dreams, and for the last three years thither he had returned. Each year he loved it more. White harled it was, set on a little promontory facing up the loch above which rose purple hills, shut in to the west by the great cone of Sgur Meadoil. It was still just as I had known it as a boy. Mr. Hodge was never tired of looking at it. To him it represented utter and complete peace. This was his reality and life in the great city a myth and an illusion.

Here, in his dreams he brought her, that shadow girl he would have married had he ever met her, forever young and ageless, whose features had assumed so many forms. Once she had had grey eyes, then brown, but now, in Mr. Hodge's imagination they were always blue, the blue of a hill loch under a July sky. Below them a straight little nose, a mouth sweet and tender, with a tiny quirk at one corner, lent her smile the radiance of Dawn. She always smiled at Mr. Hodge. It was this habit of smiling, this and her tenderness and understanding which had first appealed to him. She mothered him and he longed to be mothered.

It was a lovely day when Mr. Hodge awoke the following morning; not too bright, with just enough breeze to ripple the water nicely. Peter, the head stalker, offered to come with him, but Mr. Hodge on this, the first morning of his holiday, preferred to be alone. He rowed slowly up the loch, drifting down a series of little bays and catching quite a basket of golden trout. Having thoroughly enjoyed his morning, at midday he tied the boat to a birch root beneath an overhanging rock. The top made a small plateau, carpeted with bracken and fir needles. Shelving golden sands stretched to one side over which oyster catchers and curlews called. A "fairies' eiderdown" spread over the ground beyond, and here were anemones, orchises and bog-myrtle to relieve the young green of the bracken. The green of young bracken is like the green of rice fields. Through this loveliness ran a little burn which chuckled and laughed as it sang its way to the loch, between birches, alders, and willows. Here and there a stately fir tree rising above the rocks overshadowed the little white beaches which ran down to the water. Mr. Hodge lying there, thought that life had never been so perfect. He felt very lazy, almost tired. After all he was having a holiday, so why should he not lie and do nothing if he felt like it? He did, definitely, feel tired, though when he had started he had been full of energy. So he stayed as he was, looking up at the grave, blue hills.

It was very little later, or so it seemed to him, that a movement among the bracken made him glance up. It was then that he saw her. Down through the heather and the rocks towards Mr. Hodge she came and, as he looked open-mouthed, she waved her hand and smiled.

"What a long time you've been, darling!" she called.

Mr. Hodge's mouth opened still wider. No one had ever spoken like this to him before. Then he looked at her more closely.

"Why," said Mr. Hodge, "you're Celia!"

"Of course I am!" she cried, and laughed. "Who did you expect me to be?"

She looked so lovely standing there, the sun catching the gold in her hair and turning it to bronze, that Mr. Hodge just sat, gaping.

"But—but I don't understand," he gulped.

"You will soon, my darling," said she, and sat down on

the grass beside him. "It's a little difficult to explain at first, but I'm here with you and I won't leave you."

"Why do you call me that?" said Mr. Hodge. He couldn't bring himself to say the word, for he felt very shy. So he said "that." "Why do you call me that?" he repeated almost angrily, for he was rather frightened and the girl was regarding him with the sweetest look imaginable. "I don't know you. At least," he amended hastily, for his last remark had sounded almost rude, "I don't think I do."

"You mustn't say that," she answered. "Especially after I've come all this way to meet you."

"But I don't understand," almost wailed Mr. Hodge. "Where have you come from and why do you call me 'darling'?" He brought out the last word with a rush, for though he was no longer angry he was very bewildered, while his feeling of shyness was getting stronger every minute. It was true that this young lady was remarkably like the young lady he had thought about a great deal, in fact, she grew more like her with every second that passed. But after all, she was a total stranger, and to be called "darling," not only once but several times by a total stranger amid surroundings which Mr. Hodge was accustomed, for a fortnight at least in every year, to consider his very own, was most embarrassing.

"Where have I come from?" she repeated, and the little quirk that Mr. Hodge adored showed at the side of her mouth. "From over the hills and far away, sir! And why do I call you 'darling'? Well, you've called me that for ages, so I don't see why I shouldn't."

"But—but who are you?" stammered Mr. Hodge.

"I'm Celia."

"But not my Celia."

"Yes, my darling. Yours!"

"But—why? Why? I don't understand. I'm old and plain. You can't be my Celia."

She took his hand in her soft little palms. Mr. Hodge could feel them cool, and yet warm in his. He stood up and

UNDISTURBED

she led him down to the edge of the loch where the water lay, cool and still, in the little bay.

"Look!" she said.

Mr. Hodge looked. Little ripples stole in towards him and he could not see very clearly but what he did see made him look again. This could not be himself! This young face just as he had imagined it, the crisp brown hair, the grey eyes, the clear-cut profile.

"I don't understand," he said feebly and raised his eyes. She was sitting in the stern of the boat smiling at him.

"Get in and let's row for a little," she said. "Do, darling, it's lovely here!"

Mr. Hodge got into the boat rather awkwardly, took the oars and started to row.

"Where shall we go?" he said.

"Oh, just out a little way."

"Couldn't you explain?" he asked. "I don't understand and my head feels funny."

"Why are you here, and how did you get here, and who are you?" If he could get an answer to all this, Mr. Hodge felt, he would be satisfied.

She didn't answer but just looked at him, smiling, and her smile was so sweet, so kind, so tender and gentle, that Mr. Hodge really did not know where he was!

"I mean," he said, "I don't want to be rude, but this is all very strange. Of course it's heavenly, all this, the loch and the hills and the sun—and you. It's what I've dreamed of, but——"

"Heaven," she interrupted him gently, "is what we love most on earth. Someone said that."

"But I love this most on earth," said Mr. Hodge. "I adore it, there's nothing like it in the whole world, and if you'd only explain it would be perfect. But I'm frightened. It's what I've always dreamed of, this, with you! It's heaven!"

She looked at him and Mr. Hodge thought he had never seen nor imagined anything lovelier in the whole of his life.

"Yes, my darling," she said, "it is heaven."

It was Peter who saw the boat drifting down the loch with the soft evening breeze. It seemed to be empty, so he got another boat and rowed out to meet it. For some time he sat looking into it, after he had drawn alongside. Then he fastened the painter to the stern of his own boat and rowed back to the landing-stage.

It was on the following day that we drove up to Balnacoil and I asked him about the rumours we had heard down the glen.

"He was no looking well when he came," said Peter. "I feared for him then. Puir wee man! But his face when I looked into the boat! It was just fair mazed with happiness."

XXIII. SOME REFLECTIONS ON THE GENTLE ART—IN CANADA AND ELSEWHERE

"Why, any tyro can raise a salmon and hook him."
RECOLLECTIONS OF FLY-FISHING, SALMON, TROUT AND GRAYLING—
Dr. Edward Hamilton

AT times I am asked, "Are you a fisherman?" To this I invariably reply, "No, but I like catching fish!"

A man who confesses that he likes catching fish—though that, after all, is the main object of fishing—is, I fancy, rather looked down upon by the genuine master of the gentle art. When making my reply I anticipate, now, the fleeting look of contempt, the change of subject it invokes. "No use wasting time on this poor fish" (if you will pardon the Americanism), is the mental attitude, and we talk brightly, or as brightly as I can, of tiddley-winks or bimetallism.

My idea of a good day's fishing—and I hope no true disciple of the great Izaac will read these lines—is to proceed on a warm sunny day with not sufficient wind to cause any undue chill, but enough nicely to ripple the water, to a well-stocked loch in which, preferably, pink-fleshed trout running up to 2 lbs. or more are sufficiently unsophisticated greedily to engulf my fly. Here, with a pipe, an agreeable companion, and the sight of hills and woods of fir and birch, I can pass the day to my entire satisfaction. If, as specified, the trout are pink-fleshed, the evening during and after their demolition will pass no less pleasantly.

To sit in a boat in an icy wind, muffled up to the eyes in woollies, coats, and mufflers, exposed to every blast, and with only a chance, more or less remote, of catching a salmon; or to flog a high and roaring stream afloat or encased in waders in which there is every likelihood that I shall drown, is not my idea of enjoyment.

On the last occasion on which I fished for salmon it was necessary to wade. Fortunately the river was low, the month July. My host, some 8 inches below my own height, with feet to match, kindly lent me his waders. He also lent me his rod. Feeling rather like a very large sardine in a very small tin, I gingerly, with cramped toes, lowered myself into the river. A kindly but non-communicative gillie from the security of the bank gravely watched my antics. In a manner which secretly I rather fancied I got my line well out to the far bank. It then became necessary for me to retrace my steps. Lulled into a sense of security by the ease with which I had hitherto negotiated any difficulties, these, on the return journey, as I slowly forged my way across the swiftly running stream, had become considerably magnified. In the eddy caused by a large rock I stumbled, half fell, recovered, and plunged blindly forward, to find myself up to the neck in water with a broken rod in my hand. The gillie, his face showing never a trace of surprise, solemnly assisted me up the bank.

"You'll be the thir-r-d gentleman that has fa-allen in this month!" was his only remark.

Whilst I was wildly flapping my arms in a vain endeavour to dry my soaking garments, he wandered out of sight down the bank to where my host was fishing, accompanied by his wife. His portentous demeanour excited their attention and they enquired its cause.

"A ter-rible cata-a-strophee has ha-appened," was his announcement.

"What's the matter? Has Miss ——" (who was fishing another pool) "fallen in?"

"Far wor-rse than tha-at," came the answer. "It's Muster Wallace!" I was flattered on hearing this, without discovering the reason, at the relative importance a charming young lady and myself enjoyed in his estimation.

"I'll go and help him," exclaimed my host, making for the bank, with that ready solicitude for his guests which is one of his most prominent characteristics.

"Don't be a fool," said his wife sharply "Go on fishing. If he's ass enough to fall in, he can get himself out!"

How much more callous than men are women!

"Wull Muster Wallace be a relation of Mistress D——?" asked the gillie of my host later in the evening when he found him alone. The answer in the negative seemed to surprise him, for after pondering for a moment he remarked: "Och well! I was thinking he must be, for she showed verra little concairn at his predeecament!"

In spite of her brutal remark the lady in question did lend me her fur coat in which to drive home. For this I was grateful, having only a vest, a pair of knickerbockers belonging to the keeper which would have been a fit for an ill-nourished lad of fifteen, and a cap to cover my nakedness.

It always seems to me that luck plays too great a part in fishing. The experienced fisherman will no doubt in the long run catch more fish than the bungling novice. The latter, on the other hand, may, and quite frequently does, chuck in his fly anyhow and catch such a fish as fills the breast of his more skilful companion with envy, hatred and malice. The novice who is, in addition, a bad shot is unlikely to kill one of the best stags in the forest; firstly because he is a bad shot, and secondly because he is very unlikely to be taken up to the sort of stag which the experienced stalker would regard as a prize. The element of luck in stalking, to this extent, can usually, though not always, be controlled.

Fishing with a dry fly is, of course, one of the highest forms of sport, and in the case of a really fine fisherman an art to which even stalking can scarcely hold comparison.

Salmon fishing by the enthusiast is often regarded as the finest sport there is, adept though he may be at others. Indeed, there can be few greater thrills than to know that you are "in" to a big fish. My own experiences are few, but I still recall the tremor of excitement which ran through me when I hooked my first salmon. It was from no brawling Highland river overhung by birches and noisy with brown ripples and little lapping peaty swirls that I drew his silvery form. No Highland gillie triumphantly snatched him aloft and laid him gleaming in the purple heather. It was a dark deed: the recollection thrills me yet.

Thankful to leave the glaring noisiness of New York, I arrived in Quebec one Sunday morning many years ago, intending to remain a day or so before going West. Diving in my bag, I came presently upon a letter to one P., and though on presenting it I learned that he was away, a subsequent telephone message dispelled the somewhat gloomy ideas conjured up by a lonely supper at the Frontenac.

No one who has travelled in Canada will learn with surprise that the next morning found me steaming down the broad St. Lawrence in company with a man who, twenty-four hours before, had been ignorant that such a person as myself existed. The following afternoon saw us installed in one of P.'s fishing lodges, the last few miles being accomplished by means of a buckboard. He who has never journeyed in such a conveyance will fail to perceive how apposite is the name. The experienced traveller will cherish tender recollections—on his body, if not in mind.

Old Napoleon, who, on the principle of setting a thief to catch a thief, now endeavoured to prevent the younger generation from following in his own early footsteps, met us. He was a fine old sportsman, a French-Canadian. Not only did he guard the river, but in his odd moments acted as gillie, cook, housemaid, waiter and valet. Unfortunately, he spoke no English, and as my French is of the low canine or public school variety, the frequent allusions to his early poaching adventures were lost upon me.

The river ran close to the little lodge, and by five o'clock we were following our guide in single file along the narrow track fringed by thick bushes. All the fish in the river, so said Napoleon, were congregated in the pool below the dam: 120 yards long by 40 or 50 broad, with a strong run below the dam, it terminated in a narrow rapid but a foot or two deep in the shallower parts. It sounds almost unbeliev-able, but within an area of 10 square yards (and that is well above the mark, for it is nearer 5) were some seventy or eighty fish. P. estimated the entire number in the pool at between 200 and 250. Even as I made ready for my first cast broad tails and glistening fins swirled slowly into view and as majestically sank. Above the rapid they were thickest, so, starting some 60 yards up-stream, I worked conscien-tiously towards them. Almost at once I had a rise, but he came very short, and with one other exception this was the only salmon which attempted to take a fly during the four days we fished the river. And yet between us we caught nine! Have I not said the death of my first salmon was a dark deed? Those ardent anglers who annually migrate northwards in the springtime, whose thoughts at the close of winter lightly turn to sport they love, these Waltonians will, I say, hold up their hands in pious horror at my backslidings. Ah, well, they were once themselves even as I am. No excuses dare I offer, yet it was more than flesh and

blood could endure to see those lurking forms and remain
unmoved. As I neared the lower end of the pool, in all
directions dim phantoms mysteriously came and went. Oily
swirls marked where others stirred. To one whose sole
experience hitherto had lain in an indifferent autumn river
it seemed incredible that every break on the surface of the
water could mean a salmon. I cast across the stream and
gently and religiously, according to the directions of Mr.
Malloch and other experts, worked the fly across the slug-
gish current. Again I did it, and yet again, with no result.
It appeared impossible that even so small an object as a
salmon fly could cross those few yards of water without
coming into contact with one of those half-seen forms.
Three times did I industriously work the pool, and never
the suspicion of a rise. Then down the bank to me came P.
and unfolded his evil design. I cast again. The fly came
working slowly across the river. As had chanced so often
before, a heavy swirl broke just inside the line. "Strike!"
yelled P. I struck.

The next second the reel began to scream, a great silvery
form came leaping clear of the water, and I was into my first
salmon. The rod nearly leapt from my startled grasp. Even
P., that hardened sinner, was for the moment taken aback,
but by the time the salmon had crossed the pool he recovered
his wits and began to shout exhortations and advice.

"Up the bank!" he yelled. "Keep your rod up."

One side of the pool, that on which we were, sloped
steeply down to the water and, composed as it was of loose
earth and stones, formed a very insecure foothold. Scrambling and slipping, bringing down loads of earth with every
step, somehow or other I reached the narrow wooden ledge
built above the pool, which gave a somewhat firmer footing
on which to play a fish. Simultaneously off came the reel.
Trembling, perspiring and flurried by some method at
which I could not myself arrive, I was up at the far end of
the pool a minute later, the reel on the line still taut, and
beside me P. openly exultant. Across the pool 50 yards

away the line faintly cut the water. Frantically I reeled up and even whilst so doing saw the fish leap clear and fall back with a splash.

"Drop your point!" shrieked P., as the fish leaped again. I obeyed clumsily enough, but a beginner's luck was with me, and the fish still on as I reeled in. At length ever so slightly the strain began to tell. There came a series of spasmodic rushes up the pool, which finally collapsed in a fit of sulks just below the dam. P. left me and called out that he could see him plainly—"a good fifteen pounds."— close in by the side of the dam, his tail up and his head down. There he stayed for some minutes, and nothing I could do would move him. Voices came murmuring across the water and in the little village opposite lights began to glisten. A group of men sat by the water's edge below their homes and discussed my captive. The soft aromatic scent of the pines, one of the most magical of nature's perfumes, stirred softly above the waters.

For some twenty minutes we waited until that portion of the audience on my side of the pool began to urge stronger measures. But I would have none of them. He was my first salmon, how insecurely hooked none could tell, and rather than run any risks I was prepared to spend the entire night playing him. A dull splash sounded close at hand. The fish jiggled slowly out into mid-stream and as slowly returned. A second splash, and the movement was repeated. At the third splash I realised what was happening—P., mindful of his supper, throwing rocks in to stir him to action. I called a remonstrance, but it was too late. A stone better aimed than its predecessors roused him in earnest. With a dash he was off, darting up and down the pool, to the far bank and as quickly back, taking out yards of line and giving me all I could do to keep pace with him. More by good luck than anything else the hook held, and realising this he became crafty. In the shallows under the far bank were rough jagged rocks, and here and there, peering wickedly among them, he manœuvred for some moments;

but the strain was evidently wearying him, and finding his efforts useless, he made as if to return to his old refuge under the dam.

A series of stones hurled by P., whose aim was improving, convinced him of the futility of his efforts and sent him off down-stream at full speed.

Compelled to leave my platform, I hurtled down the bank and stumbled among the rocks in semi-darkness as best I could. Through the mass of fish congregated above the rapids he went. Splashes and swirls mingled with hurrying tails and fins. In a moment I held him above the rapids, but the strain was more than I dared increase, and though hesitating at the finish, he faced them bravely enough. With a plunge and a rush he was in their midst. At a stumbling trot, soon degenerating into a breathless scramble, I followed, the rod held high. In the darkness it was impossible to see where either I or the fish were going, whilst in the gloom behind I heard the encouraging chorus of those who waited for their supper.

For a moment he stopped and I got in a few feet of the slackened line, then off again for the next rapid. Beside a half-submerged rock I had a glimpse of a broad back which even in that light told me that the end, either way, was near. A black shadow crept out into the rapids, and, like some mediæval murderer lurking to deal his victim a sudden blow, I recognised Napoleon. A blur in the darkness, he crept among the boulders and made for the rock. Off went the fish, and Napoleon crept a little closer. I clattered towards him. A dull glint showed for a second above the water, the strain on the rod relaxed, and through the water towards me came the man, gaff in hand, and on it, feebly flapping, my first salmon.

Later he was followed by another. Salmon are excellent eating. I thought, in fact, that I could never tire of them. After ten days at P.'s fishing hut, during which period we lived on salmon and fried bacon and eggs for breakfast, salmon and fried bacon and eggs for lunch, and salmon and fried bacon and eggs for supper, I felt that life without salmon would be bearable for some time to come. It was just as well that I did, for it was twenty years before I caught another—in that delightful little river, the Helmsdale. That was in 1926, and I have caught only two salmon since.

However, as we had time to spare before starting on the hunting trip which we had planned in the States, we decided to explore the further fishing possibilities of the Province of Quebec. The difficulty was to know where to go.

"Why don't you try for ouananiche?" asked P., and continued to dilate on their sporting qualities.

Tucked away in the north-east corner of the Province of Quebec lies a small irregular blue patch, labelled on the maps Lake St. John. Should curiosity or interest prompt further enquiry on a map of larger scale, the investigator will discover a tiny black dot, one of many which cluster at the eastern end of the lake, marked Island House Hotel. It is a quiet little spot set down there in the blue patch, as far removed from the roar and bustle of the world as are the eddying backwaters which indirectly attract the wandering fisherman to so remote a locality.

I had heard much of the fighting qualities of the fish which lurk beneath those foam-covered eddies: that for his size the ouananiche was more than the equal of his cousin the great sea-going salmon, and, too, with all his finery of dress. I confess that I was disappointed, not in his appearance, for he is a beautiful fish, but I have seen many a burn trout fight as hard for his life, and harder, once he felt the fatal hook in his jaws. It may be I had been led to expect too much. There had been no rain for months; the river was low; the fish were not taking well; I never caught a big one; and last, but not least, wherein I expect lies the truth of the whole matter, I am not, as I have said, a fisherman. Not to me has it been given to flog the water contentedly all day and take nothing, which is a matter of self-pity.

So it came about that I would lie back in the canoe with a

contemplative pipe and, at peace with all the world, watch Johnnie cast dexterously across the swirling currents, his look of eager delight as the fish came scuttering along the top of the water in a final struggle to be free, his mouth open and his tail feebly beating the elusive foam. I enjoyed, too, Lessaid's accompaniment of strange cries; his brandished net, the sight of which gave the fish strength for yet another plunge below the surface; his exhortations to Johnnie to keep his rod up; his low fat chuckle as he drew the silvery form into the canoe, so that in the actual sport what did it matter if I was disappointed, with all this and more to charm me?

Every morning we would start early, for the world is young then, and in those small hours you may see many things for which you will look in vain as the day draws on. Only at its close from out of the west a reflection of one's earlier mood will come, lacking, it is true, the glad joyousness which then sent you on your way rejoicing, yet tinged with a faint, half-pleasurable regret, as the perfume of lavender which has lain long in some unopened drawer.

Once, as we went gliding down the river round a rocky point, we came on that which turned my thoughts into a more sombre channel and for a time struck the smile from even Johnnie's cheerful face. Above, the sun seemed to call on all things to make merry. The river went crying and laughing past "clear and cool, by laughing shallow and dreaming pool." Beautiful wild flowers came shyly treading to the water's edge, and there, crushing their beauty, half in, half out of the water, lay a grisly horror which had once been a man. His yellow clawlike hand was twisted under his head; a wisp of lank black hair floated this way and that as the rippling waters bore it, and covered his puffed and swollen features distorted out of all human significance. I only gave one look, but I shall never forget what I saw, and to give a kind of grotesque horror, that one glance told me that his nose was a bright scarlet like that of a funny man in a pantomime. A poor Indian working in a lumber camp the preceding winter, he had been swept under the ice and so drowned. I wondered what strange scenes the poor battered derelict had encountered on its long companionless voyage through the weary months ere it made its silent advent into the world of sunshine it had left.

So presently we went on down the glittering river. I could not at once banish the scene from my mind, but Johnnie and Lessaid talked away in their queer French-Canadian patois, and before ten minutes had passed were laughing and chattering like children.

For all their gaiety and lightheartedness they did not forget the business in hand. From down below came a low booming. Johnnie motioned me to reel up my trailing flies. In the distance I could see a cloud of spray, whilst the smooth surface of the river seemed broken by a dull, uneven line. Low evil-looking rocks began to appear. For a second or so the paddles stopped and we wavered uncertainly; but it was only for a second. With a long stealthy glide we slid out from the oily calm above the rapids into their very midst, the broken waters tossing and roaring all around. A great swirling wave broke suddenly close to the canoe; a foot off was a big brown crest. Johnnie gave a quick calculating glance the while, holding his blade wide, he steadied himself on his knees. The canoe jibbed like a living thing, then, as Johnnie, suddenly galvanised into life, gave a quick sharp turn of his wrist, shot between the two as if she herself were a sentient being.

The river went shouting and rioting past, throwing itself into a myriad twists and curves, rejoicing in the exuberance of its own strength; but we lay quiet in an eddy, or so it seemed, till, as a black sinister-looking rock slid past, I realised that we were still being borne swiftly forward, and the next second were twisting in a miniature whirlpool. More rocks, some covered with heavy drift-logs, and all looking absurdly like bad stage scenery, slid past. Lessaid suddenly gave a sharp cry, the paddles flashed, we gave a great leap, and lay in calm water, though how we passed through that tossing foaming chaos every morning without even a wetting I could never say.

Through floating lily pads the canoe sidled up to a little spit of sand. Johnnie, his face all aglow, his merry black eyes twinkling, cracked jokes, to which Lessaid, his snub nose tilted high, his grey whiskers fiercely bristling, gave passing recognition by a ponderous grunt. They motioned me to disembark, for we had come to a portage, and, as I steered my rod through the thick pendant boughs which shut in the narrow pathway and clutched with vicious claw-like talons at my line, shouldered the canoe. Like some uncouth monster rising from a sea of lovely flowers it followed me. Great masses of berries, pink and red, barred our way and mingled with the iris and reminiscent bluebell. The smell of the pines struck softly in my face, bringing with it vague indefinable longings, and tremulously stirred with unseen fingers the latent hopes which I longed to, and yet could not, express. Involuntarily I raised my eyes, conscious of some presence flitting behind the watchful stems; but the time had not yet come, and before me the wide sunlit glade basked tenantless save for the whispering of the morning breeze. Perhaps the rustling which I had heard was caused by the passage of some unseen presence. Beyond the sun-bathed opening gutted pine stems reached down to the water's edge. The fresh green of young foliage crept about their trunks and strove to cover their nakedness. But the pines, one rank above another, stood there stiff and erect, as though resenting an intrusion they were powerless to prevent. The lily pads came rippling in on tiny waves to watch them. The river widened out into a little lake, and through the green discs we slid out once again on to its calm bosom. Round a bend came the flash of a rod. A silvery form splashed and glittered in the water. "Good win-an-eesh!" said Johnnie, and paddled on. Where the foam curved in strange shapes and half-circles I could see lazy fins and vanishing tails disturb the eddies. All the long glorious morning we would drift lazily from one big pool to another.

Hardly the fins and tails would show themselves, despite the black shadow of the canoe; or, as was more frequent, there would come a swirl in the water out of reach of the fly (and you may be sure that it was at the more distant swirls that Johnnie would ejaculate: "Beeg win-an-eesh!"), as though to tantalise us.

On some little wooded islet we would take our lunch—ouananiche fried over a fire of fir splinters—and as the blue smoke rose on the still air above the sweet-smelling pine needles I dreamed those dreams which the breath of a city kills.

Ismaquhes, the fish hawk, came sweeping from his blasted pine stem, uttering a shrill cry, curiously plaintive for so large a bird, as though to assure the young ones he had left that they at least were safe, and then, as he swept over our heads, a grating defiance to the disturbers of his peace. Meeko the squirrel peeked and peered through the long grasses as though to find out what it was all about. Butterflies black and white, orange and blue, flitted here and there about the splashes of sunlight. A woodpecker popped his head around a tree trunk, as though to pass the time of day, and then, astonished at his own temerity, popped back again. Reassured at the immobility of the strange object lying on the fir boughs, he was back again directly, and soon I heard him hammering gaily away as he climbed out of sight among the fir tops. The great aisles of the wood stretched away into the distance. A thousand cobwebs, perplexing to the eye, like jewelled threads, stretched about the bushes and filled the shadows with light; there was a sound of many waters in my ears; the wood seemed on a sudden to grow very still. The pipe fell from my mouth and lay unheeded.

When I awoke it was already late, and a little pile of still, silver bodies testified to my laziness and Johnnie's energy. So we adventured forth again, a spoon substituted for a fly, and paddled along close in about the reeds. Presently there came a terrific tug; the reel began to scream. I suspected a weed, but Johnnie cried: "Beeg pike!" and sure enough it was. For ten minutes we saw nothing. Then we coaxed him into a small bay and I reeled cautiously up. Directly below the canoe against the white sandy bottom I saw a wicked shark-like monster. He turned his head and saw the canoe above him. In a flash he was gone, and the line began to sing. Again he came gliding past, this time a little nearer, his flat ugly head and gaping jaws plainly to be seen. Then the rod broke. I knew it was weak, Johnnie having obligingly broken it for me on a wretched perch a few days previously. Now a light trout rod with a badly spliced top is not the best thing in the world with which to catch 18-lb. pike. However, it was all we had, and fortunately the line held. The monster struggled feebly on the surface of the shallows; a deft finger closed over each wicked little eye; he was heaved on to the shelving sand, and that was the end of him.

So in the evening light we paddled gently back over the darkening water. Kehonka, the wild goose, went winging his way up the river, over the wild duck softly calling her brood around her, and the reeds wherein she had made her home. On either bank long luxuriant grasses rose, cut off from the river by narrow spits of sand. Beyond them lay a tangled mass of undergrowth, dark spruces rising above, with here and there the pathetic skeleton of a fallen trunk. Through an inlet I had a glimpse over the salmon and green of the water of faint blue hills; up past a little sandy isthmus rocky islands caught my eye; while round a bend everything lay hidden in the blue haze of a forest fire. Wild roses shyly greeted the passing canoe from amid the rocks and shaggy thickets. Across the water a dragon-fly went booming and hung on vibrant wings above us, then, dissatisfied with his inspection, betook himself off and vanished amid the clustering roses. Ahead I caught the deadened whisper of the rapids, which drew level as we crossed the portage, until finally their murmur died behind.

And so in the velvet hush of the darkening twilight, a star or two winking palely in the evening sky, we came to

THE GENTLE
ART—RIVER
FINDHORN

the little landing stage and to our voyage's end. But the great river went gliding quietly and silently by, never stopping until it had finished its ceaseless journeying and stilled the call which sent it hurrying to the vast bosom of the St. Lawrence and to the grey seas beyond.

XXIV. THE REQUITAL OF PODBY

"The memory of an unasked, fruitless kiss."
LIFE AND DEATH OF JASON—William Morris

"I'VE heard from Podby, to say he'll be delighted to come on the eighteenth," said George Ogilvie.

"Oh, George! That dreadful little man!" exclaimed Marjorie.

"Well, he was very good to us in Ceylon," replied her husband. "The least I could do was to ask him here for a few days when he was up for the Meetings."

"Whoever can be bothered to ask him to the Meetings?" said his wife. "For goodness' sake, send him out shooting all day. I don't want to be stuck with him."

These remarks, I thought, did not augur well for the enjoyment Mr. Podby was likely to derive from his visit to Invercra. Marjorie is a dear thing, but subject to violent likes and dislikes. Podby apparently was one of the latter.

"Well, he professes to be a great sportsman; so he can have a go at the lochs, and if the stags are coming in, he can go out early," said George.

On the 18th Podby arrived. I was out trying for a certain cunning old roebuck which had hitherto eluded my efforts; but the hum of a motor down the strath caught my ear, and I saw it swing into the drive, as I kept my glass on it, piled high with luggage.

"He's here!" said Marjorie, as I put my rifle in the gun-room.

"So I observe," I remarked, glancing at the various sporting implements which surrounded us. There was a brand-new leg-of-mutton guncase labelled "L. P."— "Lancelot Podby," I afterwards discovered—a rifle, a bundle of rods, another of golf clubs, a tennis racket and a cartridge magazine, all suspiciously lacking in signs of wear. "He's evidently come prepared for the fray!"

"What on earth he wants to bring all that stuff for, I don't know," said Marjorie, intolerantly. "Who wants golf clubs and tennis rackets up here? They're all right in the south, but an utter waste of time when you might be shooting or fishing." Marjorie, by the way, throws a beautiful line and is an excellent shot with a rifle.

I met Podby in the hall before dinner. He was a little, fat, podgy man, who looked as if he had done himself uncommonly well from birth. He had a toothbrush moustache and round, protruding eyes, like boiled gooseberries. An irritating trick of constantly clearing his throat before a remark, and a nervous fiddling with his tie, helped me to an incipient understanding of Marjorie's dislike. I thought he seemed apprehensive of my hostess from the sidelong glances he kept shooting at her. Helen, George's sister, a very pretty girl with her hair still down, he treated with the greatest deference and attention. He talked incessantly, in a low monotone on every subject under the sun.

"Well, Daddy, did you get your buck?" said Helen. Such is the name by which I have been known in the family circle since an occasion when, chiefly owing to a patriarchal appearance, due to glasses and prematurely grey hair, Helen was taken for my daughter. "I bet you didn't," she went on, without waiting for an answer. "He's too clever for the complete little stalker. Mr. Podby has just been telling us he always stalked by himself in India. You ought to let him have a try."

I detected a meaning skilfully concealed in this remark, and was not surprised when Marjorie struck in:

"Yes, Mr. Podby, you ought to go out early and try for it. It's a very good head."

"Well, but roe, Lady Ogilvie!" said Podby. "Hardly a sporting animal, is it? Always poking about in woods and things. Now, I like a stalk in the open. No fun in a wood, can't see what you're doing! I remember when I was staying with the Maharajah——" And off he went into a long account of some wonderful bit of stalking he had done in India.

"Perhaps you'd like to try for a stag, Podby?" said George. "They ought to be coming in now. There are plenty of hinds on the ground. I was up at Loch an Targ yesterday and saw about sixty."

"Thanks very much, Sir George!" said Podby. "I'm never behindhand in a bit of sport." (I saw George wince.) "Shooting, fishing, hunting—it's all the same to me."

"Or tiddley-winks or hunt-the-slipper," murmured Helen, stretching across me for salted almonds.

After dinner I heard George giving the head stalker, Archie MacDougall, instructions that Mr. Podby was to be taken out the next day. When I came down to breakfast he had not returned.

Marjorie was there; Helen, as usual, was late.

"Marjorie," I said, "why do you dislike Podby so much?"

"Swear you won't tell George?" said she.

I agreed.

"Well, when we were in Ceylon he was staying at the Galle Face, and he made a great fuss of George, and gave him introductions to people who got him a good deal of sport. You know what George is like—good-natured, mad on shooting, and loves being buttered up. He's a dear old thing, but never sees an inch beyond his nose. We went on to Rajputana from Ceylon, and there was Podby again. George went off to shoot black-buck, and I dined alone. After dinner I was having coffee on the verandah, when the little beast came up. I didn't want him, but he sat down and made himself at home. Then, to my horror, he began making love to me. In fact, he tried to kiss me before I knew what he was doing. I slapped his face and bolted indoors. He kept out of my way after that; we left in a day or two, and I never saw him again till he came here. George doesn't know anything about it."

"By Jove! He's got some nerve!" I exclaimed. "But I thought——"

Then George came in.

"Podby had any luck?" he enquired.

"None," I answered, glancing at Marjorie, who gave me a glance of scorn and coloured faintly. "At least—that is, I haven't seen him this morning."

Half-way through breakfast Podby arrived.

"No, Sir George, not a thing!" he answered, to our enquiries. "I had a shot, but the beast was moving. No chance at all really. That man of yours, hardly up to the mark, I think. If I'd been alone I could have got in much closer. But he showed himself, and the stag bolted."

"I've never had any fault to find with him," said George, rather dryly. "You'd call him a good stalker, wouldn't you?" he added, turning to me.

"First-rate!" I answered. "If he couldn't get in closer it would have to be a very good stalker who would."

"That's just it!" said Podby complacently, and without Marjorie's explanation I felt the less I saw of him the better I should be pleased.

We interviewed Archie later. He was very wroth, but

calmed down when George told him he was quite certain
Podby's failure was in no way due to him.

Podby's idea of stalking, it appeared, was to walk straight
up to the deer. He seemed to think they would wait for him.
Archie explained that a prone position was more suitable
when a near approach became necessary, and much against
his will induced Podby to go down on his hands and toes.
Anything more drastic he utterly refused. When they came
on the stag he had missed he was standing among some peat
hags; a low knoll would have given a shot at about eighty
yards. To reach it a flat crawl was imperative. Archie
wormed his way towards it, but, glancing round, discovered
that portion of Podby's anatomy which should have been
most inconspicuous elevated towards heaven, while its
owner progressed awkwardly and crab-like across a patch
of soaking moss. It was too late to rectify so glaring an
error; the stag had already seen them. Hastily thrusting the
rifle into the culprit's hands, Archie had bidden him shoot,
and a spatter of peat high over their stag's retreating form
testified to the inaccuracy of his aim. That afternoon Podby
was sent off to fish.

"Frank," said Marjorie, in a peculiarly meek voice, "Helen
and I want to ask you something!"

I knew the tone and scented trouble.

"You know," she began, "how beastly the Poblet was to
Archie this morning? Well, we've thought of a plan!"

"O Lord!" I thought. I know these plans of old; this one,
I had no doubt, would involve me in trouble.

"You know how he's always bucking. He ought to be
taken down a peg or two!" This from Helen.

"Go on," I said.

"We thought," said Helen, "you might go out with him
to-morrow morning."

"I might!" I answered non-committally.

"He'll be sure to get a shot if you do," said Marjorie
sweetly.

"Come on, out with it!" I said.

They were both bubbling with laughter, and I was quite aware that this apparently simple plan harboured a catch of some kind.

"Let's show him," said Helen. "Come on! Bring your glass."

They each seized an arm and led me through the garden. The gate from the garden leads through a small wood to the fringe of the moor. Beyond the bog myrtle and heather is a hoary birchwood—even now its scent comes back to me—and along the sky-line are plantations of fir, a quarter of a mile apart, set there by George when he first bought the place. They led me through the birchwood and presently stopped.

"Now spy!" said Helen.

"Spy?" I asked. "There won't be anything there now!"

"Look and see," said Marjorie.

I took out my glass and began to spy.

"More to the right," said Helen, her eyes dancing with excitement. "There, just beyond the plantation!"

As my glass swung slowly round into the little circle suddenly came a stag's head.

He was lying down in the long heather, staring with a rather fixed regard over the wood. A wall of grey stone, moss-grown and lichened, ran past within a hundred yards.

"Now do you see?" said Marjorie.

"I see a stag," I answered obtusely.

"We put it there," said Helen proudly.

"You put—— Great Scott!" I exclaimed, the plot dawning on me.

"Yes!" cried Marjorie. "It's a stuffed head out of the hall, and a skin and some sticks and heather," she tailed off, excitedly.

At a distance the deception was really extraordinarily good. They had propped it up with some stones and sticks in the long heather, and at first glance it looked exactly like a stag, somewhat stiffly lying down.

"You can take him up to that pile of rocks, and he can have a shot from there," said Marjorie.

"But he'll murder me when he finds out!" I cried weakly.

"Don't be silly," said my hostess.

"You're the only person who can do it!"

"But I hardly know the man!" I exclaimed. "He'll never speak to me again!"

"A jolly good job if he doesn't!" said Helen slangily.

Well, there it was! I had to give in, and as we left the wood I stood committed.

"Frank will go out with you to-morrow morning, Mr. Podby," said my hostess at dinner that night.

"Oh, Archie will go, Marjorie," said George.

"No; Frank knows the ground just as well, and I know you want Mr. Podby to get a stag," said Marjorie firmly. I hadn't realised that George was in ignorance, but I couldn't disillusion him then, and Marjorie carried her point.

"Oh, very well, Frank, if you'd like to," said her husband. "You know the ground. I should go up through the wood."

"Donald told me the Altbea people wounded a stag which came our way yesterday," said Helen, twinkling at me. "You may find him in one of the plantations. Wounded stags often make for them," she added, turning to Podby.

In the cold, grey light of a September morning I gently opened Podby's door. It had been arranged that I should call him. The window was shut, and the place smelt like a hairdresser's shop.

Podby was snoring loudly. I shook him, feeling as I should imagine the warder feels on entering the condemned cell for the last time. He grunted.

"Ooh-urgh! Urrgh!" groaned Podby, reluctantly crawling out of bed.

Half an hour later we were skirting the wood, for my instructions were to give the Poblet a good walk first. I did. We walked miles. I left no likely corrie, no secluded gully unspied. Podby had no glass, and refused the use of mine.

We saw hinds in plenty, but no stag. Podby, chilled and miserable at the start, gradually thawed, and by the time the sun was up chattered volubly of his past exploits till I shut him up, I fear, rather brutally. By 6.30 a.m. we had reached a spot from which we could spy the wood. I am no actor, and I fear my dramatic start and sudden exclamation would not have deceived a less unsuspicious person than Podby.

"What is it, old chap?" he exclaimed.

If there is one thing more than another I loathe, it is being called "old chap" on a two days' acquaintanceship. I began to warm to my task.

"I can see a stag!" I replied.

"Where, old man?" said Podby.

"Near that plantation," I answered. "He's lying down. Here! Have a look!"

"No, thanks," said my companion. "Can't see with those things. I always use binoculars."

Very well, thought I. Your blood be upon your own head. It was the one thing that might have saved him, for even an inexperienced stalker could have detected something unreal in the rigid pose of our quarry.

"How far is it?" said Podby.

"About three-quarters of a mile," I replied. "We'll go down the burn through that plantation and along the wall to that heap of stones; but I must warn you, Podby," I added firmly, fixing him with a stony eye, "that the last part of the stalk will be very flat crawling indeed!"

Podby gave a feeble and reluctant gesture of acquiescence.

I carried out our programme to the letter.

I dragged Podby down the burn. I got him very wet. I crawled through an unnecessary peat bog and got him wetter still. I also got him very dirty. He perspired freely. I made him crawl over burnt heather roots, which are painful if you have tender knees. I rather skilfully made him bark his shin on a rock, and finally dragged him, panting and limp, behind the shelter of the rocks.

"He's still there!" I announced, peering through a crack.

Then in a hissing whisper, "I think very likely he's the wounded stag from over the march."

Podby now had the rifle, and the crucial moment had arrived. He had put in his eyeglass—I should have mentioned that he confessed to short-sight—and was peering excitedly over the rocks. As he caught sight of the stag he flung up the rifle, and, hardly pausing for a second, fired.

"Quick, again!" I cried. Podby fired again.

As he lowered the rifle, from the plantation behind us came the sound, as when a bull's-eye is secured in a shooting gallery, of a bell!

"What's that?" he cried.

I knew what it was, but I wasn't going to tell him—Helen or Marjorie elaborating their masterpiece!

"What the devil's that?" cried Podby again. Then he clambered over the rocks and marched up to the stag. He gazed at it for a second; then, with a violent kick, tore the wretched animal's head from its body.

"Damn!" shouted Podby explosively. I have never known so much concentrated fury condensed into one syllable. And turning, with one savage glance at me, he strode down the hill.

I have never seen him since.

XXV. THE BIG STAG OF GLEN ALASTAIR

"What a noble beast! What a stretch of antler!"
THE MUCKLE HART—Charles St. John

WHEN Harry Brockton opened a letter signed Sheila
Campbell-Taylor, he was in two minds whether to
accept his aunt's invitation to stalk. He knew her
for an eccentric and imperious old lady with a sardonic
sense of humour. How far these qualities would go towards
making a holiday enjoyable, he doubted. Finally, his love
for Scotland conquered and he wrote accepting.

"Anyhow, I shall be on the hill, and she's bound to let
me shoot something," he reflected.

On the day fixed for his visit he arrived late in the evening,
tired after his long journey by train, boat and "machine."
His aunt did not believe in motors, and prided herself on
doing things in the old Highland style. He was conducted
to his room by a red-headed old butler, who wore a kilt—
which somehow struck Harry as incongruous—and later

through a hall hung with fine heads to the dining-room.
The room was dark, the tartan curtains and tartan-covered
chairs aiding the impression of gloom. His aunt's restrained
greeting had not inspired him with a feeling of warmth.
"I shall never stick it for a week!" he thought to himself.

"Are there many good heads on the ground this year,
aunt?" he inquired desperately.

"There are always good heads at Glen Alastair," replied
the lady.

"I hope I shall get one to-morrow," answered her nephew
hopefully—a remark which was greeted with an enigmatic
smile.

The dreary meal ended at last, and, longing for the
morrow, Harry followed his aunt into the drawing-room.
The old lady played patience, leaving her nephew to his own
devices, and as the clock struck ten gathered up her cards,
remarking, "Will you be ready for an early start in the
morning?"

Without waiting for a reply, she went on: "You'll be on
the far beat with this wind. The ponies will leave at seven,
and if you start an hour later you will be on the ground by
10.30. You'll have to walk. I don't allow any of these new-
fangled ideas about riding or driving here. We do things in
the old Highland way. You'll be back for dinner at eight."

"I can start with the ponies," said her nephew, thinking
that the day's stalking would not be a long one, with a
twenty-mile walk thrown in.

"The arrangements are all made," was the answer. "I'll
ask you to give this note to Donald," and she handed him
an envelope.

He slept well, and woke to the sound of voices coming
through the open window. He made them out to belong to
two gillies.

"I wonder will the young gentleman be getting a shot?"
said one. "It's a graand day."

"Ay, he'll be getting a shot, but I doot will he get a gude
staag," replied the other.

"Hm! Hm! A peety, too. There's no many gentleman that will be leaving Glen Alastair wi' a gude heid."

"Maybe he'll be seeing the big staag," went on the other voice. "To-day's the 8th, and ye mind he always moves in on the 8th."

They both laughed.

"I'm no' thinking the big staag will be coming down the glen on Rory's back the nicht." Their brogues sounded on the stones of the courtyard as they went to the ponies.

Harry pondered these cryptic utterances while dressing, but could arrive at no definite conclusion, and as the clock struck eight started off on his long walk. His guide was a lad of eighteen, named Dugald, shy and uncommunicative. Harry essayed a tentative question with regard to the "big stag," but beyond the information that it was a big beast which appeared on October 8th every year, bore a charmed life, was seen until the end of the season, and afterwards mysteriously vanished, none knew whither, he remained as much in the dark as when he started.

The scenery was magnificent. At first shaggy, hanging woods of fir and birch clothed the hillsides, which converged sharply on a brown, swirling torrent. Steep grey rocks shut in one side, the other merged into narrow meadows of lush grass, broken by peat hags and knolls covered with bog myrtle and heather. Presently the glen widened, the heather disappeared, and high, grass-covered hills strewn with rocks showed beyond. As they left the birches a hoarse bark sounded. At first Harry thought it was an old collie, but turned to see a roe, startled at their approach, flashing through the silver stems. Now and again an old blackcock rose from the river flats, and flew swiftly and silently across the river. The wind, which had been blowing gently on their backs, changed when they had gone half-way. A little later, as they turned a corner, a cluster at the foot of some rocks resolved itself into a group of men and ponies.

"Donald will be changing his plans," said Dugald shyly,

as an elderly man, with a shrewd, wrinkled face and peaceful eyes, came forward, raising his cap.

"Good-morning, sir," he said. "The wind is after changing, so we'll be going up to Corrie Ghorkill. It will be a long walk back for Captain Brockton, but there's no ither way."

"That's all right, Donald," said Harry. "By the way, I've a note for you from Mrs. Campbell-Taylor."

Donald took the note and fumbled in his pocket. "'Deed, sir," he exclaimed, "is this no' vexatious? I've no' ma glasses wi' me, and I canna see wi'oot; though I'm a' richt for the deer," he added hastily. "Would Captain Brockton read it for me?"

Tearing open the envelope, Harry ran hastily down the angular writing. This is what he saw: "Dear Donald,—This is my nephew, Captain Brockton. Give him a good walk, but see that he does not shoot anything of any consequence."

"You mean old devil!" he thought angrily. A sudden inspiration seized him.

"Dear Donald," he read aloud, "this is my nephew, Captain Brockton. Give him a good day, and see that he gets a really good stag."

Donald's face lighted. "Weel, sir, that's fine," he exclaimed. "It's no' every gentleman that gets a gude staag here. We'll just start at once, as we've no' much time." He gave a few rapid directions to the gillies, and started at the easy stalker's stride up the hill.

"We will just go along the edge of the sanctuary, and have a spy," he said. "There should be a good beast or two there the day."

Harry's temper was still simmering at the treatment he had received.

"I don't want to shoot her beastly stags," he thought, "but if she asks me she might at least give me the chance. Anyway, she can't blame Donald, and it serves her jolly well right if I get a good one."

"What's this big stag, Donald?" he said aloud. Donald stopped and leaned forward. "It's just a wonderful staag, sir," he replied. "We've seen him for five seasons. He was a royal last year. He comes into the ground every year on this very day. I'm thinking his home is away down in the woods by Corrie Nig; he's away again by the month's end, and no one sees him in the winter. I mind several gentlemen having shots at him—a gentleman last year missed him in this very Corrie Ghorkill at eighty yards—but no one has ever touched him. He's no' canny, that beast," he concluded.

"Well, perhaps we'll get him to-day," said Harry, laughing.

"'Deed, sir, I wish we might. But he's aaful cunning, and I'm no' sure we'll be seeing him at aal"; and Donald shook his head.

They had now reached the top, and a magnificent panorama spread before them. Far to the east lay a smiling strath, edged by a silver strip of sea. All around was a majestic assemblage of high, rocky peaks and deep corries. Deer there were in plenty. In the sanctuary itself stags were roaring freely, and below some rocks a mile away, on its edge, was a fine ten-pointer with about twenty hinds.

Donald pronounced it a good place for a stalk, and half an hour later, after an almost perpendicular shot, Harry was wondering what the expression on his aunt's face would be like when she saw its head outside the larder.

"Sixteen stones, sir! No' a pound less," said Donald.

A second stalk later in the day resulted in the death of a good nine-pointer. Not so fine a head, it was none the less a beast which any stalker would have been glad to kill. Harry's anger had evaporated, and he began to ponder on the meeting with an infuriated aunt. That it was his last day's stalking in Glen Alastair he never doubted!

"May as well be hung for a sheep as a lamb," he reflected, as he spied the hillside. It was getting late in the afternoon when, working round some rocks at the foot of the glen which led to the sanctuary, Donald spotted a wide eleven-pointer, roaring lustily as he rounded up his hinds. He was routing among some peat hags by a little burn, and, though the stalk was not really difficult, there was some tricky crawling on bare open ground before they could get within shot.

At length, panting and peat-stained, feeling very moist and happy, Harry lay within a hundred and fifty yards of his quarry. The stag was standing stern on, roaring, whilst the hinds fed quietly down the burn side, some of them within fifty yards of the stalkers. Their field of vision was limited, for to the right rose some high rocks which hid the lower end of the burn from view. The stag turned, and Harry gripped his rifle, when several of the hinds trotted past the stag, and they all looked intently in one direction. At the same instant a loud grunting roar came from behind the rocks. The stag was broadside on, and Harry, thrusting his rifle over a bunch of deer grass, prepared to shoot. Donald seized his arm, his face working, inarticulate noises coming from his throat. He was very pale, and his lips twitched.

"Stop, stop!" he whispered.

"What on earth's the matter?" said Harry.

"Ma Gord!" Another roar shook the silence.

"What is it?"

"Look, look!"

Harry peered over the knoll, and his heart began to thump. He had not seen many stags, but there was no mistaking royalty. Walking slowly up the burn came a stag whose very poise held menace to a lesser beast. His head, held slightly forward, drooped a little, as though unable to sustain the weight of his rough, massive horns. He roared again, turning his head slightly, and even a novice could not have failed to be impressed by the weight and symmetry of the massive antlers. They carried twelve points in all, thick, black, and rough, with points like needles, and their span was over three feet.

"It's him," croaked Donald. "It's the big staag." His hands trembled with excitement as they clutched Harry's arm.

Slowly the stag advanced. The eleven-pointer, dwarfed to

THE BIG TREE OF GLEN MALLIE, ACHNACARRY

insignificance, gave vent to a subdued roar, then, as the intruder, evenly pacing, was within twenty yards of him incontinently turned tail and trotted off.

A prolonged and deeper roar hastened his departure, while the fickle hinds tacitly accepted their new lord.

"Wait till he turns," said Donald; then, in a plaintive bleat, "Oh, man, dinna miss!"

A more experienced stalker might have been forgiven for missing, for to very few does such a stag present himself even once in a lifetime. Inexperience was bliss, and at the crack of Harry's rifle the great stag gave a convulsive leap, galloped madly through the startled hinds, and collapsed, with kicking legs, by the side of the burn.

Without pausing, Donald dashed wildly forward, fell headlong, scrambled to his feet, lugged out his knife, and plunged it into the stag's throat.

"Oh, the bonnie, bonnie beast!" he crooned, removing his cap and gazing reverently at the fallen monarch. He turned solemnly to Harry. "Sir," he said, "you're young, and I'm an auld mon. You'll never kill sic anither staag in aal a lifetime."

Harry felt rather inclined to laugh, and a little awed, but he recognised true feeling when he saw it, and made a suitable reply.

There is no need to dwell on his thoughts, nor the long walk home. The visage of his terrific aunt when confronted with the slayer of so epic and legendary a monster quite overwhelmed him. He arrived at the lodge tired, hungry, and footsore at eleven o'clock, to be greeted by the majestic butler with the news that his aunt had retired for the night, and would see him (this ominously!) in the morning.

He felt better after a cold meal, but when Mrs. Campbell-Taylor swept into the room on the following morning he was not there. A frown gathered on the lady's brow as she noticed a letter on her plate, and she hastily tore it open.

"Dear Aunt Sheila," she read, "when you asked me to stalk I concluded you really wanted me. I shouldn't in the

s

least mind shooting rubbish if you'd told me, but you will forgive me for saying that you scarcely carry out the old style of Highland hospitality." (Here the reader winced.) "So I altered your meaning a bit, as Donald hadn't got his glasses, and I had to read your letter to him. He is in no way to blame. It's all my fault. We killed the big royal, also two other stags. Will you send my things on, please? I'm walking down to the boat.—Your affec. nephew, Harry."

Mrs. Campbell-Taylor's brow grew even blacker as she read this ingenuous document. Then, as the meaning of it dawned on her, she did something which would have surprised her nephew, could he have seen her. Her brow relaxed, and she lay back in her chair and gave a cracked, but none the less genuine, laugh. Later in the day she interviewed Donald, who was scarcely coherent, and obtained a complete history from him of the events narrated. Recognising that he was in no way to blame, she said nothing to him beyond a dry remark that he had been very lucky.

Harry did not hear from her, and concluded that she had done with him for good and all. About Christmas time a large packing-case arrived, which, somewhat mystified, he proceeded to open. In it was a head, which he had no difficulty in recognising, and tied to the horns a letter:

"Dear Harry,—You're right, though you were a coward to sneak off like that! They didn't do things like that in the old days either, so that's one for you! You don't deserve it, but I'm sending you the head. You won't get another like it, if you live to be a hundred, but if you care to come up next season you might have a try—Your affec. aunt, Sheila Campbell-Taylor."

XXVI. A GROUSE DRIVE

"I heard the black and the red grouse crow."
Duncan Ban Macintyre

Nor so often as I could wish does a grouse drive come my way, and for that reason I appreciate one, when it does, the more. Unquestionably he is the finest bird we have. He is our very own—a native. The pheasant, that exotic fowl, does not so fit into his surroundings, having somewhat the appearance of a profiteer at, say, Claridge's. The partridge, small and always sporting, holds our affections for these very reasons. The blackcock has a nobility all his own, and, apart from the actual shot, to successfully circumvent him gives one a feeling of satisfaction which no other bird can provide. But the grouse is unique. His surroundings are unsurpassed, and to be present at a good grouse drive on a warm September day is to experience the highest luxury of sport. Weather apart, the time, of course, to meet him at his best is November. A right and left at driven grouse, high and fast at this time of year, is to present oneself with a memory which time can never dim. If the gods are kind and they come to you on a bright and frosty morning, with perhaps the stags roaring over the shoulder of the hill, it is enough, even though middle-age has you in his grip, to render you delirious with the mere joy of living. One such day was my good fortune a few years ago. As I waited the hills were spread in a panorama which no artist could hope to paint, the Beauly firth stretching below.

There are high-sounding names which go to the head like
wine. They burst upon you like a flash of trumpets. Of these
not a few belong to my own country and, as from my butt
I conned them over, I felt a mounting exhilaration which
played upon my senses like an organ.

Wyvis and Little Wyvis to the north; Fannich, Loch
Luichart; Strathconan; Monar; Benula, and Affaric, they
went almost like the line of an hexameter. This side of
Riabachan and Sgur-na-lapaich rose the hills above Struy;
Beinn a' Bha'ach Ard small and foreshortened amid such
giants. Far in the distance was the pointed top of Ben
Attow, and then a straggled mass of tops I could not
name. Guisachan was there and Ceannacroc, with, to the
south, the humped shoulder of Mealfourvonie. Lying in
between me and this vast amphitheatre—comprising as it
did half the North of Scotland—were brown moors and
purple hollows, yellow fields and green fir woods with
golden splashes of birch and larch, for the leaves were late
in falling.

Far away from the strath below came the faint thin
whistle of a train, and a slender plume of smoke marked
where it crawled leisurely along the edge of the firth. So distant was it that it seemed one of those trains which gather
a fascinated crowd to shop windows as they wind in and
out of miniature tunnels and gorges. Indeed the whole
panorama for all its size appeared curiously minute. It
created a sensation hard to describe. I knew it so intimately
and yet it seemed aloof and full of surprises. It was like
meeting a friend whom you know very well in the company of a stranger. The features are the same but there is
something hidden because a stranger is there. He does not
realise it because he is a stranger; but you do and it makes
you speculate as to what your friend is refusing to reveal.
I felt that there was something hidden which I could not
fathom. Little harled cottages nestled in the folds of the
hills, and from them, straight into the air, rose blue plumes
of smoke. So friendly and welcoming did they appear that

nothing in the world seemed so desirable as to own one and dwell in it!

Even as I thus mused there came from beyond the knoll to my right a flicker. So quick and fleeting it was that it might never have been, but that it was real I knew, and even as a cry of "Mark" came to my ears three grouse swung over to my left front, swerved, and crossed the line of butts below me. A puff of feathers floating in the air showed that they had not passed unscathed. A single grouse swinging far out beyond the right-hand gun finished the drive and presently we passed to the next row of butts.

The sky-line here was more distant, and the ground fell behind me to a wide, damp hollow covered with rushes and tufts of coarse yellow grass. The high hills were hidden by the ridge beyond, though far away I could see the blue tops and hollows which marked Strath Errick, and, beyond, the deep rift which marked the line of the Great Glen. It was very still, and presently there came a faint "pop," "pop" which showed that others were intent on the same business as ourselves. As we listened, over the ridge in front, very fast and high came two grouse. In the butt to my left I could see my host's cap, and between us they flew. There was no time to poke and I swung my gun to the leading bird. As he checked, crumbled, and fell on the far side of the flat below, the day, for me, at any rate, was made. I felt, when, at the end of the drive, my host called out to me, "If I had three hats I'd take them all off to you," that I might pat myself on the back, though self-laudation is a tiresome trait. It mattered not that later on I fired at the leading bird of three and killed the second; it mattered not that in the afternoon I had a blank drive. That one shot made me happy for days, and still makes me happy whenever I think of it.

The last rays of the sun turned the birches and larch stems to gold as we lined a strip of wood clinging steeply to the side of a gully. The hills beyond had changed their blues for purple, and the hollows they held were full of the mystery of evening. Grouse were finished for the year, but there was a chance of a blackcock. There came a distant cry of "Forward." Fast and low through the wood their dim shapes showed, grey against the paler fields, but alas! they were all hens save one old cock, and he, with the cunning of his kind, swung wide over the flats until, a shadow himself, he blended with the shadows which hid the distance.

I read with a touch of human envy of hundreds of brace killed in a day. Compared with such bags our modest fifteen brace may seem laughable; yet I wonder if those who participate in such totals, take it all in all, extract the same savour that we less favoured mortals do from our day's sport? Thirty years ago I should certainly have said "Sour grapes," and perhaps it is sour grapes still. As age creeps on one's lust for killing undoubtedly diminishes, though one's satisfaction at a good shot is, if anything, increased. I know that I would not have changed places with anyone as I drove home up the glen that night. For after such a day a man may forget his age and feel again the ardour and sensations of his youth. When he begins to enter the details in his game book and realises with a sigh that these stretch back for fifty years, he may feel correspondingly depressed. Yet after a good dinner before a cosy fire with a pipe between his teeth he may perhaps recapture something of the old ardour, and with the old zest ride once again, as he first rode so many years ago with M. de Marsac to the gloomy castle of Blois; or lay his heart with Rudolf's at the feet of the loveliest Queen who ever reigned in Zenda.

XXVII. AN AFRICAN MEMORY

"The game ranges of the Sudan are the largest and most varied of all similar British Possessions."

GAME ANIMALS OF THE SUDAN—H. C. Brocklehurst

WANDERING holds a fascination difficult to explain to those who have not known the joys of the hunting trail, and we who have tasted of its past glories know that, although life is so short, at least we have lived and sometimes touched the high tops of human enjoyment.

So wrote my dear old friend, Johnnie Millais, who knew "the high tops of human enjoyment" better than most men, and in his many writings communicated much of that joy to his readers.

Whether it be the hot sun of Africa which beats upon him as he peers with puckered eyes across the plains; whether it be an icy wind from the battlemented crags of some vast mountain range in the heart of Asia which blows upon him as he cowers "where the boulders and the snow lie, while the head of heads is feeding out of range"; whether he struggles through some tropical jungle, or moves stealthily amid forests of birch and pine, there will in the heart of the born wanderer be joy, in his ears the echo of an ageless song, and on his lips a pæan of thanksgiving.

Some there are who throughout their lives know nothing of such an uplifting. They are to be pitied. Deep in those who have lies an ache which never can be satisfied.

"You'd better come!" said Brock. "You'd better go!" said my wife, so go I did, having arranged that she should join me later in Khartoum.

It was several months later that, steaming down the Red Sea, I looked with a new interest at the range of hills which ran behind the seaboard to the west. I had seen them before, but never had they beckoned with such alluring possibilities. "The Kashmir of Africa," in Major Maydon's happy phrase, they are "the only true mountain district with its own special game which Africa offers to the hunter." Nine or ten different species are to be found in these hills between Port Sudan and Eritrea. The only one which I was intent on securing was the ibex.

So to Port Sudan we came. It is on record that an American tourist after landing encountered a resident. "Say, Bo, do you live here?" was his query. On being given an answer in the affirmative, he gazed around, pondered a moment, and asked: "Does it hurt?"

Some, I suppose, might share his feelings. To me it was the gateway to the happy hunting grounds from which I had so long been absent.

Thirty years ago, in the bad old days, Port Sudan was non-existent. Suakin, 37 miles distant down the coast, was then a flourishing harbour town, but it was unsuited to large ships, so by order of the Government was created Port Sudan. It may in the future develop into one of the great air stations of Africa, for here the routes from north to south and from east to west converge.

I only remained a couple of days, as I wished to reach Khartoum by the end of January, and had but three weeks in which to do all I wanted. My stay was made pleasant by much hospitality. Of no shooting trip which I have been lucky enough to undertake do I cherish more happy recollections than of that in the Sudan. It is difficult to write with moderation of all the kindness, help, and sympathy which I received from officials and others. Cheery and keen on their work, they welcome the stranger within their gates in a manner which suggests that it gives them real pleasure to do so. On my return I wrote:—

In no place is the system of British rule better exemplified than in the Sudan. The Sudan political service could justly claim to be one of the finest in the world. Not a little of its distinction is due to the fact that at its inception its members were recruited from the best material the universities could produce.

In the course of varied wanderings I have met many officials. Some—indeed, the majority—like those of the Sudan, do all they can to make the visitor feel at home and render him every help in their power. Others become so obsessed with the idea of their own importance, clothed as they are with a brief authority, that they lose not only all sense of proportion, but any latent humour with which they may have once been blessed. Pompous, jaundiced, and obese, they appear to think that they bestow a benefit on those with whom they confer by allowing them to breathe the same air as that which they expel in the ponderous periods deemed by them a substitute for conversation. Not once in the Sudan did I meet with any of this type, nor do I believe that there they are to be found. In other places such do exist. I only trust it may never be the misfortune of the reader to encounter this comparatively rare, but unmistakable, species.

In the house of one official I noticed a splendid pair of horns, which to me appeared to be those of a domestic ox. I enquired as to their origin.

"That," said my host, with a perfectly grave face, "is the head of a Peruvian kudu." Then, seeing my sceptical look, he told me that he often took in tourists with this explanation. If they were acquainted with the fauna of Peru he transferred the locality to Ecuador. One lady, who ought to have known better, exclaimed ecstatically to her husband: "My, Martin! Say, aren't those just the most perfectly matched pair of kudu horns you ever saw!"

I recollect one evening sitting on the roof of a house, gaily lit with coloured lights and awnings, watching a gorgeous sunset over the hills. It was exactly like a stage setting. They looked so close that it seemed one could reach their outskirts by a gentle stroll. In reality they are distant 10 miles. In rarefied air such appearances are very deceptive, as was proved by the visitor to Calgary who started to walk to the Rockies before breakfast, only to find that they were 80 miles away.

It had been bitterly cold at Port Said, but the weather now was pleasantly warm, though with a good deal of wind. Indeed, the constant wind is one of my chief recollections of the time I spent in this part of Africa. Whilst waiting in the passes for ibex I have often been as cold as on a Scottish hillside.

It was twelve days after leaving England that I started southward by motor lorry. Averaging about 10 miles an hour, we passed Suakin when the morning was well advanced. Quite deserted, it is now a city of the dead. Here pilgrims, who may have spent years preparing for the journey, embark for Mecca. Its houses stand empty, its wharves are deserted, yet a curious impression is left on the mind of the traveller. It seems that only temporarily are they vacated; that just beyond one's vision over the sky-line are waiting caravans and strings of camels; that at a given signal they will approach to throng once more its busy streets and people once again the empty houses. It is but an illusion. The houses, sound though they may appear, are crumbling into decay; the glory has departed.

Our way for the most part ran through flat and featureless country. Low, straight-topped thorn trees, scrub and tussocky grass at times broke the monotony of the view with an occasional glimpse of gazelle. Those wayfarers we met had intelligent open faces, and walked with an air of independence. Some carried swords or spears.

A GORGE—THE RED SEA HILLS

Late in the afternoon we reached Tokar, about 100 miles from Port Sudan. Sandstorms are continuous here from May to September; but there are no malarial mosquitoes.

The most appalling place which it has ever been my lot to visit is Butte, Montana. Tokar runs it pretty close! Those who are at all hazy as to the exact meaning of the phrase "the abomination of desolation" will gain a very fair idea of it if they approach Tokar in a sandstorm. Though not in an actual storm, we were enveloped in sand. How the driver knew the road I am unable to surmise. It was marked at intervals by pieces of railway line sticking from the sand. Here and there direction posts marked "Tokar" seemed to elucidate the puzzle, but as the majority of these pointed directly upwards, one ignorant of the locality might have been forgiven for thinking the word a synonym of heaven. Others lay buried in sand, but the apparently endless detours in which my Jehu indulged were not so conjectureless as they appeared. Always eventually we struck again the line of direction. We seemed to hang on the world's edge, and that, having advanced but a few hundred yards, should crash into infinite space. The horizon swam, nebulous and indefinite, set about with formless fir woods and misty lagoons. Through the vague immensity a row of stems would appear which the eye failed to focus. A glass revealed their tops solidified into the fixed and solid shapes of men, small but definite. Under their minute figures swayed and minced the legs of camels, fluid and uncertain, as the forms of fish seen dimly in a tank.

I was not sorry when a few buildings appearing through the gloom heralded our arrival, and the dinner to which the District Commissioner was kind enough to invite me soon obliterated all unpleasant memories.

He had already arranged for my shikari to meet me, and a day later we started for the hills. It was my first experience of riding a camel for a journey of any length. Once accustomed to it, there are many more uncomfortable modes of progression; but it is advisable to have something soft on which to sit!

"The Arabs are reputed to have ninety-nine ways of calling on Allah. The camel knows the hundredth; hence the look on his face of self-conscious superiority," so writes H. W. in *Something New out of Africa*, a fascinating book which emphasises the difference between the old and new works on travel, for this deals entirely with journeying by air.

I had hoped to be able to obtain an ibex by stalking, but as my time was limited and this procedure would have involved a good deal of delay, I decided to employ the more usual method and "move" them. This, of course, meant that I should need more men. The number originally fixed by my shikari as being necessary was twelve, but at each fresh place in which we pitched camp and strange Hadendowa appeared, the number seemed to expand until another dozen had been added. For this I was prepared. They were a nice crowd and extraordinarily active. I felt like a drayhorse among a lot of polo ponies when once we got among the hills.

To recapitulate the details of each drive would be wearisome; many were failures, but one at last brought success.

The hills stretched north and south, a panorama of sharp-pointed peaks and spires, sliding steeply into narrow khors. Below the precipice which dropped sheer from the summit of one of the higher peaks, 4,000 or 5,000 feet above the wady below, an old ibex was feeding. The sun was not yet up, and he seemed but a grey shadow in the gloom of the hills. That he was old could be seen by the worn smoothness of the ridges of his horns, which curved outwards and backwards over his sturdy shoulders. His knees, too, were worn and calloused, and above one eye the scalp had been torn in a fight with another ibex.

A few hundred yards from where he fed another male was trying to find his morning meal in the company of a small band of ewes. It was a mystery to know what they could pick up on that bare hillside, and still more when and where they found water, though at times their footprints could be seen in the dry sand at the foot of the hills. A yellow-headed vulture swept on noiseless black-tipped wings above them.

On the tops the mist still lay, its upper edge straight and heavy against the lighter sky, its lower torn and carded by the sharp-pointed crags into wisps of shredded cotton-wool. Here it seemed scarcely to stir; there rolled sluggishly into the depths of some gloomy chasm. So grey and lifeless did the whole prospect appear, the only movements the silent circling of the vulture and the sullen drift of the mist, that it seemed unreal, the figment of some great poet's sombre imaginings. In such awful surroundings the souls of the lost might wander for ever amid those lonely crags, expiating with the bitterness of remorse the sins of which they had been guilty in some fairer clime.

Then on a sudden the whole world seemed to stir. There came a wakening movement among the hills and the sun rose on another day. In the wady the shadows still clustered thickly. The tamarisk trees and tufts of yellow grass, even the sparse bushes higher up the hillside, held no colour and differed but little in tone from the rocks which gave them so precarious a hold. The wady widened where a narrow gorge crept furtively into the hills, and here small rings of stones, each circled by a larger ring topped with white rocks, marked the resting-places of those who slept with their fathers. Three camels, with their mincing, supercilious gait, padded softly past. They were too far off for the ibex to betray any interest in their movements, and these fed on unconcernedly as the sun rose higher. Near the graves the camels stopped and, in the disjointed and unexpected manner of their kind, lay down. Dismounting, we moved silently up the gorge, and for an hour climbed and struggled amid the huge boulders and frowning precipices which barred our upward progress.

Presently, having reached a spur which commanded a
wide view of the corrie stretching beyond, we halted. The
khor twisted 100 feet below, rounded a sharp corner, and
climbed the hill behind some projecting rocks. To the right
a slide of shale and rubble drove down beneath the high
sharp pinnacles of rock whose tops glowed red and yellow
in the increasing warmth of the sun. Pinnacle topped pinnacle as though arranged by some giant hand; whilst in
places so symmetrically and in such ordered rows were the
tiers of rock disposed that it seemed they had been set there
by some human agency, and not the vast and immeasurable
forces of nature.

As the sun grew stronger the old ibex, having eaten his
fill, lay down; the others almost at the same moment followed his example, and peace settled down upon the
mountains.

It was over an hour later that the tinkle of a stone falling
among the rocks caused one of the ewes to raise her head and
gaze intently at the spot whence the sound had come. Her
stare revealed nothing, and soon she fell to dozing again.
There were but few shadows at the foot of the hill when a
second stone fell clattering above the ewe and brought her
to her feet. The others raised their heads, watching, but the
old ibex from where he lay could see no movement and the
sound had not disturbed him. Though no further stones
fell, the ewe was palpably uneasy, and continued to stare
intently up the hillside. Presently she stamped her foot, and
the others rose, following the direction of her gaze. As they
did so a long-drawn cry shattered the stillness and broke
and re-echoed among the rocks. It was taken up, flung back
and tossed from peak to peak in falling cadences as the now
thoroughly startled animals dashed down the hillside. The
old ibex, roused at last, followed their headlong rush.

The ewe which had first given the alarm led them.
Straight across the corrie, swerving upward, she went, while
the cries and yells behind her redoubled.

She made for a narrow pass which led through a cleft in

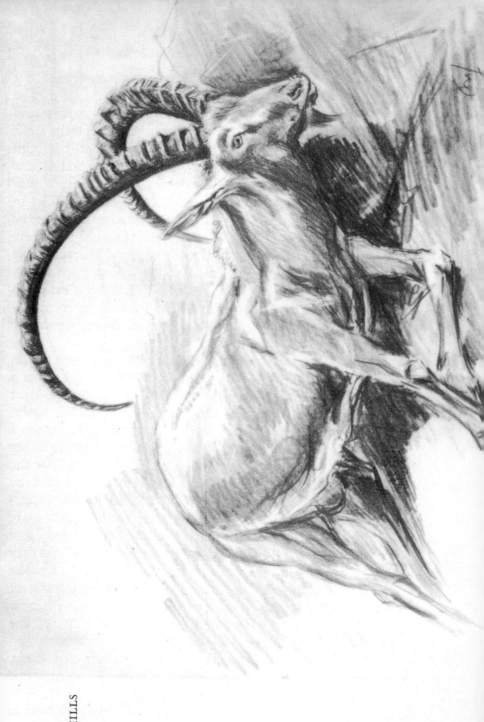

IBEX.
RED SEA HILLS

the rocks, and up which it seemed that no living thing could find foothold. As she neared it a cataract of stones poured down from the tops commanding it. Clouds of dust and fine splintered rock filled the air, and to us who watched it seemed that the hillside was on fire and that the lines, "Touch the mountains and they shall smoke," were becoming true before our very eyes.

Deafened by the crash and roar, the long-drawn cries which menaced them from three sides, bewildered by the puffs of splintered rock which sprang as though at the touch of invisible fingers wherever a boulder struck, the ibex made for the one side which seemed open to them, and, led by the ewe, turned at right angles to their previous course. From rock to rock they sprang, along ledges which seemed sheer, across gaps which seemed impassable. Poised for a moment on a point needle-like in sharpness, they seemed to float rather than leap to the next landing-place.

The turn downhill had given the old ibex the lead some distance ahead of the others, and as he reached a crest he paused. Silhouetted against the sky-line, very grand he looked. His curving horns, thrown into sharp relief, appeared enormous; the vision of them, as he leaped down among the rocks, all too fleeting. Vanishing, he reappeared, vanished again, and came into view almost opposite the point where we lay.

Again he paused. At the same moment, on the hillside above, the other ibex came into view. Turning, he moved slowly down the ravine beneath the slope of shale.

The hillside was in an uproar. It was impossible to tell from whence the cries and yells which filled the air came. Echoes seemed real; realities, echoes. Rocks thundered and crashed in all directions. On every peak appeared a figure, minute as though seen through the wrong end of a telescope. Paying no attention to the pandemonium which raged around him, the figures which seemed to encircle him, the avalanches of rock which threatened to overwhelm him, or the cries which rang in his ears, the old ibex, appear-

T

ing to my despairing eyes to grow smaller and smaller every
moment, made steadily forward with an occasional, it
seemed a calculated, pause.

The last he made upon a shelving rock, beneath a cliff
rose-red and menacing. It was his undoing. A sharp crack
and a roar filled the hills, silencing every other sound. He
stumbled and almost fell, then disappeared from sight. A
friendly bush hid him, sprung apparently from the rock
itself. As he stood there a movement among the rocks opposite caught his eye, and with a desperate effort he struggled
on. Thunder filled his ears. He stumbled, swayed on the
ledge which held him, then crashed blindly on to the rocks
far below.

Though in no sense a record, he carried a nice head, the
horns measuring 39 inches. The record is 47 inches. Ibex
suffer a good deal of persecution, and this there seems no
method of stopping. It is a pity that native shikaris cannot
be licensed as such, and at any rate made responsible that
heads below a certain measurement are not killed. I saw
some miserable specimens brought in by one party.

Having got my ibex, I returned to Port Sudan as quickly
as I could. From here I travelled to Khartoum. No one
who has made this journey is likely to forget it. The trains
are the best, without exception, in which I have ever been;
the food and attention beyond criticism. At Khartoum I
was welcomed by Brock and Charles, who was coming with
me to the Dinder. A charming companion, nothing ruffled
the evenness of his temper, and we never had a single dis-
agreement during the whole of the six weeks we were
together. I give him the full credit.

On the evening following my arrival Brock was giving a
dance in the gardens of the Zoo. After the three weeks which
I had spent entirely alone with nature, this re-entry into the
civilised world was not unwelcome. It was quite the prettiest dance at which I have ever been present. The warm
scented night, with no danger of its being spoiled by cold
winds or rain; the groups of people, among whom gazelles

and antelopes walked unafraid; the playing fountains; the throbbing music of the band pervading the air; the native servants in spotless white; the bright dresses of the ladies; one's own sense of fitness, all combined to make it a memorable evening.

The following day I visited Omdurman, and was shown over the house of the Khalifa by an old man who had lived there with him and had fought in the battle. As a boy I used to know Colonel Martin, who had led the charge of the 21st Lancers armed with a riding-cane. It all seemed very long ago.

Early the next morning Charles and I left by train for Makwar, and on February 3 reached Singa, having crossed the Sennar Dam. This is a wonderful piece of engineering, and good fishing is to be had here. From Singa we travelled by lorry to Abou Hashim, where we picked up our "hamleh" and my shikari, El Nur Ibrahim. A first-class hunter, he produced a wonderful recommendation from Brock which he thoroughly deserved.

The first few days of trekking are always a little difficult. Unexpected obstacles crop up; there are disputes among the men; the cook never has everything he wants; and it is apparently quite impossible for the camels to complete the day's journey on which you have determined. However, these troubles are soon smoothed over and, as in our case, everything settles down into a comparatively regular routine.

Before leaving England I had been given a beautiful little ·22 H.V. double-barrelled rifle. With this weapon I had in the Red Sea hills shot one or two gazelle. Walter Winans used to shoot the running deer at Bisley with one exactly similar. For game, I came to the conclusion that the bore was too small. I killed an ariel, a fairly big animal, stone dead, but very accurate shooting has to be made and the bullet placed in exactly the right spot. On another occasion I came across an ariel with a good head standing in the river bed. The stalk was an easy one to within 120 yards, and at ·this distance I fired. The animal never moved, and I fired again. He jumped, walked forward, and stood again. I fired nine shots without being able to make out clearly where he was hit. He then lay down, and I killed him with a final shot from my ·350. On going up to him I found nine bullet holes all on the shoulder or thereabouts, but not one had actually penetrated the heart. I only mention this to show the danger of using too small a bore. Had this beast been in bush country I might easily have lost him altogether. After this experience I never used the ·22 again.

A day or two after leaving Abou Hashim we came across roan, water-buck, reed-buck, and large herds of ariel.

Shooting in the type of country where we were is not easy. It is rarely that you can sit down with your elbows on your knees (by far the best position when it is possible) and take a steady shot. Long grass usually obscures your view of the target, and the majority of shots have to be taken off the shoulder.

The first animal of any importance which I got was a very fine water-buck, standing near the edge of the bush, partially hidden by long grass. He carried a beautiful head, measuring almost exactly 32 inches in length, with a similar measurement between the tips of the horns. Later I killed another just under 30 inches with a tip-to-tip measurement of 34 inches. The best Uganda horns of the Defassa variety, to which these belonged, are as a rule longer, but I have seldom seen a better balanced head than the first one I got. Wide span adds greatly to the appearance of a head of this type.

Another fine animal is the roan antelope. The best heads from the Sudan run to about 34 inches. I killed only one, with a length of 29 inches. He was an old bull, and I was well content. He had had, apparently, an encounter with a lion, for his neck was badly scarred. The horns of the roan— Abou Uruf, Father of the Mane—are disappointing compared to the size of the animal, and I had no wish to destroy a handsome beast for the sake of a few extra inches of horn. I saw plenty more, but none with a head much better.

We had great fun with guinea-fowl, which provided a welcome addition to the menu. If found near the banks of the river, which in some places were steep, we managed some quite sporting shots with the aid of our retainers. Made into soup, which we hung in bottles wrapped in wet cloths, these birds provided a very refreshing drink.

At Beit el Wahash we saw our first elephant. Standing on the edge of a swamp spraying himself with water, in the short dusk of the African night he was a wonderful sight.

I used rather to like elephants. They looked big and friendly, massive and unchanging in a petty and changing world. Not the Zoo elephants; they, poor brutes, appear merely ridiculous or rather pathetic with a lot of children sitting on their backs spitting stones out of a bag or munching sponge cake. I mean wild ones, walking about in their natural surroundings, their back-views looking like those of a pantomime elephant enormously magnified and their front-views—well, I am going to tell you about their front-views. It was the front-view of an elephant that made me alter my views. I am not quite sure that I like them, and I am quite sure that I no longer think them benevolent.

The Sudan elephants are very big, at least in that part of the Sudan which I visited. Unfortunately their tusks are small. Very few large tusks have been got in recent years, and I had no desire to shoot a beast which had taken years to reach maturity for the sake of some very indifferent ivory. Charles, however, wanted to take a photograph.

We had just been having a mild encounter with a herd of buffalo. By "mild" I mean that, very hot, perspiring freely, and a little dubious, we had got to the foot of a low rise which stood out from the 8-foot-high elephant grass. Charles had more or less successfully photographed three astonished-looking cows whose heads had appeared over the top of the rise. They had not seemed unduly perturbed, and, the sitting over, with two or three explosive snorts had lumbered heavily off, taking the herd, numbering about sixty, with them. They crossed a swamp through which it was difficult for us to follow, and after resting for some time in the shade of a few trees a quarter of a mile distant had moved quietly off, leaving us to our own devices.

We went leisurely on through fairly open park-like country covered with scattered trees until we reached a spot where a peninsula of bush and large trees ran out into a swamp. Here and there were dom palms rising above the surrounding bush.

We sat in what little shade there was and discussed the buffalo. It was then that the donkey boy ran up grinning from ear to ear, and announced that he had seen two "fils." The first, sometimes the only, words that the indifferent linguist picks up when engaged on a hunting trip are the names of animals. I cannot talk Arabic, but I did know that "fils" meant elephant.

We had seen traces of them, large circular holes sunk regularly in the ground and equally spaced, and had at first wondered, until we realised that these were gigantic footprints made when the ground was soft in the rainy season. They varied from 18 inches to 3 feet in depth and 2 feet and more in diameter. Some were even larger. These were the only evidence of the presence of elephants until the one we had seen at Beit el Wahash.

In a spirit of light-hearted optimism we set forth, Charles and I, with the two shikaris, El Nur and Bakit. Ibrahim, one of the boys, had a shot-gun and I carried the heavy rifle. Almost at once El Nur pointed excitedly, and we saw a large grey mass swing from behind a tree. The elephant, for it was he, moved across our front, looking the picture of perambulating benevolence. We cut in behind him and moved along parallel with the course he was taking, never getting a clear view of his whole body, but bits of back, legs, and ears. He was about 30 yards off, quite unconscious of our presence, and giving an easy shot had I meant to kill him. Presently he stopped and proceeded to shake the stem of a dom palm. He seemed to me to be putting a certain amount of vicious intensity into the performance. I was beginning to feel a little less casual than when we had started. We were by this time about 15 yards from him. He continued to shake the palm tree with great energy, and Charles, just in front of me, peered round a clump of high grass.

"I can see him beautifully," he announced. I received this information with somewhat tepid enthusiasm, while anxiously watching the top of the palm tree, which was shaking like a straw in a gale.

Charles proceeded to set his camera and peered round the grass again.

"He fills the whole of the view-finder!" was the next bulletin.

"Well, buck up!" I hissed, liking the look of the palm tree less than ever. I expected the whole thing to come down on top of me at any minute.

"Isn't this fun?" grinned Charles, fiddling about with his camera.

I raised my head to look at the palm and found to my astonishment that it was absolutely still. Not a leaf stirred. Their harsh rustle no longer came to my ears. I peered through the grass. I could see a bit of grey body. The elephant was still there standing absolutely motionless. What had happened? Next second I knew. I felt a faint, a very faint breath of wind on the back of my neck.

"Look out!" I whispered to Charles in a hoarse under-tone. "The wind's changed."

Charles was endeavouring to bring his camera into action again, but at this he stopped and raised his head.

Over the top of the grass, quite noiselessly, appeared two enormous ears. The next second the stillness was split by a sound which seemed to me to have come from the largest siren of the largest battleship ever constructed by man. In it there was an under-note of rage which no siren that I ever encountered could have achieved. The next second I was aware of an enormous bulk hurling itself at me.

At moments such as this one must act instantly; yet in

that instant I managed to my surprise, looking back on it afterwards, to do quite a lot of thinking.

The first thing I thought was, "Shall I shoot?" I was vaguely aware of El Nur shouting, "Shoot!" but all I could see over the tops of the bushes and grass were those two colossal ears and a bulging bit of trunk. "If I shoot," I thought to myself, "I shall probably blow a piece of his face away, as I can't see a vital spot. This may or may not turn him, but will in any case make him more annoyed than he is at present. If I hit him I shall have to follow him up and kill him, and the last thing in the world I want at the present moment is an encounter with a wounded bull elephant. As I am not going to shoot I had better decamp as swiftly as possible."

I heard someone shout "Imshi"; Bakit ran past me; El Nur vanished; Charles dived to the right; and as I turned and ran I saw Ibrahim, well ahead, going faster than I have ever seen a native run in my life. There came more siren squeals from behind me mingled with the crashing of branches and the breaking of trees. The ground was fairly open and flat. I did not feel frightened, but in a vaguely sub-conscious way wondered if he would catch me. I was making very good going, but the crashing and squealing was still going on behind, and I looked back, determined, if I saw the elephant, to try and turn him with a shot. I could see nothing, though I could still hear him. Ibrahim was going strong, and I saw no good reason for failing to follow his example. After another 200 yards I slowed down, and then, as all was quiet, stopped. Presently El Nur limped up, fol-lowed at intervals by Bakit and Charles. The former had dived into a bush, and the branch of a tree smashed by the elephant's headlong rush had crashed down on to his arm, giving him a severe bruise. Ibrahim had dropped the gun, cracking its stock, and had twisted his ankle, but there the casualties ended.

The reaction after a sudden strain of this kind is interest-ing to note. For no apparent reason that I could see I yawned incessantly for the next three-quarters of an hour. El Nur was very angry with me for not firing, and shook hands warmly with Charles at the reunion in the most pointed manner, entirely ignoring me.

I have often discussed the matter since with friends of mine, some of them experienced elephant hunters, including almost the last and most experienced of all, "Karamoja Bell." I am glad to say that they all, while pointing out the extreme idiocy of having got into such a position, agreed that I acted rightly in not shooting.

Meanwhile, as they used to say in the movies, the cause of all the trouble, after chasing us for about 200 yards, had retired behind an ant-heap, where he waited until the "hamleh" came past later in the morning. He then rushed upon them, giving once again his well-known imitation of a battleship siren. I was glad, when it was described to me on our return to camp, that I had not, on this occasion, been one of the audience. The "hamleh," terrified as its members were, yet welcomed the opportunity of, for once, being able unchecked to make as much noise as they liked. Bursting into loud yells and shouts, they beat every tin utensil available and succeeded in turning their aggressor, who retreated into the bush and was no more seen. I did not envy the next person he encountered.

People often say to me: "You've travelled a lot; you must have had some very exciting adventures."

When I tell them the narrowest escape I ever had was being nearly killed by a bus in Piccadilly they lose all interest.

Now I shall be able to tell them that I was charged by an elephant!

I have mentioned an encounter with buffalo. Such meetings are never lacking in excitement, for you never quite know what will be the outcome. However, on this occasion everything passed off quietly. I know one man who was less fortunate. A buffalo charged and tossed him. After his recovery it became necessary to obtain a medical certificate

stating that he was unfit to return to duty. The medical
officer had been called away and had left a native assistant
in charge. He supplied the certificate as follows: "I,
Chunder Dass, hereby certify that Captain B—— is unfit
to return to duty, having been punctured behind by some
blunt instrument."

One afternoon we left camp about four o'clock and
crossed the wady, where we encountered a fine bull giraffe.
I had no wish to shoot one of these beautiful, harmless
creatures, even had they not been on the protected list. A
little later we came on a Tora hartebeest, but he was in
thick bush and gave no chance before he moved off.

It was getting late when we emerged on a large open
space covered with high grass on which grazed a herd of
buffalo. El Nur, who had not much use for game other
than elephant, buffalo, or lion, in a state of great delight proceeded to stalk them, and got to within 100 yards. Their
heads were hidden, but on their backs, showing above the
high grass, were the white egrets by which these animals
are usually accompanied. The crawl through the long bamboo grass, which required a good deal of negotiating, the
wiry stems lying at all angles, had rendered me very hot and
my glasses were covered with steam. I wonder if those with
normal sight realise their good fortune on occasions of this
kind. To put up your rifle and to find that through the misty
haze you can see nothing, while large drops of moisture
run down your spectacles, effectively blurring the little you
can see, is a severe trial of patience. As the buffalo were
steadily advancing and I had no wish to shoot an animal
whose fate I should afterwards regret, much to El Nur's
disgust I began slowly to retreat. A cow was feeding within
40 yards, and the light at 6 p.m. was growing very bad.
The herd, about eighty in number, continued to advance.
The cow, her suspicions at last aroused, snorted loudly.
All their heads went up. To her left I could see what looked
like a big beast. El Nur whispered, "Kebeir! Kebeir!" So,
aiming at his chest, I was relieved to hear that loud smack

which betokens a hit. Falling on his knees, the bull, for a bull it was, recovered himself, and, rising, followed the herd, which was charging off in a cloud of dust. After going a little way he drew apart and stood looking back, his head up. I fired again with the ·465 lent me by Brock, which had been given to him by Selous. There was another loud smack, and he moved off into the long grass, 10 feet high. Cautiously approaching, we made out his form lying among the broken stems. When we got up to him he was quite dead. An old bull, he carried a good head for this part of the Sudan. It was entirely owing to El Nur that I got him, as in the bad light I should never have been able to distinguish the size of his horns.

Returning to camp, in the dark we ran right into another lot of buffalo, who were within 30 yards of us before a shot in the air from the 12-bore caused them to move off.

We had come across a good deal of lion spoor in the dry river bed, and found one day in the long grass on the bank above the dead body of a water-buck. Considerably cheered by this welcome sight, we decided to remain in the place where we were then camped, and devote all our time in an endeavour to find the animals responsible.

There are some things which you can only do once in this life, however long it may be, and to kill your first lion is one of them. Attempts are frequently made to dethrone him, but in spite of these he still remains, in popular imagination at any rate, the king of beasts. An aura of romance surrounds him which no other animal possesses.

Some animals may be more dangerous to pursue—the elephant, the buffalo, or the leopard—opinions varying with the experience of the individual, but to the death of a lion, particularly one's first, there is attached a thrill which can never be repeated.

Sitting here looking out of the window I can see the snow-covered lawn, streaked with blue shadows from the bare, twisted boughs of the trees. The gale which is humming through their tops throws them into fantastic designs. A disconsolate blackbird is hopping aimlessly about on the fringe of dirty-looking grass which shows where the snow has melted. Rose-bushes, ragged and forlorn, peer through the white drifts. It all looks very cold and miserable, and for that reason, I suppose, my mind goes back the more insistently to that day on the banks of the Dinder.

A lion was what I wanted to get above all else. Years ago in Kenya I had seen them. One had walked in the darkness round the outside of my tent within a foot of where I lay; but a shot at one had never been my luck. There were plenty in Kenya in those days, though men who had been in the country for years had never even seen one. Others on a short visit killed several. There is always a good deal of luck about lions, however experienced a hunter may be.

We had found their tracks; we had found their kill; and

> "When the moon rose, and her crescent white
> Made the woods blacker, then from either shore
> We heard the thundering of the lions' roar,
> Now coming nigher, dying now away."

I used to love lying on my camp bed listening to the sound which never failed to wake me. "There is no sound which issues from the throat of any creature to compare with that of the lion's voice," writes Sir Alfred Pease in his fascinating *Book of the Lion*, and I agree with him. Cold printed words give no idea of the impression which it imparts; nor does the pale simulacrum one may hear at feeding-time in the Zoo, "though the air vibrates and the sound comes thundering out of the depths of their insides." It is like hearing a scratched gramophone record of some famous singer after listening to the actual voice. In Africa the very ground itself seems to shake; awe descends on every living thing when the king announces his coming.

It was on February 20 that I told Osman my bed was coming unstitched, and that it would shortly disintegrate. Sure enough at about 2.30 a.m. it did, and I spent the rest of the night, not in the best of tempers, with my head and feet in or on the bed and the rest of my anatomy on the ground. Consequently, I did not feel any great aversion to rising with the first streaks of dawn.

Our way lay along the river bank. Pools of varying size showed below the trees and bushes which fringed it. At first all was grey and uniform but as the dawn grew brighter colour began to make itself felt, though there is but little colour in the Sudan. A few ariel flitted like shadows at our approach, and beyond them reed-buck, water-buck, and roan. Presently across the wide expanse of the river bed we saw figures moving. They turned out to be a young officer, H., on his way down to the Abyssinian border, and two native soldiers, fine, smart-looking men. He, too, was after lion, and after a short talk we separated. A long walk, during which I saw nothing I wanted to shoot, followed. The game was scattered, as, owing to the previous season being very wet, every maya or swamp was full. Consequently animals did not have to come to the river in order to get water, and were not nearly so localised as would otherwise have been the case. Some of these mayas were very beautiful, full of bird life, with water-buck and gazelle feeding round their edges.

It was very near the spot where I had first met him that I suddenly saw H., accompanied by his satellites, running towards me along the top of the river bank. He made a gesture of annoyance as he caught sight of us, nor did I wonder when I heard the reason. Just below the bank was a narrow pool some 50 yards long. Not three minutes before our unwelcome advent he had caught sight of a lion and lioness drinking at its edge. They had dashed up the bank, and must have passed within a few yards of us in the long grass. He took our arrival extremely well, and as they could not have gone far, suggested that we should endeavour to drive them out of the long grass. We accordingly drew lots for position, and waited to see the result. One of the soldiers saw the lioness poke her head out on the edge of the grass close to where I was standing, but she hastily withdrew and we saw neither.

Shooting a good reed-buck on the way, I returned to camp, where we held a council of war, and decided to move higher up the river and to try for these lions again. I was glad to hear later that H. had succeeded in getting one elsewhere.

Our next camp was close to a huge baobab tree, and I again spent a bad night, as we were invaded by an army of ants, which somehow managed to crawl under our nets and covered our bedding, our beds, and ourselves before we discovered their presence.

Some baboons played in the river bed, which stretched in a wide sweep just below the bank on which the camp was situated, and as we started in the afternoon marabout storks wandered off across the dry sand. Walking together, with hunched shoulders, they always reminded me of old club roués telling each other in raucous undertones salacious stories, and full of vain regrets that they were no longer able to indulge in the excesses of their misspent youth. A large island full of little bays and creeks of sand rose above the river bed. The grass had been burnt, and by the time we had explored its length we were all blackened from the charred stems. Crocodiles made sullen dives into the pools at whose edges they had been basking, but much as I love shooting a crocodile, we left them undisturbed.

Just after seeing two oribi in a charming little green glade which the fire had spared we came out into the bare expanse of sand which I had got to know so well. There were a good many lion tracks showing, and in the shadow of the bank El Nur motioned me to sit. The opposite bank was a good 200 yards off, some 15 feet high, and with a shallow pool stretching below it.

For some time we sat there smoking quietly. It was very still, and I revelled in the warmth and wondered when it would indeed be my luck to see a lion. There was a fly which annoyed me, and I kept striking at it with my hand.

Suddenly one of the shikaris muttered something. I felt El Nur pull at my rifle and say, "Shoot!"

I looked across at the far bank. Something big and yellow in the last dying rays of the sun flashed over its edge. Then El Nur whispered, "Etnen!" (Two!) A second great yellow form, bigger even at that distance than the first, followed.

I thought, "They're lions. I must take the second. The first was the lioness." He was crouching at the bottom of the bank above the pool, three-quarters on, facing me. I thought again, "I mustn't miss. It's a lion!" and cuddled down to the rifle. He fell over and lay growling in the mud. The lioness raised her head and stood gazing. The shot struck the bank just over her back, and in a second she was up it and out of sight. But the lion lay there. We went cautiously across to him. I fired again and struck him in the chest, but still he lived, and another shot went through his forearm lying across his chest. Then it was that I realised how even hunters of experience have been killed by wounded lions. He raised his head, which I had thought incapable of movement, and with a savage snarl gripped the forearm in his teeth. For a few seconds he growled and tore at it, and then lay still; but in those few seconds he could have done a man to death.

El Nur said he was twenty, and certainly he was a big full-grown lion in good condition. He had no mane—very few lions in the Sudan have (the finest maned lion I have ever seen is in the Zoo in Edinburgh); but he was the first lion I had ever killed, and for this alone I cherish the recollection of that evening more than that of any other.

I was very lucky. Apart from the distance, I was in an ideal position, sitting comfortably and shooting off my knees; I was not perspiring, always an added handicap to those who have to wear glasses; the light was quite good; I had an unrestricted field of fire if anything had gone wrong; and last, but not least, there was a large pool of water between me and the lion!

Looking back, the things which struck me most were

the bright, blazing gold of the two as they came over the bank; the very much larger size of the lion as compared with his mate; and the ease and speed with which they negotiated the 15-foot bank, especially the rapidity with which the lioness disappeared after the shot.

There is a verse in Proverbs, which reads: "The slothful man saith, There is a lion without; I shall be slain in the streets." I wish he would say it now.

XXVIII. MY FAVOURITE AUTHOR

"Shall this fellow come into my house?"—1 SAM. xii. 15

M Y friend Cheviot, whose writing lends distinction
to any sporting topic which engages his attention,
has his favourite author. Of him I am never tired
of reading whether he is "flogging the chalk streams of
Knoydart" or "driving off the first tee in the Open Cham-
pionship at Blackmount." Indeed I live in hopes that
Cheviot will one day devote an entire volume to his doings.
It would make the world a brighter place. There is a
standard in everything and no author can hope to rival the
classic sentence which a friend of mine loved to quote. It is
this: "It was a frosty July morning. Ping! Ping! went his
trusty Remington. Two grouse lay dead in the stubble."
Short, concise and an admirable choice of words. The scene
jumps to the eye. The frosty stubble, the covey cowering
in the foreground, the eagle glance of the sportsman upon
them, and the swift and dramatic close.

Harry Graham came very near equalling it in "A Complete Sportsman," which appeared in the old *Badminton*

Magazine. In a footnote he explains that though for years past he has been a keen student of some of the leading lady novelists he has never been jealous of their fame, admitting at the same time an ardent ambition to emulate it.

Clarence Fitzluce, his hero, takes long draughts at a foaming tumbler of *crème de menthe*, while sitting in his tent waiting for Lady Milicia Carlew. The estate of the latter in Yorkshire was well stocked with game.

Woodcock, coots, bandicoots, grouse, fieldfare, ptarmigan, teal, pigeon, widgeon, nightjars, capercailzie, water-rats, and red, white and blue hares abounded. Owls and otters were also fairly numerous, while among the various forms of sport which the place provided were pea-shooting, paddling, fishing and fried fishing, trawling with a dry worm for crabs, sculling the houseboat, archery, and the use of the puff-dart.

In spite of these attractions Fitzluce is bored with the lady. Taking her for a ride in his jinrickshaw he brings her to the very brink of a precipice, and with his cold nose laid against her face, and his arms around her, hurls himself into the abyss.

With a crash the two bodies descended upon the head of the village idiot, who was tending his flocks in the valley below.
The two backbones snapped together in perfect unison.

Fitzluce, I fancy, must have been up at Oxford and Cambridge with the gentleman who stepped lightly on to his college barge and paddled rapidly down to Iffley. This was the same oar who formed one of the crew in the 'Varsity boat race "when all rowed fast, but none so fast as he." But these are heights to which but few authors on sport can attain. Cheviot's friend as a rule confines himself to chronicling the doings of those favourites of fortune who are constantly engaged in the pursuit of "the little brown bird," "the little red bird," or "the little black bird," to say nothing of "the little blue bird" for which we are all searching. He very seldom, if ever, lends his facile pen to the description of a day's stalking.

I, also, have a favourite author, but all too rarely does he appear. I fancy he must be a friend of the friend of Cheviot. He has not quite so wide a field as his colleague, yet he manages to get in some wonderfully deft touches.

He is a real sportsman, for directly he hears the "belling of the first stag, he lays his rifle in the rack." He likes a forest, too, where there are plenty of grouse. "On most of the noted deer forests the grouse has been totally eliminated, lest his startled 'Kebec—bec—bec' should give warning of the advent of an enemy. Thus the stalker scores an unfair advantage."

Having got a forest with plenty of grouse in it, he makes sure that—since "the wild goat which used to share the hilltops with the red deer has almost disappeared"—there is a fine stock of sheep on the ground. This is to ensure that when the stalkers are getting near, the sheep "may give warning to the quarry"! Otherwise it is all much too easy and anyone can go out and knock over stags like rabbits. We all know that stalking can be pretty hard work, and my favourite author believes in fortifying the inner man before leaving his real Highland lodge. "He eats the breakfast of health, hope and good conscience." I should love to know what he eats when he is not feeling quite the thing; when he is a bit pessimistic, and his conscience is pricking him.

This is what he has when things are going well and he has that Kruschen feeling. "Porridge, milk, tea *and* coffee, fried eggs, hashed venison, finnan haddock, ham (he does not confide why he eats them in the above order), and finally a glass of splendid water, with perhaps a 'wee drappie' to qualify it for the stomach's sake." The poor stomach would want a bit of qualifying after the above menu!

While he is digesting his little snack, Donal' and Sandy are sitting in the heather spying the face of the hill opposite. They know exactly what to do and have everything ready— the ponies, dogs, rifle, mackintosh coat, and "a well-furnished luncheon basket for all hands." I expect when

Donal' and Sandy knew the sort of breakfast their employer devoured they struck when he suggested they should only take sandwiches for lunch.

Anyhow, in due course he joins them, and strangely enough he finds the attendants' pace a little "too—too"!

"Practically preserved deer on private property" are "more constantly disturbed than they are likely to be on the boundless, lonely veldt," and "have their watchful faculties kept more on the alert by constant training." He means, I fancy, that if they show the slightest sign of having a bit of a slack and think they are back on the "boundless, lonely veldt," Donal' and Sandy are on to them at once and shoo them away, in case they display any likelihood of not being up to the mark in watchfulness! When the stalkers reach an elevation which commands a wide expanse of deer-haunted territory they all settle down to a spy. Some "grand heads" and "deep girths are seen"; "a royal is spotted," but "half a dozen of these pests of hinds" block the way.

My author has a great time with the royal and misses him three times, but gets him with the fourth barrel, while honest Donal's face positively "glows and effervesces with delight and pride." He must have been having a go at the "well-furnished luncheon basket."

Jamie, who I think must live in a different forest, is another henchman who attends him. He is even cleverer than Donal' or Sandy. He crosses "the track of a great hart, in fact a royal." You see, he knows at once from the slot that it is a royal!

"The sporting ardour of the Saxon deer stalker" is roused at once and at sunrise he sallies forth with rifle, attendant and dog.

"After a tedious and bucketing toil, onwards and upwards, during which every corrie in the neighbourhood is vainly searched with glasses, Jamie suddenly stops with a Gaelic exclamation, and points—merely points—but, oh! so eloquently!" and there is the largest slot master or man has ever seen!

Not having seen any other slot marks it is quite easy to realise at once that this one was made by the royal.

So they track him down to a little burn where he is "couched." You see, he knows all the technical terms! The Saxon sportsman thinks at first he is looking at a bundle of sticks, but no! "it is a great big-bodied deer with a huge head, bearing brow, bay, and tray with three 'crockets' on each side. What a stretch of antler! What a mane! Up with the rifle!" But he didn't "up" it quite quick enough and Jamie and the dog, who have gone round to a pass which he would make for if disturbed, have moved two fine stags, and alarmed by this the gentleman with the crockets and the mane is off.

The next morning at daybreak the attack is resumed. It entails "stumbling, slipping, and crawling in the beds of burns; escalading, scrambling, prostration, painful contortions, great physical exertion, sodden garments and chilled limbs; wet, weariness and abrasions." At last the spoor, track or slot (the Saxon sportsman is determined to let you see that he knows what he is talking about!) is picked up again. Animation revives. The track, spoor or slot is followed. "Valleys are crossed; hills are mastered and surmounted. From a craggy summit a deer is seen lying on a black bare hillock." With all those hills and valleys to choose from you would not expect him to select a black and bare hillock to lie on! "Out with the glass! Joy! It is the stag—the coveted prize, but in a position not easily approachable." That was his cunning in choosing the black and bare hillock!

Jamie is such a good stalker, however, that he brings the Saxon up to within two hundred yards of the noble deer. Here he takes breath and screws up his nerves. "Then he kicks a stone, upon which the stag rises, and gazing intently in the opposite direction presents his 'single' (or rudimentary tail) to the marksman." I thought all the time the Saxon was stalking a red deer, but the rudimentary tail I must confess shook me.

It was a remarkably astute move on the part of the cunning animal, whatever its species. He must have realised what a sportsman was on his track.

"This will not do. You may cruelly wound but you cannot kill a stag from the rear. Another stone is clattered. The stag throws up his beamed frontlet and wheels about, standing momentarily with his flank to the enemy." That settles it, and the Saxon and Jamie and the dog return home in triumph.

I wonder what sort of a dinner they had that night!

XXIX. NOTES ON SOME FIRST-CLASS ROE HEADS .

"Some achieve greatness." TWELFTH NIGHT—William Shakespeare

THE roe has always been the most badly treated of our game animals. As a beast of venery he ranks more highly than any of those who have studied his ways. He is far harder to stalk than the red deer and a really good roe head has always been a great rarity. The roe heads of old were no better, so far as one can ascertain, than those of their modern descendants, though it is not easy to judge, as few roe heads killed by our ancestors have been preserved.

We have to go to the Continent to learn in what manner the roe should be treated. There they are appreciated at their true worth and foreign sportsmen are horrified when they learn how the roe is estimated here. Real roe stalkers in these islands are but few. The roe is looked on, primarily, as a potential source of damage to plantations, ornamental trees and agriculture, though the damage done by them is not comparable to that caused by red deer. That they do cause damage to young plantations cannot, unfortunately, be denied, but to nothing like the same extent as do rabbits. They have no more inveterate enemy than the Forestry Commission.

It has always appeared to me wrong that in this country the preservation of game and the practice of forestry appear to be irreconcilable. On the Continent both trees and game flourish together.

A foreign sportsman once said to me, "Roe and red deer are, of course, responsible for some damage to trees, but we like to see them and if some trees are spoiled, what does it really matter in the long run when we can see the deer stealing out into the open glades in the evenings to feed in the meadows? That surely is worth something, even if it has no monetary value." It is a point of view with which I have always been in complete sympathy but one which appears to be extremely unpopular.

The numbers of roe were never, of course, comparable to those of red deer before the war. They are much more localised, are not nearly so often seen, and require much greater skill to stalk. Roe, indeed, can live quite close to human habitations without being seen at all and without their identity being recognised. They are lovely little beasts and a good roe head has always been hard to secure. I may, perhaps, speak with some experience as I have been trying to find a first-class roe head for fifty years and have never seen one in the flesh.

The nearest I ever got to it was one day at Altyre in July 1935. I was alone as my host and hostess had gone away for the night. It had been a dreadful day, pouring with rain and very muggy. In the evening it cleared and I decided to try for a buck.

From the edge of a road which skirted the woods I could look over a lot of ground. Beyond lay the woods of Darnaway, and the windings of the Findhorn, loveliest of Highland rivers; to the north the Culbin sands and the Firth, the Black Isle and the hills of Sutherland; with Wyvis and Strath Conon to the west. How my heart aches for it all when its loveliness is out of reach! Below the road the ground sloped steeply to a hollow thickly grown with bracken and birch. At one end rose a stone dyke which curved round to a bank running in a wide circle bounding a field of corn. Below the bank was a ditch and all along its edge a thick jungle of whins and junipers divided from a thicket of birch beyond by a narrow path. The cornfield sloped steeply and finished in grassy open spaces, more birches and clumps of trees, beyond which lay the keeper's cottage.

It was in the cornfield or along its edge that I hoped to find roe.

A drizzle had started again and it was very hot. Wiping my glasses, always a great drawback to a short-sighted stalker, I proceeded to spy. Above the corn a head suddenly came into view and bobbed down again before I could get my glass on it. I marked the place. Presently it reappeared. A doe, her black-tipped ears pointing forward. I could see her little black muzzle, with the two fascinating little white spots on the upper lip working regularly as she chewed. Then the head disappeared. I began to feel hopeful. A doe at the end of July should surely mean a buck was somewhere near. Carefully I spied the edge of the corn, for the buck usually feeds close to cover into which he can disappear with a bound if disturbed. Then I saw a patch of red, half-hidden, close to the ditch. It was a buck's hind-quarters, as I could tell by the size. It remained almost motionless. For several minutes I kept my glass glued on it. Then, suddenly, beyond it, a head was sharply raised, turning to where the doe fed in the corn. It was a buck and I knew from the length of horn showing above the tips of the ears, a good one. The head disappeared and again I waited.

At length, after another long wait, it showed again. It was a good head, a very good head with long, rough, thick horns, but marred by short, sharp-pointed brow points, and narrow span. The curve of the hill and the fact that he was feeding in the ditch, apart from the presence of the doe, rendered it impossible to obtain a shot from the edge of the dyke from which he was distant, perhaps, 150 yards. Had it been otherwise the stalk would not have been difficult once I had got under cover of the birches below me, as I had good cover right up to the dyke. My only course was to reach its shelter and endeavour to get through the tangle of whins above the bank at a point where the curve of the latter did not prevent me from getting a clear view.

In a quarter of an hour, after the final look to make quite sure that they were not disturbed, I reached the dyke and found, as I had expected, that I could see nothing. I crept round the curve of the field following the whins. They were very thick, interspersed with nettles, and effectively hid anything beyond. It seemed unlikely that I could get through them without disturbing the roe, but it was my only chance. Accordingly I crept slowly until I reached a spot from which I thought I might be able to see the buck within shot below me on the edge of the ditch.

It took me half an hour to advance 20 yards. I was dripping with perspiration, my glasses were thick with steam, and I was wringing wet. I had another 3 yards to go, when suddenly, 30 yards distant, straight opposite to me in the corn, shot up the head of the doe. Fortunately, although she stared intently in my direction, she did not appear to see me. Hot and miserable I glared at her blurred image. Then the head bobbed down and I breathed again, for if she remained undisturbed it was more than likely that the buck was still feeding, unconcerned. Slowly and laboriously I wormed my way forward over the remaining distance, praying that the doe would remain hidden. At last I reached the edge of the bank and peered through the bracken stems.

There was the buck, his head raised, motionless, 50 yards away. The rain was pouring down and I kept reminding myself to keep calm and aim low, for I knew that he was the best buck that I had ever seen. Then, as I fired, I knew he was mine.

His horns measured 10½ inches. Otherwise he was much

as I had estimated him. Had his brow been two or three inches longer he would have been a first-class head, though narrow. I have never had a chance of another as good since that day.

At Altyre, where I stalked roe for so many years, most of the lovely woods have vanished since 1939, and where in pre-war days one might expect to see half a dozen bucks now, possibly, you may see one.

The number of bucks that will grow a first-class head is very small. I used to think that a buck grew his best head at the age of seven or eight, but I am inclined to think that this may be wrong and that he will attain his best horn growth when younger. There is, however, a great deal still to be learned about roe provided the present system of butchery does not exterminate them here altogether.

The late Bob Hargreaves was very fond of stalking roe on the open hillside at Gaick. Once when there, at a height of 3,000 feet or more above sea level, a buck came galloping to me, after a doe. He had a very straight narrow head, but his horns were long and I should have liked to get a shot at him. It was a very cold day with a biting wind and heavy showers. The roe galloped down the hill and lay down close to a herd of red deer. We tried to stalk and had got within 500 yards when the roe jumped up and gazed intently down the hillside. A red smudge in the long grass resolved itself into a fox cub. Then another appeared. The red deer took the alarm and moved off, the foxes vanished and the roe galloped down the hill and over the next ridge. I had never seen roe on such high ground before, but at certain times they will leave the woods and take to the open hill. Hargreaves was a great enthusiast, as are all real roe stalkers, and had a large number of heads which he had killed at Gaick, though their standard, compared to first-class trophies, was not high. I have never seen a head with first-class measurements from this district, though the pursuit of the roe in country of this type takes a lot of beating.

As I have said, our attitude to the roe strikes foreign roe

stalkers with amazement. A Polish friend of mine was staying with me recently and we were talking of roe. "What I cannot understand," said he, "is that in this country where sport is rated so high the roe is looked upon as vermin and even butchered with shotguns or snared. It is dreadful! Why is he not given his proper place as one of the best of game animals? It is a crime to shoot a fox, but not to murder a roe." I told him there were quite a number of potential vulpicides about, but even this did not mitigate his condemnation of our unsportsmanlike behaviour. I have often remarked that with regard to damage by red deer, not nearly enough attention is paid to individuality in animals. Some red deer are "gangsters" in the sense that they find that they can get a good square meal off a farmer's crop and get it. Some roe may be similarly classed but not all. Not all tigers are man-eaters. Chiefly those who are pressed for food. So with deer. If they cannot find enough food in their natural surroundings they will search for it elsewhere. There are the deer which should be relentlessly hunted *when they first start their depredations*. If left unmolested, they encourage others and so the trouble spreads. It can be much mitigated if the original marauders are checked at the outset.

Roe are not difficult to poach and they have suffered much during the war. Many of the woods in which they had made their homes have been levelled. They have been constantly disturbed and with timber camps all over the country have been hard put to it to find new quarters.

In *Hunting and Stalking the Deer* I gave the measurements of most of the first-class roe heads which I have come across at different times. I had not, when this work was published, had the opportunity of summarising the collection of roe heads at Altyre, nor had I seen the late Mr. Macpherson-Grant's collection at Craigo. This chapter is really complementary to those on the roe in *Hunting and Stalking the Deer*, as it seems a pity that there should not be some permanent record of these heads. In addition to these two collections I have included the measurements of several other first-class heads which have been killed in recent years.

The Altyre collection of roe heads is certainly the best in this country, and when the late Sir William Gordon Cumming was kind enough to say that I might sketch and measure them, I was more than ready to take advantage of his offer.

There are well over 100 pairs of horns in the collection, so that it was no easy matter to make a selection. The twenty heads of which I give measurements are the best in the collection, though there are others which run them very close.

It is a great pity that records are not available of dates and owners, but no one paid very much attention to the heads of roe or red deer seventy or eighty years ago. Some of those at Altyre were shot by Roualeyn Gordon Cumming.

The measurements were carefully taken with a steel tape. I took great trouble and spent a good many hours in an endeavour to arrive at correct measurements. The only measurement of a head about which there can be no controversy is that from tip to tip of the horns; the others all leave a certain margin for human error. The most difficult, so far as roe horns are concerned, is "the beam." It is quite easy if you use a tape and not a steel measure, provided the horn is smooth and otherwise normal, but when you try to measure the beam of a horn like No. 14 or No. 34 or No. 45 it is very difficult to arrive at the correct measurement. For this reason: when measuring I am not at all certain that it is not more satisfactory to take the tape round the circumference of both coronets. Of course an otherwise good head may have poor coronets, but usually it will be found that a thin smooth horn tends to have small coronets, while a strong, massive, rough head will have large well-formed coronets.

The more modern heads do not equal the older ones as a general rule, though there are exceptions, in anything except length. They incline to thinness and are deficient alike in weight, beam, and roughness, though in many cases the points are good. The head found in 1926 is a notable exception, as it is quite equal to any roe at Altyre. Of the abnormal heads there are several with extra points, apart from the three-horned specimen. A nine-pointer has the back points forking into three and two points. There is one eight-pointer and three seven-pointers.

One buck has the back point of the left horn growing in front of the top point on the right horn.

It must not be thought that under the remarks I have made when commenting on the head I am in any way attempting to detract from the head in question. I am merely mentioning any point which strikes me when looking at it. Very nearly every head, if not every head, of which I have given measurements is first-class, and I am judging them by a first-class or super-first-class standard. Length, of course, is practically essential—I mean one could not call a 7-inch roe head first-class, though it might be thick, rough, with long points and good shape. On the other hand, an 11-inch head might be thin, smooth, with moderate points and ugly shape. Probably such a head would not be first-class. I was looking at a head recently which has all the qualities for a first-class head, save beam, and though I should call it first-class others might not. If I had shot it myself I should probably take it to bed with me, though the owner has left it lying on a shelf in Inverness for the last sixteen years! Again, the shortest head in the Macpherson-Grant collection in the "good" class is certainly the *prettiest* head he had killed; and quite one of the most attractive heads in the late Colonel Hamilton Leigh's collection of roe has a very similar length measurement, namely $8\frac{1}{2}$ inches. I am not at all sure that both these heads should not be considered first-class, though as a rule nothing under 9 inches is considered as being worthy of inclusion.

The late G. B. Macpherson-Grant's roe, of which I give measurements, were all, with the exception of the head from Aldourie, killed at Ballindalloch by himself. All the 204 bucks in the collection, with one exception, were killed by himself with the rifle. In the late 'nineties and early nineteen hundreds the woods in this locality held large numbers of roe. Thirty-seven were killed in one season by fair stalking, and General H. Pelham Burn, who knew Ballindalloch well in the old days, tells me that he has seen twenty-five bucks in a morning's stalking. Mr. Macpherson-Grant killed seventeen to his own rifle in·one season; once, between 7 p.m. and 5 a.m., killing six bucks and again, during another night, five. In this season he also killed seventeen salmon and was

SOME WEIGHTS OF ROE KILLED BY G. B. MACPHERSON-GRANT
BETWEEN 1889 AND 1910, MOSTLY AT BALLINDALLOCH

Weight when killed. (Some slight allowance can be made for loss of blood.) (lbs.)	Weight after being gralloched. (lbs.)	Carcase weight ready for larder (head, neck, and lower part of legs removed). (lbs.)
63	53	---
57	$48\frac{1}{2}$	35
62	$51\frac{1}{2}$	$34\frac{1}{2}$
58	—	33
55	46	$30\frac{1}{2}$
55	$46\frac{1}{2}$	$30\frac{1}{2}$
51	43	$29\frac{1}{2}$
50	42	29
58	—	33
54	46	30
53	$45\frac{1}{2}$	29
40	33	24
$49\frac{1}{2}$	42	28
64	—	38
62	52	—
57	48	35
53	47	$32\frac{1}{2}$
51	$45\frac{1}{2}$	29

at the death of 1,000 brace of grouse during three months' leave from the Sudan. In his best season's roe stalking he killed twenty-three bucks. The best record in weight for a Scottish roebuck which he can furnish is 66 lbs. He has been kind enough to furnish me with the weights of 100 bucks mostly killed at Ballindalloch. From this it is apparent that the average weight of the bucks in this district is roughly rather more than 50 lbs., and that from 8 lbs. to 10 lbs. may be allowed for gralloch. It is a most interesting and instructive record, for, so far as I know, no other roe hunter has ever taken the trouble to keep such exhaustive particulars.

Readers of the sporting press will recollect articles appearing at times under such headings as "Sport (*sic*) with the Roe"—"An Off-day after Roe," etc. These, as a rule, give nauseating descriptions of wholesale butcheries, usually dignified by the name of keepers' shoots, in which the wretched roe are murdered or wounded by shot-guns. These battues may be necessary, though none the less to be lamented. That they are not new, the following extracts will show, taken from the Ballimore Game Book from which I am permitted to quote.

Date.	Locality.		No. of Roe killed.
Nov. 26, 1876	Beaufort, Boblainie		32
„ 29, 1877	„	„	39
Oct. 8, 1878	Pitcroy		17
Nov. 20, 1879	Beaufort	„	35
Dec. 2, 1880	„	Farley	30
Nov. 20, 1884	„	Boblainie	19
„ 21, „	„	Ruttal	14
„ 25, 1885	„	Farley	42
„ 10, 1887	„	Fanellan	8
„ 15, „	„	Ruttal	11
„ 17, „	„	Boblainie	13
„ 18, „	„	Farley	45

I do not suppose there is a single place in Scotland where such numbers could be equalled at the present day. It makes one's mouth water to think of the sport one might have had!

Roe, foresters will tell you, have to be killed down where there are young plantations, and if no one takes the trouble to stalk them, the only means of extermination is the shot-gun. Very few of those who take part in such massacres know anything about roe, and take wild shots at any beast that is seen, quite regardless of the range. It should at least

BY THE BURN—ALTYRE

be stipulated that buck-shot should be used and that no roe should be fired at at a range exceeding 25 yards.

The rifle is, of course, the only weapon that should be aimed at a roe and, in my opinion, not a ·22. Granted that he can be easily killed with a ·22, it is also even easier to wound him with such a weapon. I have known a rhinoceros killed with a ·38 pistol, but no one would seriously consider the cultivation of their pursuit with a fire-arm of this description unless he wished to qualify for the local cemetery. I have never stalked roe with a ·22 myself, chiefly because, apart from the subsequent misery to oneself and the animal consequent on a bad shot, there has always been present the thought that I might see the buck of my dreams and that I should be unable to approach sufficiently close to make certain of killing him. And I do not like getting very close to a roebuck. A stag is different. He is a larger animal, and is blessed or cursed with that fatal feminine curiosity which has been the undoing of so many attractive creatures! A roe has one look, makes up his mind, and is off in a second. It is far better, therefore, to use a larger rifle, when, if your beast is hit, you are much more certain of getting him. After all, a stalker is not running a butcher's shop, and much as I like roe venison, I would sooner spoil a certain amount of meat with a heavier bullet than run the risk of losing a wounded animal.

I can see no really good reason for using a very light rifle for roe, and everything in favour of a larger bore. To avoid the usual massacre, a friend of mine attempted to course roe with deerhounds last year. He only had one course in which the roe had a long start. The deer and the hound travelled about the same pace, and the same distance apart after a 200 yards chase over newly-planted ground with fairly long heather. The hound probably would have caught his quarry in another hundred yards or so, but took a bad fall, rolling right over and unsighting the deer.

With regard to the few other heads whose measurements I give, there is not much to say. Mr. Ewan Macpherson-Grant has set himself a high standard to live up to with his

x

first roe. Mr. Grigor Grant's head is the best I have seen from Rothiemurchus. Mrs. Eden's massive head is interesting as, though it shows traces of shedding the horns, these were still firmly fixed to the skull on February 18. This, so far as I know, is quite exceptionally late for a roebuck to have horns. Mrs. Eden tells me that on March 14 of the same year another buck was seen still carrying his horns. Previous to this I had never heard of a roe with horns after Christmas Day, when many years ago one was killed at Erchless and the horns fell off. As regards cleaning the velvet, a roe was killed at Ballindalloch with clean horns on March 27th and had been clean some days. This again is extraordinarily early.

My best thanks are due to those who have allowed me to include measurements of their heads and, in particular, to Lady Gordon Cumming of Altyre. Prior to his lamented death in 1942 Alastair Gordon Cumming asked for my help in arranging and hanging the roe heads at Altyre. We had scarcely completed our task when the Second World War overwhelmed us. Altyre was converted into a hospital, the heads were removed and have never been rehung.

MEASUREMENTS OF SOME OF THE BEST ROE HEADS IN THE COLLECTION AT ALTYRE

	Length (in.).	Tip to tip (in.).	Circumference round both coronets (in.).	
No. 12	$11\frac{1}{2}$	$7\frac{1}{4}$	$8\frac{1}{4}$	Brows: R. $3\frac{1}{8}$, L. 4. Tops: R. 4, L. $3\frac{3}{4}$. Back: R. 3, L. $2\frac{7}{8}$. Beautiful shape. Perfect points. Smooth outside and small coronets.
No. 50	$10\frac{3}{4}$	$5\frac{7}{8}$	9	Rather thin, and the left brow short.
U.	$10\frac{1}{2}$	$2\frac{3}{4}$	8	Tops: $4\frac{1}{4}$. An old head. Back points slightly irregular.
No. 43	$10\frac{3}{8}$	$6\frac{5}{8}$	$9\frac{5}{8}$	Great length between brows and tops.
C.	$10\frac{3}{8}$	$5\frac{5}{8}$	$8\frac{1}{4}$	L. Top, 4–$5\frac{5}{8}$. Points 4×3. Rather smooth and not very massive. Extra point posterior edge of right horn between brow and back point.
No. 37	$10\frac{1}{4}$	$6\frac{1}{4}$	$8\frac{1}{2}$	Great length between brow and tops.

	Length (in.).	Tip to tip (in.).	Circumference round both coronets (in.).	
No. 45	10⅛	5⅞	8½	R. Brow, 3¾. Rough, thick, and with fine points. A perfect head.
Found 1926	10⅛	5¼	7¾	Found dead in 1926. A strong, heavy head equal to any of those in the collection. A very fine typical roebuck.
No. 7	10⅛	3⅛	8½	Good points.
No. 4	10	4	8½	Brows: R. 4½, L. 4½. Tops: R. 3½, L. 4⅛. Back: R. 3, L. 3. Points 3 × 4. Magnificent brows and all the points very fine. Not quite such good shape as No. 12.
No. 8	10	5½	6¾	A wild head with good points. Small coronets. Very long back points. The extra point on the exterior edge between top and back points forms a cup on right horn.
Collection of R.G.C.	10	6	9½	From Pittyvaich, and probably belonged to Roualeyn Gordon Cumming. Good rough horn and fine coronets.
Killed by poacher	10	5¼	7¾	Shot by a poacher and given to Sir W. Gordon Cumming, Bt., by J. G. Millais. Thin compared to some of the heads, but a perfect example.
Collection of R.G.C.	10	6½	9	Shot by Roualeyn Gordon Cumming, with the date 1866 on the back. Good shape, but rather thin.
No. 34	9¾	7¼	9	Very massive, with long points.
No. 14	9⅝	5¾	10¼	Very strong, exceptionally rough right up to the back points, and splendid coronets. The most massive head in the collection.
D.	9½	6	9½	From Roualeyn's or Col. W. Gordon Cumming's collection. Points 6 × 3. Very massive. Good-shaped right horn. The brow forks into three points.
Three-horned roe	9⅜	2¾	—	Three horns, with three distinct coronets. Third horn 7⅝ long, is much better than is usually found in the case of three-horned roe.
No. 33	9⅜	6	7½	A very pretty head, thin, but wild, and with curling points.
B.	9	3½	9½	Very thick, massive and rough.
Malformed head	—	—	—	Semi-perruque head, partially covered with velvet and partially clean, about 8 in. in length, has a large number of points, probably about 11, though it is difficult to ascertain. The coronets merge into a heavy mass of horn, the extra points forming at the posterior base of the horns themselves. The horn is quite hard and shows at the tips. No history is available, but it is quite evident that the buck was injured in the genital organs.

Measurements of some Roe Heads from the Collection of G. B. Macpherson-Grant of Craigo

Date.	Length (in.).	Tip to tip (in.).	Circumference. Both coronets. (in.).	Locality.		Weight (lbs.).
29/10/96	11	$6\frac{1}{2}$	9	Christie	A beautiful head. Thick, rough and all points good.	—
28/9/09	$10\frac{3}{8}$	4	8	Aldourie	R. top and L. brow short.	—
21/7/06	$10\frac{1}{4}$	5	8	Pitchaish Burn	Short brows, good shape.	46
8/6/13	10	4	$7\frac{3}{4}$	Weiroch	Rather smooth.	55
3/4/99	10	5	† $3\frac{1}{4}$	Christie	Good normal type, strong horn, rough and good shape.	—
29/4/01	$9\frac{3}{4}$	$4\frac{1}{2}$	$7\frac{3}{8}$	Phonas-Culfoich	Very good, normal type.	—
10/6/03	$9\frac{3}{4}$	$4\frac{3}{4}$	$8\frac{3}{8}$	Drum of Carron	Brow $3\frac{3}{4}$. Very good rough normal head. All points good.	42 clean
16/6/03	$9\frac{3}{4}$	$5\frac{1}{4}$	$8\frac{3}{8}$	Tom-na-Glein	Brows, $3\frac{1}{4}$. Rather smooth.	62
15/9/98	$9\frac{5}{8}$	$4\frac{1}{2}$	† 3	Tom-na-Glein	Similar to the buck killed 12/7/97, but rather weak back points. Good, rough horn. A strong head of nice shape.	—
7/8/03	$9\frac{1}{2}$	$5\frac{1}{4}$	† $3\frac{1}{8}$	Phonas	L. brow, $3\frac{1}{2}$. R. brow missing, but a strong "offer" below point where brow should be. Otherwise perfect and a strong, rough head.	50
9/6/03	$9\frac{3}{8}$	6	$6\frac{1}{2}$	Phonas	A very good, normal head, but rather smooth.	57
12/7/97	$9\frac{1}{4}$	$5\frac{1}{4}$	$3\frac{1}{8}$	Craigroy	Very good, normal type. Strong horn and good shape. This head, and those killed 15/9/98 and 3/4/99 are similar in type, though this has the best shape. They are possibly the three best after that killed 29/10/96.	—
19/7/98	$9\frac{1}{4}$	$6\frac{3}{4}$	9	Tom Farclas	The head of this buck was full of shot when killed. The malformed points were 4 in. and $3\frac{3}{4}$ in. long.	50
—	$9\frac{1}{4}$	8	† $2\frac{3}{4}$	Drum	Very good shape, rough but rather thin, and the back points short.	52
6/10/00	$8\frac{5}{8}$	5	† $3\frac{1}{2}$	Phonas	A perfect head, rough, thick, and of good shape. Only lacking in length. The prettiest head in the collection.	55

† Beam of horn.

Some First-Class Roe Heads—Various Owners

Date.	Length (in.).	Tip to tip (in.).	Circumference. Both coronets (in.).	Locality.		Owner.
1927	$11\frac{1}{2}$	$4\frac{7}{8}$	10	Ardoch	All good points, but rather thin horn.	Lord Kensington
1927	$10\frac{3}{8}$	$3\frac{1}{4}$	† $3\frac{1}{4}$	Inchriach	Very rough and "pearled," rather spoilt by the tops turning in and a broken brow point on the left horn, which is shorter than the right.	E. Macpherson-Grant
1922	10	7	$7\frac{1}{2}$	Rothiemurchus	Brows: R. $2\frac{3}{4}$, L. $2\frac{3}{4}$. Tops: R. $3\frac{3}{4}$, L. $3\frac{3}{8}$. Back points: R. 2, L. 2. A very symmetrical well-shaped head.	Grigor Grant
18/2/25	$9\frac{1}{2}$	4	9	Cromlix	A very strong, massive head and rough horns. The right top is rather short.	Mrs. Terence Eden
1927	$9\frac{1}{2}$	$4\frac{7}{8}$	$9\frac{1}{2}$	Kilty	Very thick horn. The left horn is the better of the two.	W. Davidson
1928	$11\frac{1}{2}$ and 11	7	$8\frac{3}{4}$	Pitgaveney	Brows, 4. Tops, 4 and $4\frac{3}{8}$. Back points $3\frac{1}{4}$. Thick, rough and beautiful shape with perfect symmetry. Equal to any Scottish roe head I have ever seen.	C. J. Tegner
1929	$10\frac{1}{2}$	—	—	Stonehill Wood —Douglas	Long perfect points. Rough. A first-class head. Equal to the biggest ever shot here by Lord Home, Sept. 19th, 1898.	Hon. W. Douglas-Home

† Beam of horn.

XXX. THE POWER OF THE HILLS

"Yet I say, never morn broke clear as those."
                              PAULINE—R. Browning

THE conditions and incidents of life have changed so
greatly during the past sixty years that we who have
lived through them might well be living in another
world. Not recently did we realise that we were being overtaken, that youth was forever pressing on our heels, that no
longer were we the pursuing but the pursued. Our little
peculiarities and foibles, part of the generation to which we
belonged and on which we may have prided ourselves when
in the company of our contemporaries, are superseded and
out of date. A settled existence, such as was enjoyed by our
fathers, can no longer be looked for by our sons; leisure,
though never so sought after, is at a discount and harassed
and bewildered we walk amid surroundings that are alien to
us. In every walk such changes are apparent—in the town
or in the country, in our streets and in our houses, in our
work and in such play as is left to us. No longer can we
regard such changes with equanimity; they have come about
too violently and too subversively and there are few brought

326

up as was I who are not *laudatores temporis acti* of the most pronounced kind, though on broad principles they may approve wholeheartedly of many of the changes which they have witnessed. In no variety of sport do such changes show more clearly than in shooting. The modern twelve-bore is as different from its predecessors as is a day's grouse-shooting with all its accessories to the day over dogs which constituted that sport for a former generation. Luxurious shooting-lodges have ousted the modest dwellings to which Brixey and Fribbles were so successfully enticed by Captain Downey; and though there are many who, from necessity or choice, still remain faithful to the old-fashioned form, wherever practicable driving has been adopted.

One may not, perhaps, clasp hands enthusiastically with the anonymous gentleman who, under the designation of "Venator," "Sport for Sport's Sake," or some similar signature, so often makes his appearance about November in the sporting papers. During the preceding ten weeks he lies low and takes whatever the gods may give; then, deriding modern sport and its appurtenances, he demands with an appearance of heroic scorn his bread and cheese, his trusty spaniel Don, and a spot to which he euphemistically alludes as his "bit of bog," concluding with "I think, Sir, you will admit that for real sport such a day is hard to beat!"

Yet he shows the right spirit, for in a desire to return to Nature lies the essence of true sport, and the more closely akin to Nature that sport is, the more inherent it is in a man to love it with the best part of himself. So it comes about that there is a touch of passivity in driving, a sense of artificiality which is lacking in other forms of shooting. No knowledge of Nature is demanded of the participant; his station is allotted him, and if he be a skilful shot, he will acquit himself as favourably in his own eyes as he whose knowledge of the habits of game avails him so little. The actual shot is far more sporting, requires far greater skill and practice, and therein lies its charm. But upon the man himself, on the individual unit, less depends. The day's bag will,

it is true, suffer from the absence of a good shot, yet where
seven or eight guns are concerned there can never be the
same sense of comradeship and personal satisfaction as when
two who know each other intimately are out together on a
good dogging moor.

The Twelfth! There is only one Twelfth in the calendar
for many of us—the other eleven are colourless dates—but
into that one Twelfth is crammed all the romance and colour
which ever our boyhood's dreams have evolved. I know
staid and sober men of middle age, from whom romance
might be thought to have fled, had they indeed ever heard
the rustle of his fairy wings, who solemnly and of set purpose head their correspondence on this date, "St. Grouse's
Day." Indeed they might burn candles at many a shrine less
worthy, for who, recalling those Twelfths that are past and
companions of old, could fail to let his better self arise?
Many a sportsman has been broken to sport on this day of
all days. Who does not remember as a boy that wonderful
journey north, school and restrictions left behind, the open
hill and the free air of heaven before him for two blissful
months, all the expectations which such thoughts aroused
focused and magnified in the almost solemn joy which took
possession of one's whole being on first stepping again
upon the purple heather? The anxious dread that the morning would be wet; that the "women"—ungallant youth and
yet how wise!—would be allowed to participate in the day's
sport; and finally, last and greatest fear of all, that we ourselves would shoot badly! If only a confiding covey would
rest peacefully in the heather until we were well within
range! Better still, if instead of one belated little coward
lurking hidden after his relations had vanished, the entire
family should share his mental attitude and rising singly,
fall, one by one, easy victims to our deadly aim!

What was the advice in some old book on shooting black-
game? "The greyhen will rise first. Aim carefully at her eye.
If your aim be true she will fall; *when the rest of the brood can
be served in like manner.*" Could anything be simpler? But

when the confiding birds did not act so obligingly? When a solitary cock rose with a defiant challenge just far enough out to make a shot difficult, and just close enough to tempt one? If your bird—what triumph if he fell! What desolation and bitter regret if he escaped unscathed or, worse still, flinched and carried on.

Who does not remember his first grouse? The thrill with which he saw it fall; the jealous fear that someone to whom such killing was a matter of everyday occurrence might claim it for his own; the restrained eagerness which strove to assume an air of careless nonchalance; and the almost reverent boyish fingers which softly stirred the red-brown feathers on the still warm breast? Each has his own particular picture to look back on as I have mine. A blue sky and a shining moor beneath. The old liver-and-white setter sedately drawing up across the flat, the rustling olive-green of the bog myrtle, the little patch of mountain salix beneath the rocks, the keeper's uplifted hand and the tense, excited boy beside his father. The breaking of the covey, the gleam of the uplifted guns below, the double report and the crisp fluttering of wings madly beating the purple ling.

Then the glorious moment when he rose, the fool of the family, ere the guns had been reloaded (designedly, I wonder?), and he, unwitting of his reputation, came to me. I hear once more the deafening report of the little gun, and with the sudden cessation of his flight realise that he is indeed mine. I hear again the dear voice which I shall never hear before I too stand at the threshold of that Pass which leads among the everlasting hills, feel his hand upon my shoulder and see the dear face brighten. *"Ah! mihi præteritos referat si Jupiter annos!"* those are the moments which we would recall, moments which are gone for ever, when all lay before and nothing lay behind, when no regrets had poisoned memory, and he whom men call "No more— Too late— Farewell," was a stranger.

These are days whose charm lingers when other and more important events are forgotten. In *Amid the High Hills* my old friend the late Sir Hugh Fraser sought to analyse the charm of Highland sport.

But underlying all these [he writes] and perhaps more often than not quite unconsciously, there is one dominant, governing motive which is surely spiritual rather than material—the desire for environment which will uplift and ennoble, and with it bring a sense of being nearer to the pure—nearer to the things which are unseen and eternal, removed from all that is coarse and material. . . .

"One thing is certain," said a Highland keeper, "and that is that no one would be an atheist if he spent his life in the mountains." It is a true saying and more than one man has been saved because he lifted up his eyes unto the hills. Some there are who scoff at the association of sport and "the things which are unseen and eternal,"—I have met them and they were exactly what I should have expected them to be. But such things were and are very intimately connected in the minds of sportsmen of the old school, though they seldom try to formulate such thoughts. That is why, or one of the reasons why, some people prefer shooting over dogs to the more modern and up-to-date methods of a driving moor.

There are other days, too, which haunt one beside that first, days which at the time were black, though viewed in the softening perspective of the present they hold a charm unrealised. Wet, miserable, dreary days when winds came howling across the moor in angry gusts, when bedraggled dogs trailed dejectedly in the rear, when the bag was small and one's feet heavy. One grumbled at the moment. How glorious it all appears when the city throws its deadening influence about us and the breeze no longer stirs musically about the tops! Each hour and each day have memories all their own. The hot, lazy summer, when the birds lay close and shots were easy, when the bluebells peered shyly from the green of the bracken, and the soft purple folds of the heather rolled like some rich mantle to the shimmering silver of the birches. The early mornings, when the mist yet lingered on the hills or rolled lazily about the river; the first covey which ran secretly by ways known only to themselves through devious paths among the roots of heather; the midday heat; the counting of the bag and the joy of a pipe, surrounded by the still noisiness of the moor. The glimpse in the glen below of uplands rich with yellow corn, where whispering trees made bold splashes against the gold, and great shining argosies of cloud careered above in all the joy of heaven.

Or those days, later in the year, when the cold Nor'-Easter blew, and the old cocks cackled admonitory commands at the intruder from each uplifted knoll; when the tops, bare and glittering with the first snows, shone beyond the river flats, thronged with marauding bands; when above the grey stone dyke, large and black against the eastern sky, the black game made bold forays on the yellow stooks.

These are the thoughts which stir a man whose golden days have lain among the Highland hills and whose youth first gloried there in its own strength. They come across him at moments which he dreams not of, reborn, it may be, at the bidding of a summer breeze, the lines of an old song, or the lilt of some half-forgotten melody. The sight of a green curved hollow recalls them; a distant hill when the day goeth away and the evening shadows are stretched out; the tinkle of a burn, or the music of an unseen bird. He may go further afield in after life, he may

"Hear the song of the blossoms and the old chant of the sea,
    And see strange lands from under the arched white sails
        of ships."

He may, in answer to some prehistoric stirring of the blood and the ancient call of the red gods, follow mightier game in far-off climes and amid unlooked-for and beautiful surroundings. Yet such memories will never fade. It is the power of the hills which is calling him, and that is the greatest thing in the world, save only the love of a woman.

A man may change as I have said; he may even sink and be no more for a season the man he might have been, battered, tossed and weary; but so long as he keeps the love of the hills in his heart he will never be a lost soul. The hills and all that they watch over will be there waiting for him, changeless yet ever-changing, to welcome him as a mother does her child, until for the last time he comes to lie within their shadow and finds at length the peace which they foretell.

XXXI. A HIGHLAND MEMORY

"Listen, listen, the hills are calling me."—W. B. Yeats

FROM the Old House, which, you may trace by the date over the doorway, had been five years built when Prince Charles landed at Loch nan Uamh, the Glen of the Cotton Flowers lies north-west. In it links a chain of lochs famous for their fish, and through them flows a river broken by brawling burns and foaming waterfalls. Golden are the trout, pink of flesh and most resolute fighters; and these transferred to your creel on a summer evening of July store up memories which time can never obliterate. For fifteen of the twenty miles you may, if you be a plutocrat, jerk and throb your way in a Ford, but not so is the best to be got out of the journey. A man's feet are there for him to use, and there is yet a better way to be discovered for passing through a country that one loves. A stretch of moorland takes you to the road. Curlews pipe and call and lure your interest by their wide and tireless sweeps. Plovers wheel and tumble in the blue; while ever and anon the white scuts of rabbits bob and vanish in the heather. Presently the road leads to the top of the brae, a little lochan set like a jewel in the crest, a brae so steep that you seem poised on air above the strath at your feet. Precipitous, and clothed with shaggy woods, in which little green en-chanting glens peer shyly at you from the thicket, it lies so remote and inaccessible that the Reformation stopped short at your starting-point and the little church lying below in the centre of wide fields is of the old Faith, to serve the needs of those who dwell around.

You drop half a thousand feet in the space of a mile, cross a river with wide, deep pools of gold and amber, and find the strath stretch calm and peaceful on either side. To the west a tangled huddle of hills shuts it in, but eastward it spreads almost unbroken to the shores of the firth. Above you, as the road mounts beyond, rises Acharain, looking much as it did on that August day a hundred and eighty years ago, save that the trees are fewer and the bracken has increased. Poor Charles! His hopes had been shattered four months earlier, and his heart must have been heavy as he lay on the crest of the ridge, his eyes turned westward. We read that

About two o'clock on the morning of the eleventh they scrambled up a hill on the north side of the glen, and sending two of their number to find some provisions, they stayed two days in a neighbouring sheiling, waiting the return of their express to Pollewe, who at last brought them notice that a French ship had been upon the coast and that two gentlemen from on board had gone to Lochiel's country in search of H.R.H.

The house still stands which, tradition says, gave him shelter, its walls gleaming white against the surrounding fields. Beyond Acharain the glen narrows ere it opens out to a small loch; the confusion of rocks, spreading fanwise down the slope, marks a cloudburst which nearly overwhelmed the cottage standing on its brink.

Round a turn of the road you see the whole of the beautiful glen lying before you. Great green hills rise steeply on either side, widening into huge corries, in some of which the late snow still lingers, and may linger all through the hot summer days. Sheep feed on the lower slopes, but in the evenings a keen eye may pick out more than one herd of deer trooping in dignified array across the sky-line. For some miles a loch stretches, broken at the end by a series of cascades, the outlet from the larger loch beyond.

It is here that I always think of Archie, for it is here at Shallavanach—"The Happy Place"—that he was born. From Lochaber to Kintail, from Wyvis to Benula he was known to stalkers all over the North of Scotland. Something of the sweetness and happiness of his birthplace must have entered into his nature, for no man was born with a sweeter or a kinder disposition. A harsh word against anyone never passed his lips. Children of all classes loved him, and followed him with that trusting devotion which was a part of his own nature. It is pleasant to think that half an hour before his sudden death his laughter had mingled with theirs. Shy and unversed in the ways of the world, he possessed what many an efficient and esteemed citizen lacks, for the kingdom of God was within him. If ever a man was born to the hills it was Archie. The love of the hills was in his blood. Away from them he was miserable, and to them, like those of another hillman long ago, his eyes were ever uplifted. William the Red, it is written, "loved the tall deer as if he had been their father," but to Archie they were father and mother, wife and child. It is no exaggeration to say that for them he lived. He was for ever talking of them, and but few stalkers had his knowledge of their ways. On the day of his death he sat outside the Old House recalling old stalks and stalkers and days which had been among the happiest of his life. As a stalker he was unsurpassed, and to see him approaching a herd in full view over an exposed face was an education in itself. He literally melted into his surroundings. It was up the Glen of the Cotton Flowers that I walked with Archie on one of the last occasions that we were together.

"I mind I did my first stalk on yon toppie." His soft Highland voice makes music in my memories. "Barefoot I was, and the two gentlemen was saying I was too young. But I got the stag, and me feyther was aaful pleassed." Well he might be, for the child was about ten. "I was a wee thing then. I saa a man come stooping over the sky-line. I thocht it was that he would be hitting his heid against the sky." True it is, alas! that heaven lies nearest in our infancy.

The road here sweeps round a bend, the north side bare of trees, crosses the river and toils steeply up the brae. To the south is a wide corrie, thick as to its lower slopes with firs, old as the hills themselves. They crowd down to the water's edge, leaving bare little sandy bays, whose silver sands gleam white against the deep amber of the silent pools. Anon the shores creep bravely forth in promontories and jutting islands. Ashamed at their temerity they shrink back; and later regaining courage, essay further encroachments. Now and again the ground falls away and the river breaks into tempestuous falls which delight the eye of the traveller on the road above. They surge and batter their way through rockset passes, the gnarled and grizzled pines still gravely aloof. Rabbits burrow in the sandy knolls and work ingenious routes among the boulders.

"I was digging in yon holes," droned Archie, "och! thirty years ago. I was trying for a rabbit, and I struck a piece of iron. I dug away, and at last I dug out a sword. It had a basket hilt. They was telling me it was very old. I was but a boy, and a man, a keeper, took the sword from me. He got three pounds for it in the toon. Me feyther was very vexed at me for no keepin' the sword." It is curious how his trivial remarks have laid stored in my memory.

Beyond is the natural rocky seat where long ago the chief used to sit and view the confines of his heritage, so Archie told me. Right up the far loch could he see, to where, set in the gullet of the pass, now stands a lodge built to shelter

EVENING BY
THE LOCH SIDE

for a while some visiting Sassenach. Below it slides and ripples the river, merging from shallows into wide reed-fringed pools. Everyone, I suppose, has his ideal home pictured in his mind. In an emerald-green hollow by the loch side would I set mine. Close to it a peaty burn ends its long journey from the heights of Carn Eige, and all around are the wide unchanging hills. There, if anywhere, lies peace.

It is that peace which I recapture as I walk down the glen, the peace which Archie had and which he kept far from the bustle and turmoil of the modern world and its ever-growing problems. The place is not the same without him, but whenever I look at the hills, and more particularly at the hills of home, I have a memory of a little bent figure, tired but happy, returning in the gloaming, his spyglass on his back, a stag's horns black against the sky swaying on the pony behind us. Alas, it is now only a memory, for the hunter is home from the hill for the last time; but it is a memory which will never fade.

XXXII. AN ISLAND OF DREAMS

"We sail to seek those isles,
Those isles of yesterday."—Alfred Noyes

IT has always seemed to me one of the most surprising and romantic things in the world to find the coloured outlines and boundaries of a map transformed before one's eyes to solid and unassailable fact. It matters nothing whether you regard a presentment of the British Isles, Africa, or unknown Asia, save that in the former there is no room nowadays for speculation. Each little islet, each lonely loch is set down, figured with the most meticulous care. It is romance hedged and bound. No outlet is there for the play of wandering imagination save within circumscribed limits. And yet, illogically enough, there hangs a fine smack of mystery about it. A road winds here; there rises a hill-top; a belt of woodland fringes the twistings of a mountain burn and the blue sea-water frets for ever at the fronting

cliffs. It is all precise and definite. You hold it clear within
your brain. On a sudden you come upon a photograph or
sketch of the country which your map presents; at once you
are all abroad. A brown woodland borders upon the road;
corries, grave, austere and strewn with rocks, swell with
heather; little sunlit dells peer between the birch stems;
pools, cool and overhung with ferns, are starred with rising
trout; of such details a map takes no account, nor of the
wide and open sky which stretches above each and all of
them. They cannot be set on paper, ruled and measured
with mathematical exactitude. A cleverly arranged com-
position of colours, an inspired catalogue of words may
conjure them before you, but no map, unless you know the
country. You come to a spot, out comes the map. There it
is, set down as accurately and precisely as man can master
such things by figure and line. But the romance has slipped
out.

You lift your eyes, it smiles and beckons from every
thicket and bend, intangible yet ever present, and then, if
you have the right stuff in you, you lift up your eyes and
thank the Maker of it all that He has created something
which man cannot bottle and pin and label and classify.

Such thoughts as these came to my mind, sitting on a
grass-covered knoll fronting the western isles which lie off
the coast of Scotland. On a map, should you chance to
inspect the north-west corner of the British Isles, may be
seen an irregularly shaped dot labelled "Handa." On a
portion of it are clearly inscribed the figures 428. But little
consideration is necessary to conjure up an island, a mile
or so in length, whose highest point is 428 feet above the
Atlantic waters which roll and heave beneath. There you
come to a full stop. What the island contains, how it strikes
one at the outset, are left to the imagination. Nor was I in
much better case, for though I strained my eyes seaward
I could see no island.

It had been a long drive. Narrow lochs, wind-twisted
birch woods, frowning cliffs and corries to delight a stalker's

heart lay between us and Lairg. Knoll after knoll, grass-covered and of a surprising similarity, surrounded us, with one common characteristic, an abundance of rock.

Of every imaginable shape and size, long and thin, short and squat, round and angular, grey with the grey of countless years, they shut us in on three sides. Into the sea they stretched in wicked-looking points or scattered islets, whilst the spray and the breakers roared impotently against their impassive sides and the cormorants preened themselves and gazed with cold fish-like eyes across the waste of waters.

To the west a promontory stretched, against which the surf broke in a brawling uproar. Beyond again, some three miles distant, stretched another point, squarely bitten as though by some sharp-edged tool driven by a mighty hand. It flattened away to the north in low heathery slopes which rose in turn to a not inconsiderable hill crowned with a cairn of stones. I had imagined an island with great fronting cliffs facing the coast in a solid and immovable line, but for these and my island I looked in vain. Yet there it was, set down on the irreproachable map but a few hundred yards from shore.

Not until two days had passed did I realise that the square-bitten promontory marked the southernmost limit of the island. I had fallen into an error such as is commonly the case with those who look for the famous rock on nearing, for the first time, the Straits of Gibraltar. There, ocular demonstration shows the great rock face, so familiar an object in pictures, to be facing north towards the land of the Dons, and not, as one previously supposed, the coast of Africa. Similarly the cliffs of Handa are invisible from the shore, fronting as they do the Atlantic tides.

For long the skies were grey and lowering whilst a blustering, boisterous wind sent a succession of white-capped breakers following each other into the bay. Then it cleared and we danced out in a fishing boat on rippling wavelets which sparkled and glittered in the sun. The brown sail bellied to the breeze and our little craft tugged and strained as the rocks slid past. We rounded the rocky promontory on which cormorants blinked and swooped, and there lay the island. It sloped from the cairn in a succession of undulating heather-clad knolls to green banks and sandy beaches on which the transparent greenness of the sea broke into spray. Through the straits it came lapping, of a sapphire blue. Overhead herring gulls screamed and wheeled; little gentle-eyed kittiwakes hovered within arm's length and even plucked at crumbs from outstretched fingers.

Presently we tacked, slipped between two crouching rocks, guarding the entrance to a sandy cove, and landed. An eiderduck dived into the shadows leaving a widening ripple, came up, bobbed again, and presently swam silhouetted against the wavelets at the opening of the bay. A cottage—the sole dwelling on the island—sheltered in the lee of a bank. Tenantless at our advent, it held during the spring months a shepherd who watched over the young lambs. Rabbits had destroyed the pastures, but they had been killed down until only a few remained. I saw one hopping among the bents.

"Ay!" said Mackenzie, "that'll be Aa-nn-ie!" The other, he volunteered, was Lizzie, which accounted for the declining birthrate.

There are lochs in the folds of the tiny hills, some holding good trout, and, peering from the surrounding purple, clump after clump of white heather.

It is the northern, or rather north-western, side which has made Handa famous, for here in the earlier part of the year, on the high cliffs, ledged, terraced, streaked and weather-worn, birds collect and fill every inch, crack and crevice giving foothold. Here they lay their eggs and, a fact which delighted the Exception, in rows. The cliffs were empty when we saw them save for a few kittiwakes. At the foot of the cliff, ubiquitous cormorants dotted every rock and craned writhing, snaky necks in an endeavour to ascertain what was going on in their immediate vicinity.

From the Stack, a great block of rock which rises detached from the island, flew a skein of geese which went honking on their way across the straits.

Gannets on powerful, black-tipped wings, alert and agile, coasted the cliffs. Now and again one would suddenly arrest his flight and shoot, a veritable bolt from the blue, into the shimmering sparkle of the sea to reappear a moment later with a fish.

The summit of the island disclosed a view to dream of on a summer's night. The sea was of a living blue. It stretched away to sapphire islets in the north and a misty haze; far, far out lay the Butt of Lewis and a low hint of land. South, the eye followed a cluster of rocky points to Badcall Bay, wandered seawards to the Old Man of Storr and the rocky landmarks of the Reay Forest. Suilven, the Sugar Loaf, was the most distant, then Quinaig, the dominating cone of Stack, the rocky slopes of Foinavon and Arkle and so northward again to Kinlochbervie, where once died a goat. Promontories launched themselves seaward to shrink into indentations and clefts. Then as if ashamed of their cowardice they sprang boldly out once more, only to shrink again into still wider inlets. Sandy beaches slipped slyly to meet the waves, which glowed at their coming into wonderful transparent emeralds and greens. Everywhere dotting the wide expanse of blue were little points of rock fretting it to white.

"We'll now go to the Seals' Cave!" cried Mackenzie with the magnificent air of an official guide. Thither accordingly we went.

Great red cliffs, split and ridged in terraced lines, rose frowning over a wide, deep pool. A cave it was in no sense, merely a shallow indentation a quarter of a mile across. The waves called and clamoured on the boulders which fringed the foot of the cliff. A great mass of seaweed rose and fell in the transparent water.

The Exception and I lay on a ledge and overlooked the pool while the waves ceaselessly shattered themselves on the rocks and the seaweed swayed like a woman's hair.

From its centre rose a black head with bristling whiskers. It turned alertly, looking for all the world like the sleek head of a bather. Then with the celerity of a conjuring trick it was gone and the seaweed waved and slid in the sunlight.

"Oh!" cried the Exception. "Did you see it?" And almost before the words were out the seal was up again.

A moment later a second broke the surface of the water and the two lay rolling together. Through the glass I could see a brown eye turning from side to side; then they dived and their pale undersides flickered as they sank to the bottom of the pool. The Exception was in ecstasies, and indeed the sight justified them.

For long we lay there. Then the Exception peered beyond the ledge.

"Look!" she breathed.

Immediately below us the water glittered clear and deep of a wonderful transparency. Through the greens and blues which coalesced, mingled, and showed, dim and undefined, strange nebulous shapes, from amid the writhing, swaying roots of seaweed to the clear sunlit surface came floating the great grey phantom.

At first it seemed but a hint of life, an uncertain flicker. It developed, grew and then burst to the upper air, a great spotted seal.

It lay in the sunlit ripples, floating easily, lazily, with now and again a quick turn of the head, a being from another world. I had but to stretch my hand for the rifle and the rest would have been easy. But I could not. I wanted to watch him, to see him dive again into the grey waving tentacles of weed and come shooting back like a great grey ghost. So I lost my chance. He paddled out a few yards, curved gracefully downwards, flickered and died away. We never saw him again. Late in the evening a black head bobbed in the surf and presently ceased to bob, though all in vain, for the boat failed to reach him ere he sank. But it is not of that I like to think, nor of the two great lythe that broke my tackle and departed to cope with the red phantoms which adorned their jaws. Even the rush and scurry of the return journey before a favouring breeze lingers but faintly in my mind. The map of Handa brings before me with photographic distinctness a grey form, with wandering brown eyes, swaying gently in an azure sea.

XXXIII. THE FORGOTTEN FLEET

> "You'll never lift again
> Our purple-painted headlands, or the lordly keeps of Spain,
> They're just beyond your sky-line, howe'er so far you cruise."
>
> THE THREE-DECKER—Rudyard Kipling

No three-decker bore a happier band to the Islands of the Blest than did the Forgotten Fleet. No deep greybearded seas did its keels furrow; no lordly keeps of Spain did its helmsmen descry, but beyond every turn and bend rose purple-painted headlands, each one lovelier than the last. Of three stout vessels was the fleet composed (though one, it is true, was but a conveyance for cargo), with high-sounding names which still ring in my ear like bells, *Loch Ness*, *Glengarry* and *The Chevalier*. Motor-cars and evil-smelling charabancs have ousted them, and of their former glory but a remnant endures. It is a sad and gloomy affair to step across their gang-planks nowadays; a painful admission that your plans have gone awry; that a connection has failed, or that a car has broken down.

Of old it was a different matter, I see the red funnel against a background of trees; the bustle about the gangways; the "touries" easily recognisable to the expert eye; the jerseyed sailors, each an old friend, getting the baggage on board; the blue-clad figure of the captain gazing, aloof, from his august eminence on the bridge, far down the dusty road. I hear again the warning blast from the siren, the signal which warned the onlookers of a certain lull in the activities preceding departure. The tourists stopped perambulating the deck; the golden eagle, set with outstretched wings above the saloon, continued to glitter impassively; all eyes turned to the road, following the gaze of the captain. We, the initiate, knew what to expect. Scarcely ever were we disappointed. A cloud of dust, no bigger than a man's hand, would arise above the scattered roofs. A spasm of excitement communicated itself to the onlookers. From the shelter of the distant houses a fly would suddenly shoot forth. Again the siren blared. The driver of the vehicle could be seen redoubling his efforts. The dust increased. The whip cracked. Everyone stood agog. Would it be in time? It was as exciting as the rescue scene in a cinema ere the heroine arrives with the police just as the hero is about to be done in by the chief gangster! And all the while the captain stood Jove-like, omnipotent, aloof; in his hands alone the success or failure of the flyman's gallant effort. It never failed. We knew that. At times even a doubt assailed us as to whether the fly's belated arrival was not a clever piece of stage management arranged to enhance the pomp of our departure. Often we wondered what would happen, supposing our vessel swung into mid-stream after that first awe-inspiring blast! Would the flyman tamely accept defeat; or, flinging all considerations to the winds, would he gallop madly down the towpath in pursuit, hurling objurgations at that god-like figure on the bridge? We never had an opportunity of settling our doubts. In a final cloud of dust the fly dashed up to the quay, the passengers were hustled on board, ropes were flung off and majestically, to the solemn chug, chug of revolving paddles, we swung down the canal.

On rare occasions, realising that he was too late to attempt to catch our vessel at its starting-place, a belated traveller would go to the reckless extravagance of driving all the way to the lock at Dochgarroch. Their arrival drew one's attention from the fascinating spectacle of the captain, the mate, the crew and certain of the more able-bodied passengers slowly revolving round the capstans which opened and shut the lock gates. Many a time have I seen the gigantic form of "Gub," arrayed in the loudest of loud checks, dwarfing his companions at this self-imposed task.

The arrival, too, was no less exciting. Far down the canal bank a string of flymen would walk to meet the incoming vessel. Never does one see now clothes such as they wore. Even their bowler hats seemed dedicated in some mysterious fashion to that noble animal, the horse, though they were not in the least horsy. Cracking their whips and uttering strange monosyllabic cries they paraded along the bank, keeping pace with the steamer and balefully eyeing the passengers until they had located a victim. The art in selecting a Jehu from our point of view lay in gazing steadily from one to another, occasionally giving an almost imperceptible nod, until quite certain that our own particular friend was not present. At his advent we ostentatiously turned our backs, leaving our cast-offs to less experienced travellers.

I have dined at the Ritz and Claridge's. The food, of course, is quite good and the cooking passable; but to compare the meals served at these establishments with the ambrosial fare provided in the Forgotten Fleet is to bring into contrast earthly and celestial matters. Breakfast we indulged in on the outward, and tea on the homeward voyage. I do not really know, on looking back, which was the better, though each had common factors; triangular slabs of the most delicious golden-brown toast, and tea out of inordinately thick cups. No tea or toast has ever tasted as good. Breakfast was the more stately affair. The captain sat at the head of the table. On his right was the purser; and on his left, when the difficulties of navigation permitted, the chief engineer. This great triumvirate maintained a gloomy silence, broken occasionally by an almost inaudible and unintelligible growl from the captain. The steward would skip briskly along one side of the table, murmuring a strange formula which sounded like "Chorpherringharma'neggs." Resolved into its constituent parts you realised that your choice lay between a chop, herring or ham and eggs. I do not know who cooked those delectable viands, but the fortune of any grill-room which secured his services would be made. Their aroma still comes to me, mingled with the clinging embrace of plush settees, and the recollection of framed oval paintings of Highland scenery let into panels in the saloon.

Usually we knew many of the passengers, or at least who they were; distinguished figures in the world of sport, travelling from one shooting lodge to another. The "touries" were a race apart, pariahs in a strange land, mere passers-by with no lot or portion in so glorious a heritage. There are no snobs like the young! Usually in command until the more populous districts had been passed, the captain, after, say, Lochend, would descend from the bridge and become, despite his blue coat and gold-laced cap, a mere man. The thrill if he condescended to greet us!

The bearded first mate was in command during his superior's descent from Olympus; but it was a captain who, owing to a slight error in navigation, rammed the concrete pier at one stopping-place, instead of gliding gently alongside. A wave of horror passed through the Fleet at the degradation of one of their number, for the unfortunate, in modern phraseology, had his licence suspended. Mishaps will happen, and on another occasion the guest of an American millionaire, something of a *rara avis* in those far-off days, had the misfortune to drop his rifle case into the waters of the loch on disembarking. I know that the neighbourhood rejoiced at the arrival of real divers, suits and all, who were sent for at fabulous expense. Whether the rifle was recovered I cannot at this distance of time recollect.

Market days were always certain to produce some excitement, and it takes no effort to recall the black-faced mountain sheep being herded into temporary pens erected on the deck, the recalcitrant members being lifted bodily by their fleeces and hustled willy-nilly over the gangway. They showed plenty of fight. Calves, their pathetic faces, with wildly rolling eyes, protruding from sacks, showed none.

Looking back it seems that such scenes always took place in a glorious atmosphere of fresh air and sunshine, mingled with dreams of the Twelfth and the gorgeous and remote possibility of a stag. Interwoven into such dreams are pictures by Archibald Thorburn, *Fur and Feather*, Stevenson, Kipling, Stanley Weyman, Rudolf and Flavia. How I loved them and still do. Then I loved them for what they were. Now I love them because they bring back something which might have died. The longer we live the more we learn that it is the simple old-fashioned things which are the truest and the best.

In winter our business with the Forgotten Fleet was a more grim affair. Yet the sunshine in which my family were basking at Monte Carlo was forgotten as I made my preparations for a foray among the hinds. No explorer of unknown lands, no invader of the haunts of strange beasts ever embarked upon the preliminaries of his undertaking with a greater zest. The long drive in the machine over snowy roads, once my voyage had ended, was, to me, but the forerunner of joys to come. The stumble down the hillside in the dark, the drive down the frosty glen in the mail, the wait on the pier, the mournful farewell of the pier-master (his glory too has departed with the advent of motor-cars, and he drags out a dull existence beside the grass-grown pier), the dimmed lights of the *Loch Ness* as she rounded the point on which the old castle stood sentinel, these were but the sad preliminaries to the long railway journey—hard—which would take me back to the study of law and to the gloom of London.

As, now, I pass Fort Augustus in some swiftly travelling

car I see what is left of the *Loch Ness*. Charred by fire, rusted by water, she lies at the edge of the loch and I heave a sigh for her past glories. The hurrying passers-by reck little of her derelict timbers. To them, if they notice her at all, she is "just an old boat." To me she is one of those golden argosies which sailed so proudly into the setting sun, bearing a cargo of bright hopes and dreams, many of which are still unfulfilled and many, alas! charred and tarnished as she is herself.

TO A STAG'S HEAD—IN LONDON

1932.

Your horns are black with London grime,
  And grey with dust your russet hair;
The passer-by, from time to time
  Is caught by your unmeaning stare.
You're "Just a head"—and nothing more!
  No lettered tag records the date
When some old sportsman, long ago,
  Upon the hill decreed your fate.

Well! Blackened in this gloomy den
  Your glories fade—but not for me!
The monarch of a distant glen
  I see you as you used to be:
When all the world was young and fair,
  And youth and I went hand in hand,
When life—or so it seems to me—
  Was easier to understand.

1945.

Contentment, leisure, ease have gone,
  Loved ones, with whom we used to share
Our simpler pleasures—laughter—sport,
  When life ran on without a care.
We cannot tell the purpose planned,
  Nor yet the end which it fulfils,
But, like the Psalmist, long ago
  We lift our eyes unto the hills.

                                F. W.